CASSINO
The Four Battles
January – May 1944

First published in 2001 by
The Crowood Press Ltd
Ramsbury, Marlborough
Wiltshire SN8 2HR

© Ken Ford 2001
Colour plates © The Crowood Press 2001
Edited by Martin Windrow
Design by Frank Ainscough/Compendium

All rights reserved. No part of this publication may be reproduced or transmitted
in any form or by any means, electronic or mechanical, including photocopy,
recording, or in any information storage and retrieval system, without
prior permission in writing from the publishers.

British Library Cataloguing-in-Publication Data
A CIP catalogue record for this book
is available from the British Library
ISBN 1 86126 395 3

Printed and bound in Great Britain by
Alden Colour, Oxford.

CASSINO

The Four Battles
January – May 1944

Ken Ford

Colour plates by
Mike Chappell

The Crowood Press

Dedication
To my grandson Adam Callum James Ford
Born 9 April 1999

Acknowledgements
I should like to thank all the individuals and
institutions that helped me during the preparation of this book.

In particular I am very grateful to the following
for giving me permission to quote from their published works:
the late Ian McKee, *The 5th Battalion Northamptonshire Regiment in Italy;*
Sir Paul Bryan, *Wool War and Westminster;*
Sir Denis Forman, *The Reason Why;*
Col John Horsfall, *Fling Our Banners to the Wind;*
and to Mrs Marian S.Porter for allowing me to use
the late Brig John Mackenzie's *CO 2LF.*

The photographs are reproduced through the kind permission of the
Trustees of the Imperial War Museum, London;
the National Archives, Washington DC;
and the Budesarchiv, Koblenz

I should also like to express my gratitude to
Mike Chappell for his splendid colour plates,
researched by Martin Windrow and himself.

CONTENTS

CHAPTER ONE — 7

The Road to Cassino

The Allied landings in Calabria and at Salerno. Churchill, the architect of the Italian campaign. Differences between the Allies over the strategy of the war in Italy. Kesselring's optimistic assessment of German strategy. From Salerno to the Gustav Line - slow progress through the mountains. The commanders - Wilson, Alexander, Harding, Leese; Devers, Clark; Kesselring, Von Vietinghoff, Von Senger und Etterlin, Von Mackensen. The significance of 'Ultra'. The rival armies: Allied and German divisions - terminology and brief summary of strengths. The Allied and German air forces.

CHAPTER TWO — 18

The First Battle: 12 January-8 February 1944

The competing demands of the Italian campaign and the preparations for Operation 'Overlord' in Normandy. The Allied plan to outflank the Gustav Line by an amphibious landing at Anzio. General Clark's intentions for US Fifth Army's offensive against the Gustav Line. The French and British attacks, 12-18 January - Gen Juin's French Expeditionary Corps drives through the mountains north of Cassino against the German 5.Gebirgs-Division; British X Corps breaks through the 94.Infanterie-Division on the River Garigliano barrier. Kesselring moves his reserves from the Anzio area to counter the advance. The US 36th Division clears Monte Trocchio and moves up to the River Rapido. General Walker's misgivings over orders for an assault crossing; the 'Texas' Division torn to pieces.

CHAPTER THREE — 32

Anzio - Battle on Two Fronts: 22 January-8 February 1944

Anzio, 22-27 January - Gen Lucas' US VI Corps make an unopposed landing. Kesselring marshals his forces to stifle the Allied lodgement without significantly weakening the Gustav Line. VI Corps inactive while the Germans surround the beachhead. Cassino - the 'Red Bull' across the Rapido, 24 January-4 February - US 34th Division cross upstream of Cassino and fight their way into the northern foothills. All attempts on Monte Cassino fail in the face of resolute defence, appalling weather and hostile terrain. The French success on Monte Belvedere, 25 January-4 February - Juin's supportive attack on the American right flank.

CHAPTER FOUR — 43

Anzio - Build-Up, Check and Recoil: 28 January-4 February 1944

After seven days of inaction Gen Lucas makes his move inland. British 1st Division creates a 2,000-yard salient, and US 3rd Division also make some gains, but both are halted by well-entrenched enemy. After four days the attacks are called off with very small gains - VI Corps threatens to become a liability rather than an asset. German Fourteenth Army starts to probe the perimeter; Kesselring and Von Mackensen plan a counter-offensive to drive VI Corps into the sea. Lucas organises a final defence line.

CHAPTER FIVE — 50

The Second Battle: 15-18 February 1944

The arrival of New Zealand II Corps. German dispositions in the Cassino sector. General Freyberg's plans for a new attack against Cassino and Monastery Hill. The bombing of the monastery. The failed attacks by 4th Indian Division around Point 593. 2nd New Zealand Division in the town - the Maoris of 28th Bn briefly capture Cassino railway station. The second battle for Cassino ends without gains.

CHAPTER SIX — 63

Counter-Attack and Stalemate: 4 February-14 March 1944

Anzio: probing attacks herald the start of the German counter-offensive. Von Mackensen strikes against VI Corps with six divisions. The beachhead contracts under the fury of the German onslaught - VI Corps is forced back to the final defence line. German attacks begin to falter under the weight of Allied artillery and air bombardment. The Allied line holds; Kesselring calls off the attack after four days.
The Gustav Line: Clark's US Fifth Army stalled. Fifteenth Army Group staff rethink the strategy, and plan a massive spring offensive including Leese's British Eighth Army. The paratroopers of 1.Fallschirmjäger-Division take over responsibility for the Cassino feature. Further German attacks at Anzio gain little new ground.

CHAPTER SEVEN   87
The Third Battle: 15-23 March 1944

Freyberg's New Zealand II Corps prepare to try again. Cassino town is bombed, destroying all buildings and cratering all approaches; Freyberg's piecemeal opening attack makes little progress through the rubble. The capture of Castle Hill - 4th Indian Division move on to the slopes of Monte Cassino. The New Zealanders are unable to drive Heidrich's Fallschirmjäger from the south-west corner of the town. The Indians get on to Hangman's Hill and hold out for nine days. Further attempts by 4th Indian Division on the mountains to the north achieve little. The battle slows to a standstill.

CHAPTER EIGHT   99
An Infantry Division in the Line: March-April 1944

British 78th Division take over the Cassino sector - 'As we stood together looking at his map I heard a sharp crack, he fell at my side'. Life in the line on the exposed mountains; Great War-style logistics. Hide and seek among the rocks - 'It seemed illogical to have to defend such vulnerable positions.' Morale; patrolling; Allied and German artillery and mortar fire; casualty evacuation. Holding the ruins of the town, and the castle. Polish II Corps units relieve 78th Division - 'They only wished to kill Germans ... They were quite imperturbable'.

CHAPTER NINE   108
The Fourth Battle: Operation 'Diadem', 11-18 May 1944

Alexander's spring offensive takes shape; the Germans strengthen their defences in preparation. US Fifth Army and British Eighth Army launch Operation 'Diadem'. Polish II Corps beaten back at Monte Cassino. The French break through the Aurunci Mountains and into the Liri valley from the south. British XIII Corps cross the Rapido and penetrate the Gustav Line. US II Corps strike down Route 7 towards the Anzio beachhead. The Poles capture Monte Cassino at the second attempt.

CHAPTER TEN   117
Break-Out: 19 May-4 June 1944

Kesselring unleashes his reserves. US VI Corps break out of the Anzio beachhead. The French, Canadians and British close on the Hitler Line in the Liri valley, and break through after two days' costly fighting. German Tenth Army begin to retreat towards Rome. General Clark changes the direction of US Fifth Army's drive and makes for Rome himself, allowing the bulk of Tenth Army to escape. The remainder of the war in Italy.

APPENDIX I: Allied Orders of Battle 121
APPENDIX II: German Orders of Battle 124
COLOUR PLATES & COMMENTARIES   65-76
MAPS   8, 21, 25, 33, 54, 90, 110, 115
BIBLIOGRAPHY   126
INDEX   127

CHAPTER ONE

The Road To Cassino

On 3 September 1943, the fourth anniversary of the outbreak of the Second World War, British and Commonwealth troops returned in force to the mainland of Europe. The Eighth Army, under the command of Gen Bernard Montgomery, landed its XIII Corps at Reggio on the 'toe' of Italy opposite Messina in Sicily. British 5th Division and Canadian 1st Division waded safely ashore after a mighty artillery bombardment, meeting little opposition. The landings were the start of a campaign which in some senses would come to match the worst days of the Great War.

The scale of destruction of men, equipment and landscape, and the squalor of the battlefield, would often recall the old Wesern Front in miniature. The desolation brought down on the civilian population, and the seemingly wanton devastation of cultural treasures, marked a tragic episode in Italian history. And nowhere was this tragedy played out with such intensity and under the appalled eyes of a larger world-wide audience than at Monte Cassino. It took almost six months and four great battles before the Allied armies could move past this medieval strongpoint.

The landings in southern Italy seemed to many people to be just a continuation of the long trek across North Africa and Sicily – a natural progression towards Germany through the Fascist empire in the Mediterranean. To others, most notably the Americans, the decision to carry the war into Italy was a mistake. They argued that the best route was the most direct: across the English Channel, through France and the Low Countries and into the heart of Hitler's Germany. Italy could only be a sideshow, a diversion that would suck in men and matériel which could be put to better use in the main thrust across the battlefields of North-West Europe. So why did the Allies decide to invade Italy and embroil themselves in a theatre of war that took almost

Late-model PzKw IV tank abandoned north of the River Trigno during British Eighth Army's advance from Calabria in autumn 1943. The Panzer divisions of 1943-44 had a tank regiment of two battalions; I.Abteilung was supposed to be equipped with the much more powerful PzKw V Panther, II.Abteilung with this elderly, if up-gunned and up-armoured design. Note the extra spaced armour plates fitted around the turret, and the hull racks for large plates to protect the thinner hull sides and the suspension.

two years to subdue? The answer probably lies in the strength of will of one man: Winston Churchill.

After the Allied victory in North Africa in May 1943 Britain's wartime Prime Minister was convinced that the momentum of attack should be maintained by keeping in close contact with German forces who were still reeling from their eviction from Tunisia. It seemed natural that Sicily should be invaded almost immediately, its capture being followed by a swift invasion of Italy. Such moves would have two immediate benefits: first, Mussolini and his Fascist state could be eliminated from the war, and second, the conquest of Italy would allow a direct route into Hitler's occupied Europe. Such initiatives would also be welcomed by the third of the great Allied nations, Soviet Russia. Stalin had long been calling for action in Europe to ease the German pressure on the western regions of the USSR. He was not happy that the promised cross-Channel invasion had been postponed until 1944, and was demanding that British and American forces should open a 'second front' immediately.

While they were sympathetic to Stalin's pleas, the American Chiefs of Staff believed that the main Western thrust against Hitler's 'Fortress Europe' should be launched

The heavy rains during the winter period in Italy reduced all secondary highways and tracks into seas of glutinous mud. American four-wheel drive vehicles were better able to deal with these conditions than the often outdated transport used by the British. (US National Archives)

7

ability, and enough strength and manufacturing power, to carry through the will of its leaders. To the United States concentration of effort was a prerequisite for victory.

The Allied landings

In the event, Churchill got his own way. He appealed to President Roosevelt on the grounds that the Western Allies could not just sit back and watch the Russians struggle until they were ready to invade France; they had to fight the Germans somewhere, and it might as well be in Italy. In addition, the capture of the great airfields on the Foggia Plain would allow Allied bombers to reach strategic targets in southern Germany and the occupied territories. The seizure of major Italian ports such as Naples and Taranto would assist the Allied navies in completely clearing the whole of the Mediterranean, and allow assistance to be given to partisans struggling against the Nazis in the Balkan states. Reluctantly, the Americans agreed to the campaign, but only in a limited sense: it was a sideshow and was to be treated as such – preparation for the cross-Channel attack was always to take priority.

With the political decision taken for the invasion to go ahead, Allied planners were confronted with the topographical problem of how to wage war in Italy. The country is almost one thousand miles long, with a backbone of mountains running down its entire length and splitting the long peninsula into two halves. These mountains rise to over 6,000 feet in many places and are traversed by few lateral roads. On either side of this long Apennine range only narrow coastal plains divide the mountains from the sea. These strips of flat land nowhere exceed twenty-five miles in width and are often as little as five miles wide. Draining the mountains are numerous rivers running down to the sea, each carving out a precipitous route through the rocky ground. The Allied march from the south to the north of the country would be confronted by scores of these rivers, each an ideal natural obstacle which a resolute defender might convert into a serious military barrier. Tactically, Italy was not a place where any military commander would wish to wage war, and any strategist who chose to land in the south and march northwards along the whole length of the country would need something more than brute force to achieve a victory.

The initial landings in Italy (Operation 'Baytown') were carried out by troops of the veteran British Eighth Army. They crossed the narrow Straits of Messina from Sicily on 3 September 1943 and created a lodgement on the coast of Calabria. A few days later, on 9 September, a much larger Allied force landed on the wide beaches which stretched for twenty miles to the south of Salerno (Operation 'Avalanche'). The evening before Marshal Bodoglio, head of the Italian government since the fall of Mussolini a few days earlier, announced Italy's surrender and informed his countrymen that they were now pledged to fight on the side of the Allies. In response to this capitulation of its Axis ally Germany acted with supreme alacrity and ruthlessness – the Wehrmacht took over the coast defences, disarmed the Italian garrisons, and moved its own troops into key areas. The despised Italians may have given up the fight, but the Germans were adamant that Italy would remain under their control.

The landings at Salerno were carried out by Gen Mark Clark's US Fifth Army which, together with Montgomery's

against northern France with the maximum effort possible to ensure a successful lodgement. The Allied armies could not be brought to a convincing state of readiness for such a massive operation in 1943. It should be remembered that American forces were fully engaged in the Pacific. The war in the Far East covered vast areas, and though primarily dependent upon naval forces it none the less required great numbers of troops to capture and garrison the myriad islands along the ocean path leading to Japan.

In Europe, the land war would require that the Allies assemble a great superiority of men and equipment over German forces if they were to break through Hitler's Atlantic Wall defences. The Americans were convinced that Nazi Germany could only be defeated by a concentration of effort along the shortest route to Berlin, placing overwhelming numbers of troops on the mainland of Europe via a cross-Channel invasion. Everything else could only be a distraction and would serve to dilute or postpone that invasion. General George C. Marshall – US Army Chief-of-Staff and Chairman of the Combined Chiefs of Staff Committee – was suspicious of British motives in the Mediterranean, and his unease was shared by many of his colleagues. Marshall was of the opinion that if the Allies invaded Italy the USA's great but finite military resources were in danger of being drawn off until there was not enough left to deal the decisive blow in North-West Europe.

This difference in strategic thinking was coloured by each country's experience of the war up to that point. Britain's forces were stretched to the limit; after three years of conflict, and many defeats, they needed to husband their resources and to use them with a degree of restraint, often favouring an indirect approach to strategy. By contrast, the US Army, after a shaky start, had great confidence in its

German Sturmgeschütz III Ausf G self-propelled assault gun, mounting a long 75mm gun in a low, fixed superstructure on a PzKw III tank chassis, waiting on a bridge for word to move against the advancing Allies. Cheaper to produce than turret tanks, and as effective in the defensive warfare of 1943-45, these 'SPs' would appear in increasing numbers. The powerful Panzer Regiment 'Hermann Göring' had two battalions of tanks plus a third battalion with these assault guns. (Imperial War Museum)

Eighth Army, comprised Fifteenth Army Group under the command of Gen Sir Harold Alexander. He in turn was subordinate to the Allied Supreme Commander Mediterranean, Gen Dwight D.Eisenhower. The US VI Corps and British X Corps which came ashore at Salerno would represent the main Allied effort in Italy. Such a landing had been predicted by the enemy and the location of the landfall came as no great surprise, being the only suitable section of coastline within range of Allied fighter cover from Sicily. The landings were opposed with great vigour – not least by the 16.Panzer-Division, with spirited Luftwaffe support – and for several days things looked bad for the Allies. However, repeated German attacks were successfully repulsed; and on 16 September elements of British Eighth Army linked up with the bridgehead from the south. During the same week more British landings took place, this time at the great port of Taranto (Operation 'Slapstick'). Possession of this modern harbour, with access to a large transport network, speeded up the arrival of the rest of Eighth Army. Now British V Corps and 1st Airborne Division began to disembark and press northwards along the Adriatic coastline. All these landings helped seal the fate of the German garrisons in the south and strengthened the main effort at Salerno.

The German strategy takes shape
The commander of the German Tenth Army, Gen von Vietinghoff, whose forces were opposing the invasion, recommended that all attempts to drive the Allies back into the sea should be abandoned and a gradual withdrawal be made to a more tenable defensive line in front of Rome. His immediate superior, Field Marshal Kesselring, Commander-in-Chief (South), agreed in part. He advised Hitler that they should continue with steps to prevent the Allies taking Rome by constructing this defensive line, but should make the Allies fight for every yard of their advance up to it. Kesselring wanted to keep the Allies as far from Germany as possible. Rome and the ground before it should be denied to the invaders with all vigour. In contrast, Rommel, Commander-in-Chief (North), wanted to abandon most of Italy to the Allies and defend the route to Germany from prepared positions in the Alps. Kesselring's strategy was more in keeping with Hitler's obdurate spirit, and the Führer gave orders for the approaches to Rome to be defended. The German High Command decided to give up ground in a controlled manner, causing as much delay and destruction as possible to the advancing Allied armies. They would then choose the time and place to make a determined stand behind one of the many great rivers that crossed the Italian peninsula.

With an agreed strategy in place, Hitler sent out a clear signal that Italy was to be defended. He appointed Kesselring as Commander-in-Chief Italy and sent Rommel to France. He also sent reinforcements south to counter the Allies and gave instructions for the building of a series of stop lines along the length of Italy. To the south of Rome a formidable defensive line was to be constructed, capable of holding up the advancing British and American armies throughout the whole of the coming winter. This 'Gustav Line' was to be built across the narrowest waist of Italy; starting on the west coast it ran along the River Garigliano, then the River Rapido, over the Apennine mountains and down the River Sangro to the Adriatic coast. This line was to be defended at all costs.

The nature of the ground offered only three possible openings for an Allied attack. Two of them were along the coastal plains on either side of the country; the third, the most direct and the most suitable for an armoured thrust, was through a gap made in the mountains by the River Liri. This last route was the most obvious for any advance upon Rome: it had a good road, passed through a wide valley, and was the most direct. It did, however, have one great drawback: it passed right under the natural fortress of Monte Cassino.

Before the advancing Allies reached the Gustav Line there were, however, other formidable defensive positions to be overcome. After the lodgement at Salerno had been established beyond any serious danger of elimination, US

British 6-pounder anti-tank guns mounted on American T48 half-track gun carriages, under camouflage nets during the advance up Italy to the Gustav Line. These guns served with the support element of Eighth Army's 23rd Armoured Brigade, an independent formation equipped with Sherman tanks. Tank units were normally supported by towed or motorised anti-tank guns or self-propelled 'tank-destroyers' with longer-ranged weapons than the turret tanks. (US National Archives)

Fifth Army began its move northwards. The Germans withdrew slowly before it, using every delaying tactic possible, buying time for work to continue on their series of defensive lines. Naples fell on 6 October and the harbour became available for landing reinforcements and supplies. This triumph was short-lived, as twenty miles to the north of Naples the Allies came up against the first of the great rivers to obstruct their path, the Volturno. A set-piece attack was mounted and the river barrier was breached by six divisions on 14 October. The advance continued; but a few days later the hastily erected fortified positions of the Barbara Line barred their way once more. This defensive line was a much tougher proposition and it took until the end of the month to force a passage.

As the Allies advanced, so the Germans resisted, employing a series of classic delaying tactics. They built roadblocks, laid mines, and entrenched anti-tank positions; mobile artillery groups and self-propelled guns reinforced a few rearguard infantry elements, slowing the Allied advance to a crawl. Each mile was gained at great cost in men, machines and above all time. While their comrades delayed Clark's army the main strength of the defenders withdrew into prepared positions on the next defensive line. The Fifth Army reached the Winter (or 'Bernhardt') Line in November 1943, by which time any progress was becoming very difficult to achieve. This fortified system used the local topography to good effect, linking together the heights of several mountains so that positions on each peak might give mutually supporting fire to the others. The Fifth Army attacked along the line and initially made some penetrations, but the offensive soon became bogged down in front of the key German defensive positions on Monte Camino, Monte Maggiore and Monte La Difensa. To add to the difficulty of moving men, machines and supplies the weather had broken, and winter cold was aggravated by periods of torrential rain. General Clark decided that he had no option but to call a halt to the advance. His men were exhausted, depleted in numbers and ill-equipped for winter warfare; they needed rest and replenishment. A period of static warfare followed. Since landing at Salerno on 9 September, US Fifth Army had lost almost 22,000 men killed, wounded and missing; and they had not yet reached the main German defence line.

This pause was just what Kesselring wanted; it gave him time to complete his fortifications and to refresh and reinforce his troops. Work on the main defensive line continued at a furious pace. The Todt Organisation was brought in to help with the construction of concrete pillboxes and strongpoints, using conscripted Italian labour – 44,000 Todt workers were put to work on the Gustav Line. Wehrmacht divisions nevertheless found most of the labour for their own sectors of the line, reinforced by engineer units from Corps. From Germany, 100 steel shelters, 76 armoured casemates and numbers of armoured machine gun nests were despatched to the Cassino front.

Over on the eastern side of the country, along the Adriatic coast, the difficulties faced by British Eighth Army mirrored those of US Fifth Army as it made its own increasingly painful advance up the Italian peninsula. Since landing in Calabria and at Taranto Montgomery's forces had cleared the central and eastern part of southern Italy. Progress had been relatively easy as they advanced up through the Plain of Foggia, but resistance increased when they reached the great river barriers. Set-piece battles took them over the Biferno, Trigno and Sangro and on to Ortona, which was seized by the Canadian 1st Division in a savage and very costly week-long battle over Christmas 1943 and New Year 1944. Thereafter the terrain to the north of Ortona along the narrow coastal plain became impassable, and the worsening weather and stiffening enemy resistance halted the advance. There was little room to manoeuvre large numbers of troops and little ground on which to employ the armour. A halt was called to any advance on the Adriatic front until the spring; this was not the terrain over which to fight a winter battle.

Between the Fifth and Eighth Armies lay the wall of the great Apennine mountain range. Towering peaks, precipitous cliffs and narrow, winding roads made it very difficult country in which to wage a war with a modern motorised army. In the main, this mountainous territory had been gained by obliging the Germans to fall back as they were outflanked on either side of the long range, rather than by wresting it from them by force of arms; but occasional peaks had to be captured the hard way. By the time winter came, and the snow locked in pockets of troops and made road movement impossible, both sides were content to hold a

General Sir Henry Maitland Wilson (right), Supreme Allied Commander Mediterranean, discusses the Italian campaign with his American deputy, Lt Gen Jacob Devers. (Imperial War Museum)

static line through the mountains where things were quiet save for patrols and the odd infrequent raid. By contrast the local Italian partisans refused to sit still during this period and took to skirmishing with the Germans, which brought down the predictable horrific reprisals upon the heads of the local civilian population.

In the first week of December, after rest, replenishment, and reinforcement by newly landed divisions, the US Fifth Army resumed its advance up the west side of the country. It attacked the stubborn mountain peaks guarding the Mignano Gap through the Winter Line with fresh troops and more weight behind its punch, grinding inexorably away at the enemy's fixed defences. However, the German Tenth Army expertly performed its task of holding up the Allies for as long as possible while using the minimum possible defensive force. Clark's British 56th Division finally took the bastion of Monte Camino, and his GIs forced the enemy off Monte Maggiore and Monte la Difensa, after many days of hard fighting; clearing the single village of San Pietro on Monte Sammucro cost 1,500 US casualties. At last the Fifth Army came up to the Garigliano and Rapido rivers and could finally look into the Liri valley. Ahead, concealed and strengthened after months of work, lay its next great challenge: Kesselring's formidable Gustav Line, and the great fortress of Cassino.

The commanders and their armies

By early January 1944, Gen Alexander had brought his Fifteenth Army Group up to the Gustav Line after a four-month campaign of extreme hardship. It was clear that the Italian front was not going to yield a quick victory, nor was the enemy likely to give up the country without a very stiff fight. The road to Rome and a swift occupation of the city still seemed to mesmerise the Allied high command; but the reality was that whenever this symbolic prize finally fell, it would only be as a result of many long, hard-fought battles.

In January 1944 some important changes took place among the Allied command in the Mediterranean. General Eisenhower, the Supreme Commander, had left the region and returned to Britain to take charge of the preparations for Operation 'Overlord', the invasion of France. He was replaced by a senior British general, Sir Henry Maitland Wilson, as Commander-in-Chief Mediterranean. General Montgomery also departed, leaving his beloved Eighth Army to take over command of all land forces for the assault phase of 'Overlord'. In his place, Gen Sir Oliver Lease took control of Eighth Army.

These changes at the top brought a definite British influence to the Italian campaign, with America providing just two of the five senior commanders. This lack of American command at the highest level tended to give the impression that the Italian campaign was a 'British show', and some of the decisions that were subsequently made aroused deep suspicion in the American camp. While there was mutual respect for the fighting capabilities of all sections of the Allied forces, it is undeniable - as it was inevitable - that national and personal interests sometimes outweighed sound strategic and tactical decisions.

General Sir Henry Maitland Wilson was a large, well-built, affable man who was known to his contemporaries as 'Jumbo'. He had spent most of the war in the Middle East in a variety of commands, ranging from GOC Egypt in 1939 to C-in-C Middle East in February 1943. During this period he was involved in the operational planning for Gen O'Connor's great victory in winter 1940-41 when the Italians were driven from Cyrenaica; less happily, he had commanded the British force in Greece in 1941; thereafter he had dealt with the revolt in Iraq and captured Syria from the Vichy French. Later commands included British Ninth Army and C-in-C Persia-Iraq Command. When Wilson was elevated to Supreme Allied Commander Mediterranean to replace Eisenhower it was not in recognition of his experience in conducting operations in the field, but had more to do with his long service in the region, his seniority, and his proven ability to maintain excellent relations between British and American forces. Wilson was big in both size

The always elegant Irish Guardsman Gen Sir Harold Alexander, Commander Fifteenth Army Group. A likeable man with a fine combat record, 'Alex' had diplomatic talents which enabled him to work successfully with his US colleagues in Italy despite the difficulties of inter-Allied relations. (Imperial War Museum)

(Left) General Alphonse Juin, Commander French Expeditionary Corps (left), talks to Gen Oliver Leese, Commander British Eighth Army (centre) and Gen Alexander during a visit to British Eighth Army HQ on 26 March 1944. (Imperial War Museum)

(Right) General Mark Clark, Commander US Fifth Army, on the beach at Anzio on the day of the landings, 22 January 1944; Clark had arrived in the beachhead by motor launch. (US National Archives)

and personality, but was able to exercise sound judgement and tact. His role in the Mediterranean, and in Italy in particular, was to address broad questions of policy and strategy rather than to exercise command in the field.

The strategy and tactics employed in the Italian theatre were largely the responsibility of Gen Sir Harold Alexander, Commander Fifteenth Army Group. Alexander was a capable and popular general with a great deal of experience. At the start of the war he commanded 1st Division in France as part of the British Expeditionary Force. At Dunkirk he was elevated to corps command to organise the last of the troops to be evacuated, and legend had it that he had been the last man off the beaches. In 1941 he took over Southern Command in England, facing the invasion threat, and held the post until 1942 when he was sent to Burma to organise the withdrawal of British forces back to Assam in the face of the Japanese invasion. Given the Allied experience elsewhere in the Far East it was greatly to his credit that he conducted an orderly retreat and kept most of his forces intact.

August 1942 saw him in the Middle East, where he became C-in-C and directed the finally victorious campaign in North Africa. With the American arrival and the 'Torch' landings that November, Alexander was made Deputy Supreme Commander and Commander Eighteenth Army Group (British 1st and 8th Armies). After the collapse of Axis forces in Tunisia he commanded the Allied troops in the invasions of Sicily and Italy. When Eisenhower left the Mediterranean, Alexander was not promoted to replace him even though he was his deputy, but became C-in-C Allied Armies in Italy and Commander Fifteenth Army Group. Churchill recognised that his qualities, both diplomatic and strategic, made him the ideal choice to exercise command and control over the conduct of the multinational forces fighting in the Italian theatre.

Harold Alexander was of aristocratic birth, the third son of the Earl of Caledon. He had served with distinction in the Irish Guards in the Great War; led Baltic German troops fighting the Bolsheviks in northern Russia in 1919; and later saw action as a brigadier on the North - West Frontier of India in the inter-war years. Alexander had an elegant and slightly remote air about him, his shyness sometimes appearing as aloofness. However, he was supremely confident in all that he did and was able to instil this confidence in those around him. His main forté was in fighting battles rather than planning them, being most comfortable when in the field reacting to events as they unfolded.

Alexander had as his chief-of-staff Gen John Harding, a soldier with a fine military brain and a sound reputation as a clear-thinking strategist. Harding had been on the staff of Gen Richard O'Connor during the astonishingly successful 1940/41 campaign in Cyrenaica. He had later served on the staffs of both Auchinleck and Montgomery in North Africa. Harding's arrival at Alexander's HQ reinforced the already well-organised staff structure, and he proved to be a great asset to Alexander in his conduct of the war in Italy.

The third senior British commander was Gen Oliver Leese, Commander Eighth Army. Leese had served under Montgomery as GOC British XXX Corps from El Alamein to Sicily and replaced him when 'Monty' went back to England to command Twenty-First Army Group. Leese was of large build, with a bluff and cheerful nature, but could sometimes be prone to explosive outbursts. His normally genial manner set subordinates at ease, however, and maintained the confident spirit engendered by Montgomery at Eighth Army HQ. Oliver Leese had been awarded the DSO as an officr in the Coldstream Guards during the Great War. In 1940 he was sent to France to join Lord Gort's BEF command staff; and back in England after Dunkirk he had organised and become GOC of the Guards Armoured Division. When Montgomery was clearing out the 'dead wood' before El Alamein, Leese was called out to North Africa to take command of XXX Corps. He successfully fought in most of the major battles of Eighth Army and won considerable recognition for his handling of the corps. When Montgomery left Eighth Army to return to England in January 1944, Leese became his natural successor.

Heading the American contingent in the Mediterranean was Gen Jacob Devers. When Eisenhower left to head 'Overlord', Devers was sent out from England to become Wilson's deputy. Jacob Devers had commanded both infantry and armoured formations, but lacked battle experience, although he had gained a wide reputation within the US Army as a fine administrator. Destined for high command, he was sent to the Mediterranean to gain familiarity in the handling of large formations. He was appointed as deputy Supreme Allied Commander Mediterranean, and commander of all American forces in that theatre.

General Mark Clark, the commander of the US Fifth Army, had been Eisenhower's deputy in Europe prior to the 'Torch' landings in French North Africa, in whose preparation he had played a major role. After that invasion he had continued as Eisenhower's second-in-command until he was given the Fifth Army in January 1943, at the age of 47. His army did not see action in Sicily but was kept back for the invasion of Italy, where it landed at Salerno in September 1943. This was the first active command Clark had exercised since serving in the Great War as a young captain; his meteoric rise – by the standards of the US Army of that time – was due to the impression he had made on senior American generals by his skill in training and organisation. In Europe and North Africa his duties had largely been political. Clark had a forceful personality, good looks and a great desire to be in the public eye; he welcomed publicity, and used his fame in the service of his intense ambition. He was a great patriot and was eager to ensure that he and his army received all the recognition due to them. This sometimes made him suspicious of British motives, and he was often very critical of British and Commonwealth tactics. Clark filled the role of the popular American hero and acquitted himself well, becoming one of the most successful American generals of the war.

By the end of 1943 Alexander had two armies in the field, totalling six corps. The US Fifth Army had four: US II and VI Corps, British X Corps and the French Expeditionary Corps. The British Eighth Army had two: British V and XIII Corps. Others were in the process of being formed as new divisions arrived in Italy. Before Rome was captured, three new formations had taken the field: New Zealand II Corps, Polish II Corps and Canadian I Corps. The Allied forces in Italy contained a variety of nationalities with varying experience of warfare, ranging from rather war-weary divisions who had been fighting far from home for years, through those just hitting their peak after a blooding in Tunisia and Sicily, to entirely 'green' units which had never heard an angry shot. In addition to these large organisations from various nations, other smaller contingents from many countries fought in Italy for the Allied cause, including South Africans, 'Co-Belligerent' Italians, Greeks, Palestinian Jews, even Brazilians. It was Alexander's task to weld this cosmopolitan collection of troops, all subject to the influence of their own political masters at home, into a homogeneous fighting force capable of striving for a common purpose.

The Wehrmacht in Italy

Opposing Alexander as German Commander-in-Chief Italy was Field Marshal Albrecht Kesselring, a professional soldier who had served with the artillery from the age of nineteen. He had transferred to the fledgling Luftwaffe as a career move in 1933. He had commanded Air Fleet 1 during the invasions of Poland and France, and was chief of Air

Field Marshal Albrecht Kesselring, Commander German Army Group 'C' and C-in-C Italy. Kesselring (1885-1960) entered the German Army in 1904 and served as an artillery officer in the Great War. After transferring to the newly-formed Luftwaffe in 1933 he made a name for himself in a variety of staff roles. In 1939 he was in command of Air Fleet 1 in Poland and in 1940 headed Air Fleet 2 in France during the Battle of Britain. His competent handling of air-ground co-operation on the Eastern Front was followed by various appointments in the Mediterranean, which quickly progressed beyond mere Luftwaffe commands. Kesselring, always the optimist, was nicknamed 'Smiling Albert'; in Italy this optimism was soundly based on an expert strategic grasp of his options. It was also just what Hitler wanted from his generals, and Kesselring's relationship with his leader was one of mutual respect. At the end of the war he refused to discuss surrender terms until he was convinced that Hitler was dead. Here he is photographed in Italy in 1944 wearing Luftwaffe field marshal's tropical uniform with his Knight's Cross with Oakleaves and Swords at the throat. (Bundesarchiv)

General Heinrich von Vietinghoff-Scheel, Commander German Tenth Army in Italy, was a Panzer general who had commanded an armoured division before the war. In Russia he was commander of XLVI Panzer Corps and was acting commander of Ninth Army. He formed Tenth Army in Italy in August 1943, by which time he had completed nearly forty years service in the German Army. Near the end of the war he became C-in-C Italy and commander of Army Group 'C' when Kesselring replaced Field Marshal Gerd von Rundstedt as C-in-C West.

Fleet 2 during the Battle of Britain. During service on the Russian front he had demonstrated a talent for handling air-ground operations. In 1942 he was sent to the Mediterranean, sharing the direction of the war in North Africa with Rommel and finally organising the German withdrawal from Tunisia in spring 1943. In Italy, with all forces under his direct control, he was able to employ his great skills as an accomplished strategist and a sound tactician. Kesselring's handling of the Italian campaign during the long retreat up the mainland singled him out as one of the great German commanders of the war.

German forces in Italy comprised two major formations, Tenth and Fourteenth Armies. Tenth Army held the line across the south while Fourteenth Army controlled the north of the country. At the head of German Tenth Army was Gen Heinrich von Vietinghoff, a soldier of the old school and a graduate from the Prussian Guard. A cavalry

DIVISIONS

The basic military formation mentioned most often in this book is the division, identified by an Arabic number. Two or more divisions made up a corps, identified by a Roman number; and two or more corps made up an army, whose number is spelt out. In the **Allied** armies the division normally had a field strength of between about 14,000 and 16,000 men.

The battles for Cassino and Anzio involved formations and units of so many different nationalities that there is a danger of readers becoming confused about the identity of those mentioned in any particular passage. For this reason British, Commonwealth, US, French and Polish Divisions are normally identified by nationality wherever mentioned.

Numbered Allied divisions - e.g. 'British 5th' or 'US 36th' Divisions - are always infantry formations unless otherwise identified. These normally consisted of three regiments (US) or brigades (British and Commonwealth), each of three battalions of infantry, each battalion fielding - at full strength - between 800 and 900 men. The nine infantry battalions were supported by three or four integral battalion-sized artillery units, and anti-tank, anti-aircraft, reconnaissance, engineer, signals, medical, administrative and logistic units, including generous motor transport. Organisation varied in minor details - e.g. the British division had a separate medium machine gun battalion while machine guns were dispersed between the infantry regiments of US divisions - but their combat capabilities were roughly comparable.

Before Operation 'Diadem', the breakthrough of May 1944, Allied tanks were almost entirely deployed in the infantry support role in broken terrain rather than in tank-vs-tank manoeuvres in open country, so the tank strengths of the opposing armoured divisions were not very significant on this front. The US Armored Division of 1943-44 had some 11,000 personnel, including three armoured infantry battalions carried in half-tracks and three tank battalions totalling 186 medium (M4 Sherman) and 77 light (M5 Stuart) tanks. The armoured brigades of British and Canadian divisions consisted of three battalion-sized tank regiments plus an integral motorised infantry battalion.

Many other independent armoured, artillery, engineer and other specialist units were available to the high commands at corps and army level, which were committed in support of the infantry divisions as needed. For this reason some units mentioned in this text will not be found in the brief divisional orders of battle in the Appendices.

The 2nd New Zealand Division was unique; with a strength of 20,000 men and 4,500 vehicles in one armoured and two infantry brigades and very strong artillery, this was the most powerful single Allied division on the Italian front.

German infantry divisional titles are given here in the form e.g. '44.Division'. Wehrmacht divisional titles reflected several distinct types of formation; those encountered here apart from *Infanterie* are *Jäger* (rifle, i.e. light infantry); *Gebirgs* (mountain); *Fallschirmjäger* (parachute rifle); *Panzer-Grenadier* (mechanised infantry); and *Panzer* (armoured) divisions.

By the end of 1943 the manpower of the Wehrmacht was visibly weakened by the bottomless grave of the Eastern Front. The '1944 Infantry Division', introduced by an order of November 1943, had an official establishment of just under 13,000, with only six infantry battalions - two in each of three infantry regiments. These were backed by the same range of supporting units as in Allied divisions. In fact this reduction was a retrospective move to regularise the fact that many divisions were already down to that or an even lower strength, whatever their number of battalions. The Jäger designation, supposedly indicating lightly armed mobile infantry, in practice often dignified infantry divisions which could not be supplied with heavy equipment and which were usually short of the transport needed for a mobile role. The Mountain Infantry Division also had about 13,000 men at full strength, with two Rifle regiments. The Parachute Rifle Division had a theoretical establishment of nearly 16,000 men, in three 3,200-strong Rifle regiments of three battalions plus airborne artillery and other supporting units; but the dispersed 1.Fallschirmjäger-Division could not boast this kind of field strength at Cassino.

The Panzer-Grenadier-Division of June 1943 regulations had a strength of about 14,700 in two motorised/mechanised infantry regiments each of two battalions, and one Panzer (tank) battalion, plus mechanised or motorised supporting units. The '1944 Panzer-Division' of September 1943 regulations was also just under 15,000 strong, in one two-battalion Panzer regiment with 165 tanks, two two-battalion Panzer-Grenadier regiments, and motorised supporting units. The 1st Bn of a Panzer-Grenadier regiment was supposed to have armoured half-tracks, the 2nd Bn trucks. The most powerful German division in Italy was the Luftwaffe's Panzer-Division 'Hermann Göring', whose losses in Tunisia had been made good with remarkable speed thanks to the priority it enjoyed through the sponsorship of the Reichsmarschall.

★ ★ ★

The major combat units of Allied and German divisions involved in the campaign are listed in the Appendices at the end of this book. Note that in the orders of battle infantry unit designations such as Grenadier, Fusilier and Light Infantry are purely honorific or traditional and had no tactical meaning.

German infantry machine gun crew passing a Jagdpanzer 'Elefant' by the side of the road near Nettuno during the Anzio fighting of March 1944. They wear Luftwaffe camouflaged field jackets over their greatcoats, and are thus almost certainly Panzer-Grenadiers of the 'Hermann Göring' Division. The leading man carries a 7.92mm MG42 slung from his shoulder; this fast-firing belt-fed weapon was probably the best light machine of the war, and in slightly modified form is still in use.

The SdKfz 184 'Elefant' (originally called the 'Ferdinand') was a tank-destroyer armed with the 88mm gun housed on a Tiger tank chassis. Only 90 were built; most of these first saw service in Russia with Heavy Tank-Destroyer Bns 653 and 654 in the battle of Kursk in July 1943, where they did not perform well. Hitler, the military amateur, was over-impressed by giganticism. Weighing up to 67 tons, and more than eleven feet wide, the Elefant had a cross-country speed of only 6mph (10km/h); when survivors of Kursk were - inexplicably - transferred to Italy they found the Italian roads almost unusable. This one, with a towing cable attached (left), seems to be one of the many which got bogged down. It has post-Kursk modifications: a hull machine gun for infantry defence and an extra armoured gun mantlet plate. (Bundesarchiv)

general, Von Vietinghoff had commanded XLVI Panzer Corps in the Balkans and in Russia during 1940-42. From June to December 1942 he was acting commander of German Ninth Army before taking over Fifteenth Army in France. With the deterioration of Axis fortunes in the Mediterranean, Von Vietinghoff was moved to Italy to form the new Tenth Army on 22 August 1943. Tenth Army consisted of two corps containing a total of ten divisions in the line and four in reserve: XIV Panzer Corps, commanded by Gen Fridolin von Senger und Etterlin, and LXXVI Panzer Corps, commanded by Gen Traugott Herr.

General Herr's LXXVI Panzer Corps was destined to play a static role on the Adriatic front once British Eighth Army had halted, until it was called north to counter the Allied landings at Anzio. General von Senger's XIV Panzer Corps, on the other hand, controlled the sector of the Gustav Line that lay directly in the path of the advancing US Fifth Army. Fridolin von Senger und Etterlin was a cavalry general with a sound reputation. At the beginning of the war he had been a regimental commander and was instrumental in the capture of Cherbourg during the 1940 French campaign. He had later commanded 17.Panzer-Division in Russia, and liaised with Italian Sixth Army in Sicily. He organised the withdrawal of German troops from Sardinia and Corsica before taking over XIV Panzer Corps in September 1943. In his youth he had been a Rhodes Scholar at Oxford; a dedicated professional soldier, he was not a great admirer of Hitler.

General Eberhard von Mackensen had commanded German Fourteenth Army since arriving from the Russian front in November 1943. He was another cavalry general, from a highly distinguished military family. During the early part of the war he had held a number of staff posts in Vienna and France, and was later given command of III Panzer Corps for the invasion of Russia, where he won praise for his seizure of bridgeheads across the Dnieper and Samro rivers. He demonstrated brilliant tactical skill in the fighting prior to Stalingrad, and was elevated to the command of I Panzer Army during the siege of that city. Later reverses saw him deprived of this command and sent to Italy, where he assumed control of Fourteenth Army in an anti-invasion role guarding the north of the country. His seven divisions were held partly as coastal defence troops and partly as interchangeable reserves for those divisions that were in the front line.

Competent as he was to counter Allied intentions in Italy, Kesselring laboured under a significant handicap of which he was totally unaware: almost all of his messages and reports sent by radio to Supreme Headquarters in Germany

The diminutive figures of three smartly turned-out Gurkhas from 1/5th Gurkha Rifles, 17 Indian Infantry Brigade, 8th Indian Division, one of the formations of British Eighth Army brought across the Appenine Mountains to take part in Operation 'Diadem'. Colonial troops were very much in evidence in Italy with both the British and French armies; those recruited from mountain peoples, like these Nepalese and the Berbers from French North Africa, often outperformed white troops. (Imperial War Museum)

and to his two armies in the field were intercepted by the Allies. These reports were picked up at Bletchley Park in England and deciphered by 'Ultra' teams of code-breakers. Their contents were relayed back to Italy and made available to the very few selected people at Fifteenth Army Group who were cleared to know about this most secret intellignce source. Thus it was that Alexander was able to have a clear sight of Kesselring's order of battle, his deployment of reserves and his aims and objectives just a few hours after he had made them clear to his own men. This gave the Allies a tremendous practical advantage over their enemy.

When the two belligerents faced each other across the Gustav Line in December 1943, Alexander's formations could muster eighteen divisions against Kesselring's twenty-one. Being the attacker, Alexander could choose his point of action, whereas Kesselring could only react to events. Von Mackensen's army was therefore by necessity kept in the north of the country ready to move against any further amphibious landings and to provide mobile reserves when required. This left just German Tenth Army facing the Allied Fifteenth Army Group, fourteen divisions facing eighteen. On paper this was far from the superiority of at least two to one that was theoretically required by an attacking force; but whereas the Allied divisions were more or less up to strength, most German units were well below their theoretical establishment.

The German high command had already started down a pernicious path of forming numbers of new, smaller divisions rather than replacing in full the losses suffered by mauled formations. Losses suffered in North Africa and Russia often dictated that divisional strength was reduced to two regiments rather than three, and six infantry battalions rather than nine. There was also some disparity of effectiveness, the ranks of several German infantry divisions being filled out with less than willing conscripts gathered from many of the Axis-occupied territories. These units often had poor levels of heavy weapons and equipment, while many divisions still relied on horse-drawn transport. Reinforcements were of two types: *Marsch* battalions and *Osttruppen* units. It was normal for the Germans to organise replacements into 'march battalions' which could be sent to fighting areas and either be deployed independently, absorbed by divisons, or broken up for posting to individual units. The 'East battalions' were originally made up of non-Russian 'volunteers' from the occupied regions of the USSR, but later deserters of many origins were accepted.

In contrast to the 'average' units, put into the line to make up the numbers, there were a number of divisions that were certainly equal to, or better than, most that the Allies could put into the field. Prominent among these crack formations were the four Panzer-Grenadier-Divisions - 3., 15., 29. and 90.; the two Fallschirmjäger-Divisions - 1. and 4.; and the so-called 1.Fallschirm-Panzer-Division 'Hermann Göring' (its 'parachute' title awarded in February 1944 was purely nominal; it was in fact a very strong armoured division, though in Luftwaffe uniform).

Many German divisions had already been forced to conduct long fighting retreats on the Eastern Front, in North Africa and Sicily. The 3. and 29.Panzer-Grenadier-Divisions - like the 71., 44. and 94.Infanterie - were in fact new formations replacing the original bearers of those numbers which had been wiped out at Stalingrad a year before; the 90. and much of the 'Hermann Göring' had been all but destroyed in the Tunisian redoubt. In the best of them, however, morale was high and their fighting ability seemed to remain unimpaired. These divisions were well – in some cases, superbly – equipped and led. Their officers and senior NCOs had a wealth of battle experience and great pride in their ability to handle anything that was thrown at them. All of the motorised divisions were highly mobile both in attack and defence, able to rush to any sector that required their special strengths. A mixture of fresh and highly motivated young troops and veterans, trained and led by battle-hardened cadres, made a formidable combination.

★ ★ ★

On paper, then, the two sides were more or less matched for an offensive/defensive campaign, with the superiority in numbers lying with the attacking force. However, each side had one distinct advantage over the other with which to increase its effectiveness. For the Germans this 'force multiplier' was their prepared system of strongly fortified defensive positions; for the Allies it was the strength of their air forces.

The Gustav defensive line and the immensely strong natural fortress of Monte Cassino bolstered the German

Lieutenant General Lucian Truscott (left), Commander US VI Corps, and Lt Gen Ira Eaker, Commander US Mediterranean Air Forces, discuss the Anzio situation within the protected perimeter of VI Corps' HQ in April 1944. The large walls of sandbags and barrels remind us that the whole Anzio beachhead was vulnerable to German artillery fire. (US National Archives)

Tenth Army with a determination that was hard to break down. Sheltered by their concrete bunkers on high ground, behind barbed wire and thick minefields, individual soldiers of even 'average' ability gained a moral strength that was difficult to destroy, especially when they were backed by elite troops stationed in the rear ready to counter-attack. The drawbacks of a 'defence mentality', often the result of manning static lines, can be avoided when the defence proves to be effective against attack. Each time the enemy is repulsed the defenders' confidence grows further towards a conviction of invincibility - and so does their bloody-minded determination not to give in, as their psychological investment increases. This was amply demonstrated at Cassino, where each failed Allied attack seemed to engender an even greater stubbornness among the German troops. The moral advantage normally enjoyed by the attacker was negated at Cassino by a defence that was both supremely effective and resolutely committed.

Modern warfare of the kind seen in 1944 relied heavily upon air support both as a weapon in offence and a supporting arm in defence. In this the Allies in Italy had a great advantage over their German opponents. The Luftwaffe of 1943/44 was stretched beyond its effective limit through waging war on so many fronts, against enemies who were now equally proficient in the application of airpower. The German air force was still well-led, could field many skilled aircrew, was served by an efficient manufacturing industry supplying it with effective aircraft, and had not yet lost the output of the Balkan oilfields. It had already lost many experienced flyers over Russia, the Mediterranean and the Channel, but the strain of defending the Reich against the Allied daytime bombing offensive had not yet pushed this human cost to the chronic levels it would reach later in 1944. The Luftwaffe's tactics were equal to those of the Allies. However, it was too small and too dispersed to field the numbers of aircraft required to fight an air war on three fronts.

Field Marshal Wolfram von Richthofen, Commander of Air Fleet 2, controlled the German air force in Italy. As the great 'Stuka general' of the Russian front his background lay in offensive ground-attack operations. Allied air superiority led Von Richthofen to adopt a policy of trying to keep the bulk of his offensive strength out of reach of Allied counter-strikes. After the collapse in Sicily he withdrew all his ground and technical installations to northern Italy and used airfields in the south as 'advance landing grounds'. His tactics did not lack an aggressive spirit, as was demonstrated by the lightning hit-and-run raids over the Salerno beaches, but he could not employ the mass bomber attacks and fighter patrols that the Allies were able to mount. At the end of January 1944, about the time of the Anzio landings, the Luftwaffe's strength in Italy was 474 aircraft, of which only 224 were serviceable. In contrast, the Allied air forces had 2,700 aircraft available to support the landings - twelve times the number the Germans could get into the air.

General Ira Eaker was Commander-in-Chief Mediterranean Air Forces, with both strategic and tactical air forces under his control. The strategic bombers stationed in Italy were part of the Allied Combined Bomber Offensive and were based on airfields within striking range of southern Germany and other Axis-held countries. They were part of the greater Allied strategic bombing campaign, and their targets and employment were directed from England. The air support provided to Fifteenth Army Group in Italy was delivered by the two tactical air forces based in the Mediterranean. Supporting US Fifth Army was US XII Tactical Air Force, under the command of Gen John K. Cannon, while British Eighth Army could call on the veteran Desert Air Force under the command of Air Vice Marshal Harry Broadhurst. Each of these air commands had a formidable array of aircraft at its disposal, from reconnaissance types to fighter-bombers. However, this superiority sometimes counted for little during the coming campaign, since Allied aircraft were often grounded for days on end by the atrocious winter weather.

On balance, then, Alexander had greater power at his disposal than did Kesselring. Material superiority should have dictated that the continuation of the war in Italy would end in a victory for the Allies - as indeed it did. But it was not the quick victory that many had imagined. When the two sides lined up facing each other along the Gustav Line at the end of December 1943 after four months of bloody fighting, it would still take another sixteen months of even worse carnage before the Germans could be eliminated from the long Italian peninsula.

CHAPTER TWO

The First Battle: 12 January– 8 February 1944

By the middle of November 1943 it was becoming increasingly clear that the approaching winter and the strength of resistance being offered by the Germans foreshadowed very little progress being made without a protracted and costly effort. The enemy was demonstrating how easy it was to defend the mountainous terrain of southern Italy and how difficult it would be for the Allies to achieve an early victory. This was bad news to the American high command, who were adamant that the operations in the Italian theatre should not continue at the expense of either the North-West Europe invasion (Operation 'Overlord') or the proposed landings in southern France (Operation 'Anvil').

The Italian campaign had been authorised on the understanding that its main objective was to draw into battle as many German divisions as possible to divert them from countering the planned cross-Channel invasion. With the advance reduced to a crawl, the enemy only had to commit the minimum of divisions necessary to hold his defensive lines in the south, leaving many other reserve divisions available to be sent anywhere in Europe that they might be required. It was very important that the intensity of the war in Italy be stepped up in order to force Kesselring to commit more of his units in the south. Yet this strategy would inevitably place stronger resistance in front of Alexander's armies and make their task more difficult. Alexander was in an unenviable position: first, he had to draw more Germans on to him, and second, he had to make sufficient progress in Italy to silence his detractors. In short, he had to get Kesselring to commit more troops against him and then destroy them.

Very few new divisions were earmarked to join Fifteenth Army Group in Italy; indeed, some already in action with Fifth Army would be removed in 1944 to take part in the 'Anvil' invasion. Alexander could see that unless

he made considerable progress, and quickly, the war in Italy would be reduced to a stalemate through lack of strength. Time appeared to be against him as the new year opened, for the moment would soon arrive when he had to release units to other armies for other campaigns. If he was to gain the upper hand in Italy he had to continue his campaigning throughout the cruel winter months and win a victory of substantial proportions. This was easier to see than to accomplish, for immediately in front of him was a German defensive line of greater strength than he had ever met in his whole career. Some reappraisal of strategy was called for.

At the fourth Allied conference which took place in Cairo and Teheran in November/December 1943, the question of what to do about the slow progress being achieved in Italy was discussed. Churchill implied that the straitjacket placed on Alexander by 'Overlord' denied him enough men to finish the job quickly. The Prime Minister still saw the early capture of Rome and an advance into southern Austria or France as a distinct possibility, provided Alexander was given the forces to carry it out. The Americans were unconvinced and were adamant that 'Overlord' had to remain the absolute priority, followed by 'Anvil'. They accepted that the Italian campaign could continue with the immediate aim of capturing Rome, but only as far as the release of forces to 'Anvil' would allow. However, after painstaking negotiations Churchill did secure agreement that the landing craft at present in the Mediterranean could remain there and be made available for use until mid-January, when they must be sent back to

One of the limiting factors in planning the Anzio landings was the availability of landing craft. The strength of the invasion force was curtailed by the strict timetable for their use, and the need for them to be returned to England in good time for the 'Overlord' operation. Here American tanks disembark from Landing Ship Tank (LST) 77 on 27 April, straight into Anzio town. The Shermans are from 13 Tank Bn, part of US 1st Armored Division. (US National Archives)

Panoramic view across the Rapido valley from the San Michele area, looking towards Monte Cassino in the centre of the picture. Smoke generators smother the town of Cassino, but the monastery is visible on the skyline just right of centre. The isolated feature on the left is Monte Trocchio, with the Liri valley behind. In the extreme left background of Monte Maio, dominating the southern side of the Liri valley. (Imperial War Museum)

England to prepare for the cross-Channel invasion.

With these landing craft placed at his disposal Alexander could now contemplate a landing south of Rome to outflank the Gustav Line and revitalise the whole campaign. An amphibious landing in the rear of Tenth Army could loosen Von Vietinghoff's grip on southern Italy; if it were threatening enough it might lead to a German withdrawal north of Rome. Alexander's planning team came up with a plan for Fifth Army to mount an amphibious landing at the small town of Anzio on the west coast just south of Rome. US VI Corps would hit the beaches with a strength of two infantry divisions, supported by one armoured brigade and the Special Service Force. The corps would then advance inland and threaten the rear communications of German Tenth Army. Just prior to this landing, the remainder of US Fifth Army would attack the Gustav Line in force in an attempt to draw off German reserves that might threaten the Anzio beachhead. It was hoped that the landings would cause Von Vietinghoff to pull back his army to a new line rather than have an American corps loose in his rear. Clark would then advance through the Liri valley, join up with US VI Corps from Anzio, and race for the capital with armoured forces. The main drawback to the plan was the number of landing craft available and the restricted time placed on their use. The whole operation had to be organised and implemented by early January so that the ships could be returned to England. By the middle of December it was decided that the operation was impossible within the limits placed upon it, and the plan was dropped.

Churchill was unhappy with the abandonment of what had become his pet scheme, and lobbied and coerced anyone who would listen in order to get his own way. He finally appealed to Roosevelt, and eloquently persuaded the President to consider the benefits of an amphibious landing close to Rome. Roosevelt agreed with the Prime Minister's arguments, and ordered his staff to extend the time limit for use of the landing craft until February. With this easing of the deadline the Anzio landings once again became a reality, and they were scheduled to take place on 22 January 1944.

General Mark Clark now contemplated his assault on Kesselring's well-prepared Gustav Line. He had three corps at his disposal: one British, one American and one French. He planned to put all of them to work to try to draw the enemy on to him and away from the proposed Anzio landings. Three separate attacks would go in on different parts of the line at different intervals, each of them inviting the Germans to switch troops and bring up reserves to block any penetrations.

Kicking off the offensive would be the French. General Alphonse Juin was to send his French Expeditionary Corps (CEF) on to the high ground to the north and north-west of Cassino, with Gen Dody's 2nd Moroccan Division and Gen Joseph de Monsabert's 3rd Algerian Division both attacking into the mountains towards Atina. Their aim was to force a way into the Gustav Line with a view to breaking through into the Liri valley from the right, swinging wide of the defences around Cassino.

The US II Corps, commanded by Maj Gen Geoffrey Keyes, was given the major task of US Fifth Army. First, he was to take the isolated peak of Monte Trocchio and close on the River Rapido; then he was to make an assault crossing of the river and break into the Liri valley. Major General Fred Walker's 36th Division was to secure a bridgehead across the Rapido, thus allowing an armoured thrust by a combat command of US 1st Armored Division to drive into the Liri valley. Major General Charles Ryder's 34th Division could then either attack the town of Cassino directly from the east and tie down the German defenders, or cross the river and attack Cassino from the south. If the attacks produced a solid break through the Gustav Line, 34th Division would then be available to support the 1st Armored Division's tanks and half-track infantry in their drive up the valley towards VI Corps at Anzio.

A goumier from Gen Juin's French Expeditionary Corps (CEF) and his steed. These Moroccan irregulars, initially equipped with obsolete Great War weapons, were essentially weak light infantry units, lacking the support weapons and the training given to the Tirailleur *regiments. They were, however, extremely hardy, familiar since birth with mountain terrain, and the products of an age-old culture of the blood feud; in Italy they became a byword for aggression - not to say barbarism. Each* Goum *was equivalent to a company; three were assembled with a small heaqdquarters and support element into a battalion termed a* Tabor, *and three Tabors into a regiment or Groupement de Tabors Marocains (GTM). The 4e GTM were the first unit of the CEF to reach the Italian front lines in December 1943. Most Tabors had a mounted platoon attached to the HQ company; the use of mounted patrols and pack mules by the CEF improved their ability to move easily across hostile terrain, and gave Juin's colonial troops an advantage over allies more dependent on motor transport and thus on metalled roads. (Imperial War Museum)*

General Clark's third attack would be undertaken by Lt Gen Sir Richard McCreery. He was to take his British X Corps across the River Garigliano, starting immediately the American II Corps had taken Monte Trocchio and had closed up to the Rapido. X Corps intended to make two separate crossings: the first near the mouth of the river, the second near the village of San Ambroglio close to the Liri valley. The first of these crossings was to be made by a powerful force of two divisions, with British 5th Division crossing opposite Minturno and 56th Division attacking three miles upstream on its right. Two days later, X Corps was to make another assault over the Garigliano when 46th Division crossed nine miles further up river; their goal was to gain possession of the high ground looking northwards down into the Liri valley, and to help give flank protection to US II Corps.

General Alphonse Juin, Commander French Expeditionary Corps, was pleased with the start his men had made since arriving in Italy. Their introduction to the war had begun when 2nd Moroccan Division had been assigned to US VI Corps and given a limited objective operation in the mountains to the north of Cassino. In December two regiments of the division attacked and secured Monte Pantano, a mountain that had defied the whole weight of US 34th Division. The strength and ferocity of the French attack caused consternation in the German line, where the situation was only restored by replacing the 305.Infanterie-Division with the Mountain Riflemen of Gen Ringel's specialist 5.Gebirgs-Division.

Few of the senior Allied commanders had had great hopes of the French Expeditionary Corps. It was very largely recruited from colonial troops, which they regarded as ill-disciplined and lacking in the training and experience necessary to fight effectively in a mechanised war. Allied planners envisaged that their employment in Italy would be as useful reserves to hold the line and release exhausted troops for rest, or to garrison static areas. They were also suspicious of allowing the French to fight as a unified force, in case this won them too much say in the conduct of the campaign. The suspicion with which the French were regarded by the 'Anglo-Saxons' was natural, given the memory of French collapse in 1940 and the all too obvious disunity among the new French forces then in formation.

The CEF - like the other French formations still being formed, equipped, and trained with Allied assistance during 1943 - was drawn in great part from the old Armée d'Afrique. The garrison of French North Africa had only abandoned its allegiance to the Vichy government after the Allied landings in Morocco and Algeria in November 1942 (Operation 'Torch'), and then only after episodes of bitter local resistance and a complex and ugly struggle between rival factions. Politically, the French forces included several different cliques each with their own agenda; and there was real ill will between the Gaullists, who had rallied to the Free French cause in Britain in 1940, and the more recent arrivals in the Allied camp. Their grudging co-operation, which was marred at times by vindictive acts of administrative sabotage, cost them the trust of the British and Americans - whose suspicions about French motives were reciprocated in full measure.

General Juin was perfectly aware of Allied sensitivities, but had no intention of over-reacting to perceived slights; he was content to bide his time until the CEF's performance in combat could speak for itself. The short, dark, burly Juin had passed out first in his class at St Cyr (Charles de Gaulle had been one of his classmates). In June 1940 he had distinguished himself in command of the 15th Motorised Infantry Division in the Lille pocket, where he passed into German captivity. In June 1941 Marshal Petain had secured his release; he was offered the Vichy Ministry of War, but preferred to serve under Gen Weygand in North Africa, commanding the French troops in Morocco. He succeeded Weygand as commander of land forces in French North Africa that November; and two years later was instrumental in throwing some of his units into battle alongside the Allies in Tunisia after the 'Torch' landings. Their brief but bloody involvement, armed with obsolete weapons and short of every kind of matériel, had something of a penitential flavour.

Juin had dropped a rank to take the CEF to Italy, and he had confidence in its potential. His divisions comprised a mix of European and native colonial troops who came mainly from Morocco, Algeria and Tunisia. A good proportion of them were Berber tribesmen from the barren highlands of the Atlas and Kabylia - tough mountaineers, self-sufficient and aggressive, often difficult to control but splendid fighters if well led. Most of the officers and NCOs

The two divisions of Juin's CEF were organised according to the US 'triangular' system, with three infantry regiments of Tirailleurs *(North African Rifles) each of three battalions, plus artillery, armoured recce and armoured tank-destroyer battalions and supporting divisional troops. They could thus be divided into three Combat Commands for independent operations. The theoretical divisional establishment was 16,206 all ranks, of which the non-European element of e.g. the 3rd Algerian Infantry Division was only 8,907 men. Uniforms and personal equipment were entirely US-supplied apart from the reliable French FM24/29 light machine gun, which was superior to the American BAR, and French headgear, retained when available for reasons of morale and national esprit. The Adrian helmet, recalling the glory days of the Great War* poilus, *was the most common type, and junior leaders tried to acquire them even in* Goums *issued American M1917A1 helmets. (Imperial War Museum)*

were European; but Juin's corps differed from the usual colonial model in that all units also contained a significant proportion of European rankers, raised by a general mobilisation in North Africa – between 30 and 50 per cent in most units. Juin understood the locally recruited European settlers, who were mostly of Spanish, Italian and Alsatian stock – he was himself an Algerian '*pied noir*' by birth and upbringing. In addition his command included some 13,000 Corsicans, and 20,000 men who had escaped from occupied France. Whatever the bitter divisions in the professional French officer class, many of those who now served under Juin were genuinely eager to wipe out the shame of 1940 and of the passive years under Vichy.

The criticism aimed at the CEF's lack of mechanisation and of familiarity with modern methods rebounded on the accusers when his men were sent up into the mountains around Cassino. They were not totally dependent upon metalled roads in the way the British and Americans were. Juin had equipped his units with as many pack mules as possible, even at the cost of stripping the casualty evacuation sections, in order to free them from the conventional dependence on motor transport. (It was reckoned that to keep a battalion properly supplied in the fighting line took 500 mule loads a day, though this number of animals were seldom available). Juin had seen in the early days of the campaign how whole armoured divisions were immobilised, incapable of deploying off the roads in terrain that was completely hostile to their mobility. He believed that the key to success in Italy was to take on the Germans in the mountains and outflank defensive lines rather than relying on brute force and frontal attacks. When Clark ordered Juin's corps to drive into the mountains and try to outflank Cassino, the objectives were in keeping with the Frenchman's own ideas on breaking through the Gustav Line. But Juin doubted that he had a strong enough punch to achieve the breakthrough, and thought it a great mistake that sufficient force was not given to him in order to carry out the plan.

Facing the French was the German 5.Gebirgs-Division commanded by Gen Julius Ringel. This specialist mountain division had only just arrived after a long spell on the Eastern Front, and was in the process of coming into the line when the attack took place; its Mountain Rifles battalions were sent into action piecemeal as and when they arrived. General Julius 'Papa' Ringel – an unmistakable figure, in that he was one of very few German generals to wear a beard – had commanded 5.Gebirgs-Division since its formation in 1940; its personnel were mainly Bavarians, with some later Austrian additions. It first saw action in the Greek mountains in spring 1941; and soon afterwards won great respect during the hard fighting on Crete, where the mountain troopers supported the badly mauled Luftwaffe paratroopers at Maleme. The division then moved to Norway, and finally to Russia early in 1942, taking part in the siege of Leningrad. It is believed that Ringel was on good terms with Hitler and used his influence to have his division transferred to Italy. Although they left the sub-zero temperatures of a Russian winter for the supposedly more temperate climate of Italy, the change was not necessarily for the better: Ringel's troops found that the discomfort of alternating snow, sleet, rain, frost and storm was almost unbearable.

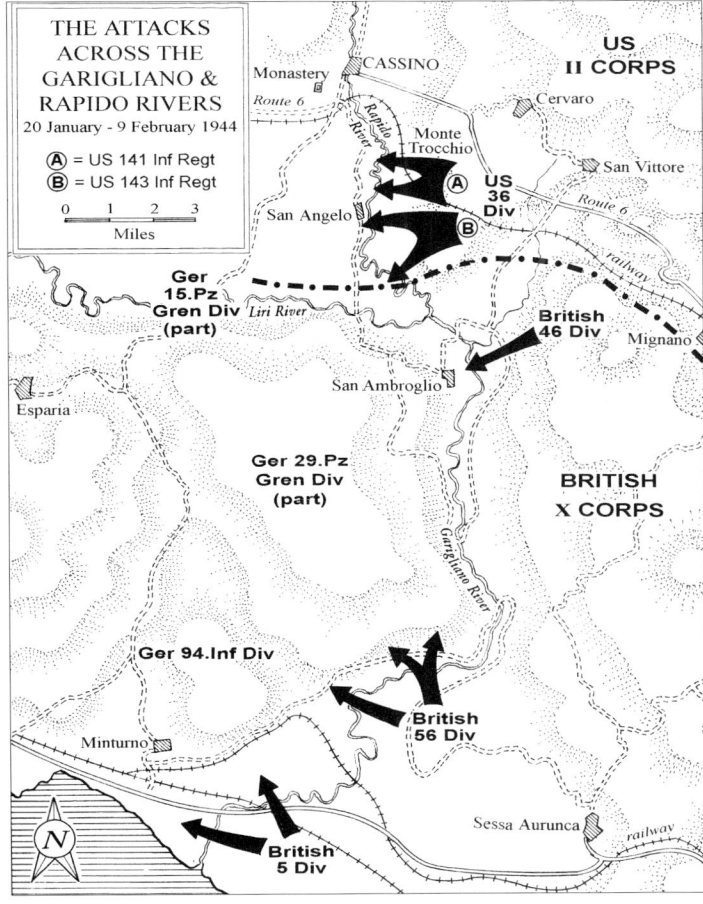

General Julius 'Papa' Ringel, commander of 5.Gebirgs-Division, decorating some of his mountain troopers with the Iron Cross 2nd Class in June 1941 in recognition of their performance in Crete (note the Edelweiss cap and sleeve badges). The division, recently arrived from Russia, held the northern part of the Cassino line against Juin's French Expeditionary Corps in late January 1944. They were shaken both by the miserable weather conditions and by the ferocity of the North Africans' attacks. (Bundesarchiv)

GIs of the 142nd Infantry Regiment, part of US 36th Division, moving forward on 21 January prior to the division's attempt to cross the River Rapido. The 142nd Infantry did not take part in the river crossings but was kept in reserve to exploit the expected lodgement over the river - which never happened. Most of the men in this photo wear the cold weather jacket and overtrousers normally associated with US Army tank crews. They are carrying improvised bedrolls rather than the lower component of the infamously inconvenient 'long pack'. (Imperial War Museum)

The French attacks

Juin's North Africans got General Clark's offensive off to an encouraging start. During the night of 11/12 January, Dody's 2nd Moroccan Division moved off without any artillery preparation and achieved immediate surprise. The Berber riflemen advanced quickly over the rough, snow-covered ground and were soon among the first of the German defences, doing great damage before the enemy had time to react. All three regiments - 4e, 5e and 8e Régiments de Tirailleurs Marocains - were in the line attacking abreast, each with a single battalion in reserve. The gains made in the first two days were held despite repeated counter-attacks by Panzer-Grenadier Regiment 115, who were sent in to support the shaken 5.Gebirgs-Division. However, as the Moroccans pressed closer to the main German defensive line and the regiments became more strung out, some of the impetus went out of their attack. Casualties mounted rapidly as battalions were torn apart by ferocious artillery and mortar fire. In the steep, rocky terrain incoming shells burst with devastating effect, showering exposed infantry with razor-sharp splinters of rock. One of the Moroccan battalions, II/8e RTM, lost three-quarters of its officers and its companies were reduced to about 40 men each.

On their left, Gen de Monsabert's untried 3rd Algerian Division struggled forward against considerable opposition in an attempt to seize the high ground overlooking the route to San Elia. Its first main objective, the important heights of Monna Casale, were reached and taken by the 7e Tirailleurs Algériens (7e RTA), but the position was vigorously counter-attacked and retaken almost immediately. During the day the summit changed hands four times in savage close-quarter battles with bayonets and grenades. The defenders from Gebirgsjäger - Regiment 85 called upon all their skill and experience, hard-earned in the Balkans and Russia, to keep the Algerians off the mountain; but the Kabylie infantry continued to attack with a fervour bordering on madness.

The French officers led by example, inspiring their men to go forward regardless; the Tirailleurs responded, following their leaders blindly, seeking out more of the enemy to kill. When officers fell, as most of them did, then the NCOs continued to lead attacks. Gradually the Bavarians pulled back, giving up ground reluctantly. Over the next four days the French applied constant pressure, following hard on the enemy's heels as they relinquished each peak, gully and ridge. This was fighting North African-style, with small units constantly infiltrating, exploiting forward, coming up in support on each others' flanks without waiting for orders. All along the CEF's front the enemy units shuddered, and Juin never allowed them time to re-establish themselves.

It was too much for the Germans; shocked into disarray, they fell back off the mountains and retreated across the upper reaches of the River Rapido into the main defences of the Gustav Line. All hope of making an intermediate stand on the river was abandoned. The 5.Gebirgs-Division quickly established itself in the prepared positions and waited for the French to renew their attack; but the fighting of the previous few days had taken a harsh toll of Juin's forces. Ideally, he would have liked to mount a major assault on the Gustav Line before the enemy had time to consolidate, but his depleted divisions needed time to regroup. Juin was convinced that one fresh division thrown into the attack at this point would have ensured a breakthrough, allowing a broad flanking movement above Monte Cairo and Cassino into the Liri valley. But Gen Clark was not convinced, and was reluctant to redeploy any divisions from Fifth Army over to the French sector of the line.

Four days later, on 21 January, Juin tried again. His two divisions continued to press right up to the Gustav defences but faltered at the final hurdle. The German defenders, shut tightly in their concrete pillboxes and bunkers, poured small arms and mortar fire on every forward movement. As the French troops closed on the enemy line their artillery support dwindled - the two sides were so close together that there was a danger of bracketing friendly troops with shells. Free of this inhibition, the Germans could use their artillery to great effect, bombarding the known and previously 'zeroed in' approaches to their fixed defences. Fighting over

The First Battle: 12 January-8 February 1944

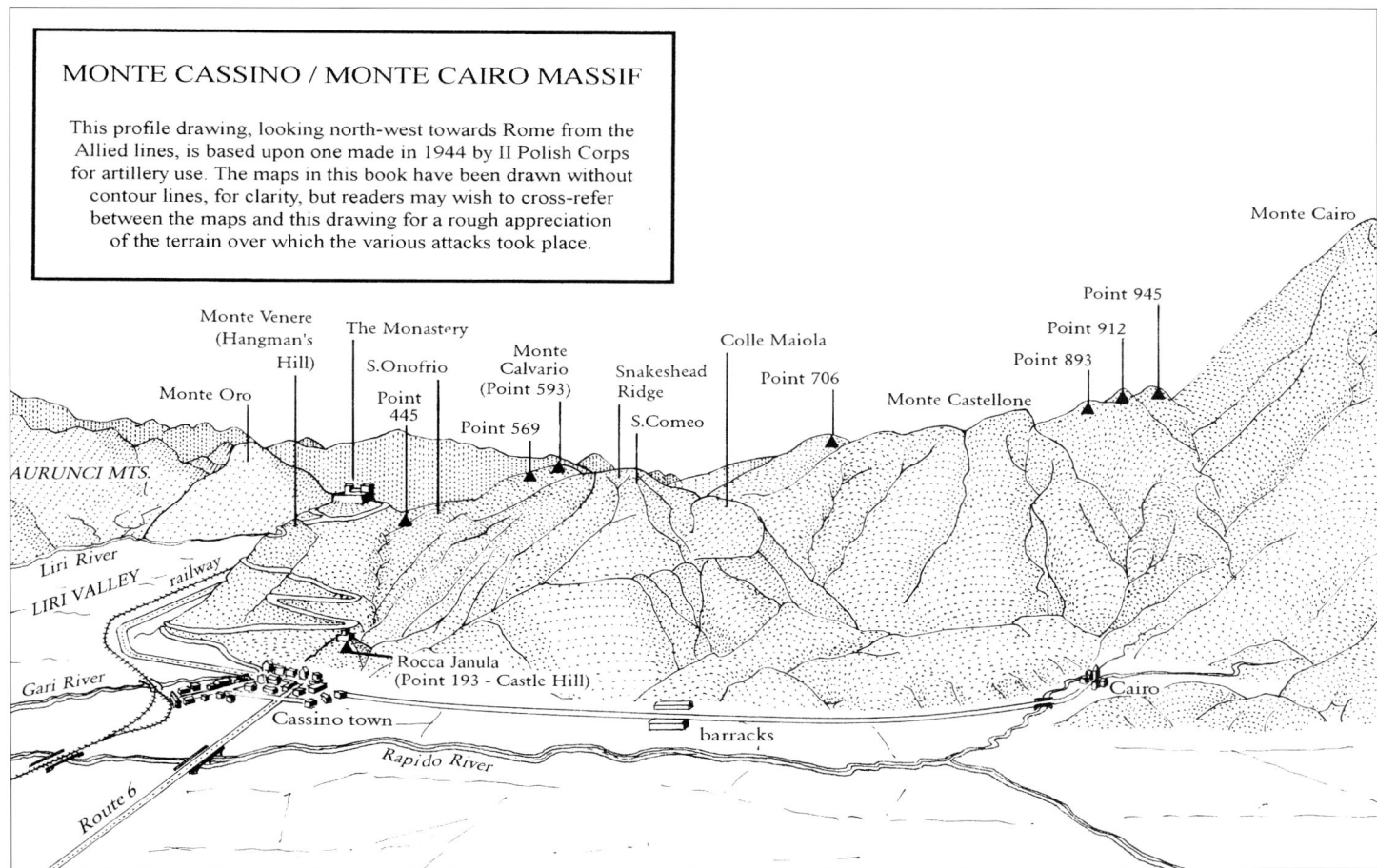

MONTE CASSINO / MONTE CAIRO MASSIF

This profile drawing, looking north-west towards Rome from the Allied lines, is based upon one made in 1944 by II Polish Corps for artillery use. The maps in this book have been drawn without contour lines, for clarity, but readers may wish to cross-refer between the maps and this drawing for a rough appreciation of the terrain over which the various attacks took place.

terrain that often reached heights of over 5,000 feet, in snow, sleet and bitter winds, mere survival became a test of endurance. The two sides became locked in short-range local infantry battles with rifles, sub-machine guns and grenades. Movement gradually became impossible under the constant lash of machine gun fire from prepared emplacements. Over the next few days Juin's attack gradually lost its impetus and finally petered out, stalled by a resolute defensive line and drained by exhaustion. By 25 January the right hand element of Clark's triple offensive had shot its bolt.

The French attack had originally given the commander of XIV Panzer Corps some concern. General von Senger und Etterlin could see the dangers inherent in the French assault when he personally visited the front and watched the strength and direction of Juin's forces. Once he had ascertained the axis of the attacks he brought forward and concentrated a large proportion of his artillery onto this sector in order to frustrate and break up the CEF's advance. It was a textbook use of artillery, delivering the right amount of punch just where it was needed.

Meanwhile, down on the flat land alongside Route 6, Gen Keyes's US II Corps was making its assault on the isolated knoll of Monte Trocchio, the last German stronghold before the Rapido. On 16 January one regiment each from the US 34th and 36th Divisions moved against the hill. Aerial photos had shown many prepared emplacements, weapons pits, wire entanglements and minefields; no one underestimated the effort that would be required to shift the enemy from his well-entrenched positions. In the event, when the Americans pressed home their attack they found that the German defenders had gone. Three hours after the assault began Monte Trocchio was in Allied hands and the engineers were moving about clearing enemy mines and boobytraps from the summit of the hill. By nightfall all German forces had withdrawn back across the River Rapido.

General von Vietinghoff had given up Monte Trocchio because he decided that it was too isolated to defend in strength. He therefore shortened his line, regrouping the divisions of Von Senger's XIV Panzer Corps behind the river line in the already-prepared fortifications. With control of the heights on either side of the Liri valley - Cassino on his left and Monte Maio on his right - he could effectively bar the way through the centre of the Gustav Line, and create a pool of locally available reserves. With this plan in mind, Tenth Army conducted a timed and controlled withdrawal into the defensive positions along the west bank of the Rapido.

The British on the Garigliano

On 17 January it was time for British X Corps to join in Clark's offensive. Since December Gen McCreery's corps had been engaged in only minor operations and had been reinforced by a new formation, 5th Division, brought over from British Eighth Army's Adriatic front by 6 January. This pre-war Regular division, commanded by Maj Gen G.C.Bucknall, was the most travelled in the whole British Army, having seen service in both Norway and France in 1940, in Madagascar, India, Iraq, Persia, Syria and Egypt in 1942-1943, in Sicily and finally Italy. (After service in Italy it was still on the move, via Egypt and Palestine to join

General Oliver Leese, Commander British Eighth Army (left), with Gen Jacob Devers, Deputy Supreme Commander Mediterranean (centre), and Lt Gen Richard McCreery, Commander British X Corps. (Imperial War Museum)

Montgomery's British Twenty-First Army Group in North-West Europe for the last months of the war.)

McCreery's other two formations were the British 46th and 56th Divisions. Major General J.Hawksworth had taken over command of the 46th just before the landings at Salerno. In 1940 the division had been part of the British Expeditionary Force in France and was severely handled during the German invasion of Belgium. Two brigades were pulled out through Dunkirk, while the scattered troops of the third trekked westwards across France to find their escape to England via Cherbourg, St Malo and St Nazaire. The division, whose shoulder patch was a Sherwood Forest oak tree, was rebuilt and re-equipped; it retained two brigades from Northern and Midland regiments, but now included a brigade formed from three battalions of the Hampshire Regiment. It had joined British First Army in the Tunisian campaign; after the German collapse in Africa the 46th was prepared for the Italian campaign and joined British X Corps as part of US Fifth Army for the Salerno operation.

British X Corps' third formation, 56th Division, was commanded by Maj Gen Gerald Templer. Called the 'London Division', it had as its sign Dick Wittington's lucky black cat. As a Territorial division it had formed part of Home Forces until mid-1942 when it was posted to the Middle East. The division had seen action in Tunisia and later landed with US Fifth Army at Salerno. Also available to McCreery to exploit any breakthrough were two independent brigades: the elite infantry of 201 Guards Brigade, and the Sherman tanks of 23 Armoured Brigade, veterans of battlefields from El Alamein to Sicily.

Facing X Corps across the Garigliano was the German 94.Infanterie-Division which had recently arrived in the area, joining the defences of the Bernhadt/Winter Line in November 1943. Originally mobilised in September 1939, the 94. had taken part in the French campaign of May 1940 and the invasion of the USSR in June 1941, fighting in the Ukraine. In November 1942 it was surrounded at Stalingrad and captured, but not before the divisional headquarters had escaped. The division was reformed in France in 1943 under its old staff and was sent to Italy to take up garrison and coast defence duties after the collapse of the Mussolini regime. Although not fully trained or equipped - its transport was mainly horse-drawn - it was up to strength and fresh, and Kesselring found it necessary to send the division into the line to face the Allied drive. The division was commanded by Gen Bernard Steinmetz, considered by his corps commander Von Senger to be 'a competent officer, thoroughly grounded in the General Staff, who saw things as they really were.'

Steinmetz's division held a long sector of the Garigliano stretching from the sea to the Liri valley, where 15.Panzer-Grenadier-Division took over the line. It also had responsibility for part of the coast defences along the Tyrrhenian shore. General von Senger was under no illusions as to the vulnerability of this section of his corps' defensive line. He knew that 94.Infanterie-Division lacked combat experience, but trusted the commander to make good any shortcomings. He also knew that the line of the Garigliano was overlooked by high mountains; it was difficult terrain to cover, but he had massed artillery on call to contain any breakthrough. He also decided to place the 2nd Battalion of the 'Hermann Göring' Division's tank regiment behind the line to act as a local reserve.

On the evening of 17 January British X Corps attacked. All of its guns opened up with concentrated fire on the front opposite 56th Division. British artillery of three divisions supported by corps and army guns laid a barrage to cover the advancing brigades and provide interdictory fire on known enemy targets. The 'London Division' swept across the river with two brigades, losing many boats and men to German mortar fire on the way. Engineers followed closely behind to build the necessary bridges and ferries under close observation by the enemy. Some of the assaulting battalions made good headway, while others, especially 9th Royal Fusiliers, had a difficult time. The battalion ran into stiff opposition near the ruined railway bridge and lost its colonel. Casualties during the whole assault were significant, but not severe. By the morning the greater part of two brigades were over the river, fanning out and expanding the bridgehead inland. By noon on 18 January a raft was ferrying tanks into the lodgement.

In contrast to 56th Division's noisy start, 5th Division had slipped into the right hand sector of the Garigliano positions two days before unknown to the Germans, and intended to make a silent crossing, with 13 and 17 Brigades leading its assault. The 'silent' attack by 13 Brigade met with mixed success. The 2nd Wiltshires passed across with little opposition and took their objectives by early morning; but a second battalion, 2nd Royal Iniskilling Fusiliers, were halted on their section of the river by the loss of a number of their assault boats. The 'Skins' withdrew down river to cross at the site used by the Wiltshires, and then marched upstream again on the far bank to take their objective.

The crossing by 17 Brigade was less successful. The plan had been to land 2nd Royal Scots Fusiliers from the sea near the mouth of the Garigliano to outflank the German defenders on the river. Unfortunately, while some troops made it to the correct landing place they found themselves boxed in by a considerable minefield. To make matters worse, the DUKWs (amphibious American $2\frac{1}{2}$-ton trucks) carrying the other infantry and engineers mistook their landfall and beached on the wrong side of the estuary. The

The First Battle: 12 January-8 February 1944

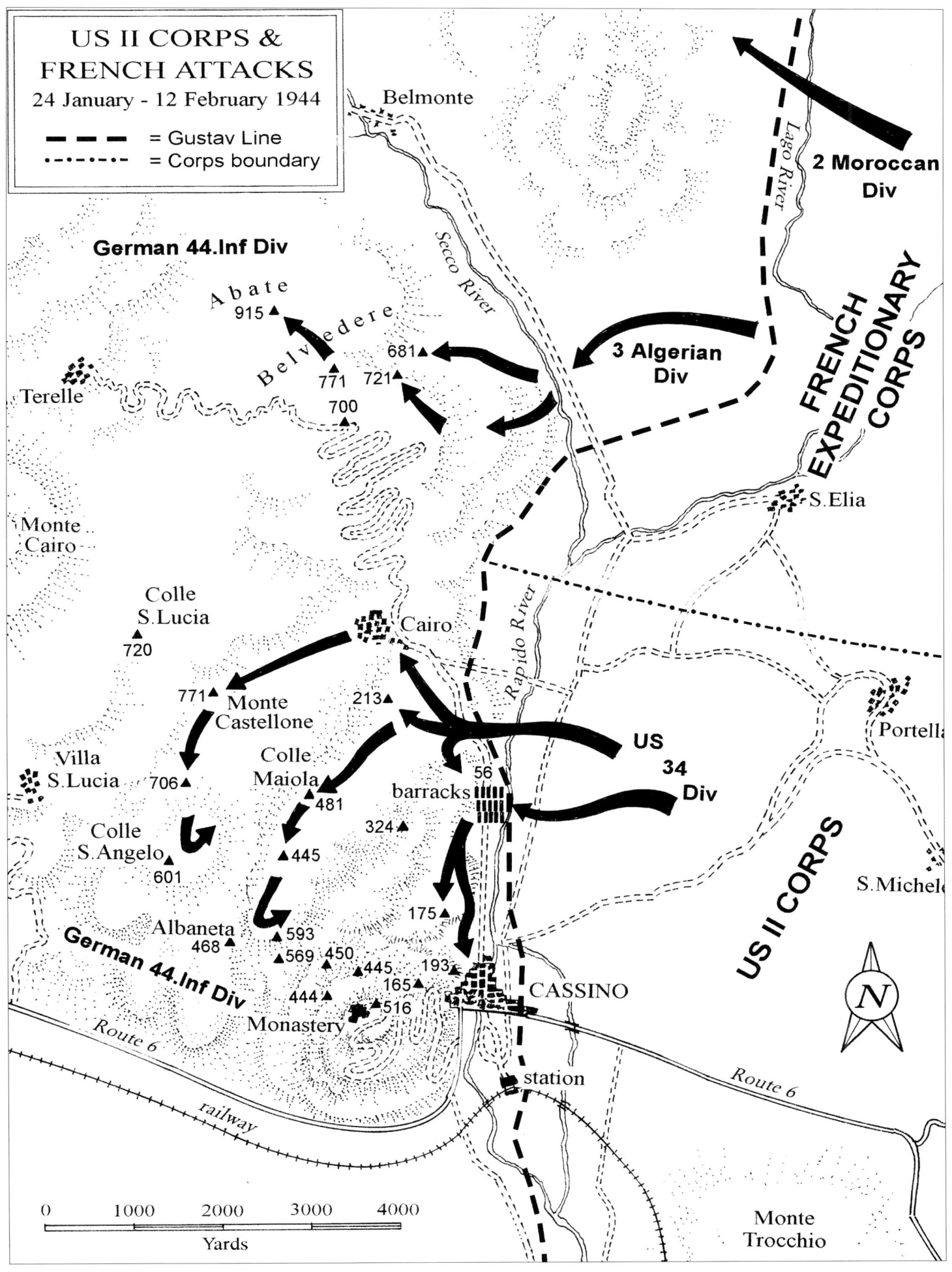

An American-made 155mm 'Long Tom' with 14 Battery, British 54th Heavy Regiment RA, firing in support of British troops. (Imperial War Museum)

landing craft carrying the anti-tank guns could not find any landing marks at all and returned their loads to base. Unable to clear the minefield without the sappers, the Royal Scots Fusiliers were stranded on the enemy beach. The other two battalions of 17 Brigade made successful crossings of the river, but were also confronted with extensive minefields, some extending over a mile in depth. Swift progress out of the bridgehead was impossible, but by the middle of the next morning the assaulting battalions had formed up and began to slowly extricate themselves from the minefields and advance inland.

At around 1000 hours on 18 January, 5th Division's bridgehead was counter-attacked by tanks of the 'Hermann Göring' Panzer Regiment which approached along Route 7. This armoured response to the lodgement was beaten off by the concentrated fire of five regiments of field artillery. Other counter-attacks then developed all along X Corps front, and 94.Division began laying defensive artillery fire down against any movement inland. Every British attack was met with a German counter-attack. Gains were made by McCreery's corps, but only after extremely stiff fighting. By the end of the second day, however, X Corps had successfully carved out a significant bridgehead over the Garigliano, and showed every intention of moving through the foothills bordering the river up into the mountains that led to the Liri valley. The main effort would be made by troops passing along 56th Division's axis.

On the night of 19/20 January the third of X Corps' divisions made its attack across the river. Nine miles upstream from 56th Division's crossing place, 46th Division attempted to get over the Garigliano in darkness. Leading the division was 128 Brigade - the Hampshire Brigade, consisting of 1/4th, 2nd and 5th Bns of the Hampshire Regiment. The crossing was designed to protect the left flank of US II Corps when it attempted its own crossing of the Rapido five miles to the north on 20 January.

Opposite 46th Division the line was held by Panzer-Grenadier Regiment 129, part of 15.Panzer-Grenadier-Division. The main defence line was back from the river, along the low hills that bordered the Garigliano. All of the crossing places were overlooked and vulnerable, so the assault was planned to go in under cover of darkness. The river at this point was narrow and fast-flowing. Just before the attack, perhaps in response to X Corps' earlier crossings, the Germans opened sluice gates on the River Liri at San Giovanni; the Garigliano downstream became a raging torrent, with a swirling current that swept everything before it. This was the downfall of the Hampshire Brigade, for although it achieved surprise with its approach march to the river every attempt to get troops across came to nothing.

The 2nd Hampshires on the left managed to get a cable across and two boats made it to the far shore before the rope snapped, but little else followed. The right hand attempt fared a little better when boats were launched way upstream and used the river's momentum to carry the craft to the far bank. Almost a whole company got across in this way; the boats failed to return safely to the near shore, however, being smashed on landing or swept violently away downstream. The efforts of 1/4th Hampshires met with the same disappointment; all attempts to get a line across failed, as it proved impossible to paddle boats across the fast current. Those brave swimmers who tried were all swept away. Fourteen separate attempts were made, but they all failed. By this time the Panzer-Grenadiers had been alerted to the crossings and began to attack the Hampshires' isolated company. With the coming of daylight the frantic activity on the riverbank was exposed to the enemy's view. Retaliatory fire caused many casualties, and Gen Hawksworth was forced to suspend the operation, calling his troops back from the Garigliano and abandoning the men of the marooned company to extricate themselves as best they could. The complete failure of 46th Division's attempt to cross the river stripped US II Corps of any flank protection for its own proposed crossing of the Rapido planned for the next day just a few miles upstream. The US 36th Division was on its own.

The gains which X Corps had achieved spread some consternation in the German camp, however. When news reached Kesselring of the British crossings he viewed the development with alarm. 'This is the greatest crisis that we have so far experienced', he said; 'exceptional measures must be taken.' He could see that X Corps' attack could be developed to carry it into Liri valley and outflank the Gustav Line; it was unmistakably a first step by US Fifth Army in their campaign to break the German defences at Cassino. He immediately decided to reinforce Von Senger's corps by the addition of the 29. and 90.Panzer-Grenadier-Divisions which were held in army reserve near Rome. In the meantime, 94.Division was to be reinforced locally by a regiment from 15.Panzer-Grenadier-Division.

This release by Kesselring of German divisions from army reserve was just what Clark was hoping for. The two Panzer-Grenadier-Divisions were located at a point where they could have moved directly against the imminent landings at Anzio. With this operation set to begin in just two days' time, it was welcome news for Fifth Army's commander. Not so for McCreery, however: when the crack German reinforcements arrived on his front and counter-attacked X Corps, his excursions on the western bank of

The First Battle: 12 January-8 February 1944

All the battles in the Rapido and Garigliano valleys would depend at their outset on the ability of Allied engineers to bridge the rivers, usually under direct enemy observation and artillery fire. This Class 40 pontoon Bailey bridge across the River Garigliano in British X Corps' sector was able to take loads of up to 40 tons - i.e. tanks, but not loaded tank transporters. The photo was taken on 21 January, the fifth day of US Fifth Army's first offensive to break into the Gustav Line. (Imperial WarMuseum)

the Garigliano were stopped stone dead. The British advance would finally peter out into a posture of 'active defence' in front of Monte Faito and Monte Ceresola on 8 February.

The Texans on the Rapido

With the French attack pressing forward on the Allied right flank and British X Corps tying up German units on the left, it was time to launch Gen Clark's main thrust in the centre. US II Corps was to move across the Rapido opposite San Angelo and break into the Liri valley, to allow the deployment of armour which would attempt to link up with the Anzio landings once they had been established. General Keyes, commander of II Corps, had given the task of the Rapido crossings to Gen Walker's US 36th Division. This formation had already had a punishing campaign, fighting almost continually since its arrival on the Salerno beaches.

The US 36th 'Texas' Division was a National Guard division made up of part-time soldiers inducted into federal service in November 1940. In September 1941 a regular officer, Brig Gen Fred Walker, arrived to take command. Walker had been in the US Army since 1911 and had been decorated while serving with the AEF in France during the Great War. He had a reputation as an inspired trainer of troops, and set about bringing his civilian soldiers up to the standard of performance expected of regulars. In doing so he made the 'Texas' Division his own. He was impressed by the calibre of the men and kept all of his senior National Guard officers rather than replacing them with professionals, as was then usual. In 1943 the division left for North Africa but did not see combat there, nor in the campaign in Sicily, where Eisenhower preferred to commit combat-hardened units.

In September the division's moment arrived when it was chosen, with 34th Division, for the invasion of Italy. Its landing at Salerno was, after a shaky start, a success; the 36th quickly established a safe bridgehead and beat off a strong enemy counter-attack. It held the perimeter through twelve days of fierce combat and helped secure a safe lodgement for follow-up troops. Walker fought his division well, receiving a Distinguished Service Medal for his actions. After Salerno the division came out of the line to rest and reform in preparation for the difficult slog through the Bernhardt/Winter Line and up to the Rapido.

After coming back into the line in November the 36th fought a series of hard battles through the German-held mountains and achieved some important victories, most notably the taking of Monte la Difensa and the capture of San Pietro Infine. But it had become a tired division in the process, taking severe casualties in all of its battles; each task that it had been given was a tough one. At the end of 1943 it was again pulled out of the line for rest and replenishment. Then came Monte Trocchio and the move to the Rapido. By this time Gen Walker had been briefed to carry out the assault crossing of the river, and he viewed the forthcoming attack with grave misgivings.

The problems confronting Walker's division were immense. The approaches to the river were across open ground, littered with barbed wire and thickly sown with mines. The ground was soft and marshy, incapable of carrying wheeled traffic. Every yard of the approach from the slopes of Monte Trocchio to the river bank was under direct observation from the heights above Cassino. The river itself, although of no great size (being only fifty feet wide), was twelve feet deep, with steep, muddy banks and a fast-flowing current. On the far side there were more minefields, more wire and more fixed defences which covered every foot of the wide open spaces that led back from the river. Waiting expectantly, carefully sited and protected by concrete emplacements and deep entrenchments, were the first class troops of 15.Panzer-Grenadier-Division.

The keys to the operation were the engineers, who had a number of important tasks to perform. They had to clear the minefields on the near bank before the assault and on the far side once the advance waves were over the river. They had to supply and man the craft to ferry the troops over, both rubber dinghies and wooden paddle boats (there were no amphibious DUKWs available to the division); provide a ferry service to get supplies and reinforcements across; build catwalks and bridges for the follow-up troops, tanks and guns; and all the while keep the approaches open and serviceable. All of these tasks, each difficult enough under perfect conditions, had to be performed on schedule, in the dark, and under enemy fire.

Fred Walker could see that the attack had all the makings of a disaster. The whole idea of crossing a water obstacle and attacking a line of fortifications head-on while being overlooked by the enemy from high ground on both flanks was not a sound military enterprise. Walker felt that history was repeating itself in reverse, as he compared his present position to that of his opponents in World War One: as a battalion commander in 1918 he had been awarded the Distinguished Service Cross for his part in destroying a

The First Battle: 12 January–8 February 1944

British Sherman tanks wait to go into action in the muddy Garigliano valley. A tank was its crew's home as well as their fighting machine; note the mass of jerrycans, bedrolls, cooking tins and ammunition boxes used to stow their kit.

complete German unit as it tried to cross the River Marne. General Keyes was also doubtful of the operation's chances of success. He had earlier expressed his misgivings about attacking through the valley while the high ground dominating each side of the axis of advance was still held by the enemy. At a commanders' conference earlier in January Keyes had proposed that instead of crossing the Rapido, US II Corps and British X Corps should cross the lower Garigliano together and drive through the mountains to enter the valley behind the Gustav Line. This was immediately vetoed by McCreery as being impractical. General Clark also knew that the attack was going to be a very difficult proposition, but was anxious that the drive up the Liri valley should not be delayed. It was imperative that a strong move was made to put pressure on the enemy, both to draw reinforcements into the valley away from Anzio and to break through the Gustav Line to link up with the bridgehead.

It was a wretched situation for the commander of the 36th Division to be put in; none of his senior commanders really believed that the attack would succeed, but it had to be made regardless. Lower down, the junior officers and men of the 'Texas' Division could see for themselves the reality of the situation as they surveyed the mud-brown river from their observation points on Monte Trocchio. They were being asked to enter what could only be called a death trap. They were not being called upon to make a death-or-glory charge, but to carry out a stumbling, painfully slow advance across enemy-dominated open ground, perform a dangerous and difficult water crossing, and then occupy an exposed bridgehead ready to repulse an almost certain armoured counter-attack, armed with only the small arms they had carried across with them. They fully expected to be slaughtered.

When a battle begins with such negative portents it is inevitable that things go wrong from the start. The operation was a nightmare. The assault was a two-regiment attack, with 141st Infantry crossing above San Angelo and 143rd below, to the south of the village. At 2000 hours on the evening of 20 January the six battalions of infantry began their approach to the river, covered by an artillery barrage on known German positions. It did little damage to the deeply entrenched enemy, but did stir up retaliatory fire which hit the American infantry as they moved through the open fields bordering the river. Continuous wet weather and German manipulation of water levels had turned the ground into a quagmire. Thick mud slowed the approach to a crawl, clinging in great balls around the GIs' boots and preventing the use of any wheeled transport. Everything required for the crossing had to be manhandled forward to the river bank. To make matters worse a thick fog descended and blanketed the crossing places, confusing the stumbling infantry – but not the German gunners, whose weapons were zeroed in on all the routes down to the water's edge. The approach to the river quickly became disorganised as men lost their way, were blown up by mines or dispersed by shellfire.

The initial attempts at crossing were sporadic and disjointed. Artillery support ceased as the infantry closed on the enemy, who were less than a hundred yards away across the water. German machine gun fire raked the river as dug-in enemy grenadiers probed through the mist, registering the crossing sites by sound alone. Few boats arrived intact on the river bank, many of the rubber craft being damaged by shell splinters. Those that were launched were swirled away by the current and torn by bullets. Confusion and panic gripped the disoriented troops, and some of the men who did make it to the far bank arrived in a poor state to launch an assault.

On the northern part of the river the 141st Infantry managed to get a few boatloads of two companies over, and these quickly got off the deadly river bank and began attacking the enemy. Behind them, engineers worked long and hard to erect footbridges so that the follow-up troops could race across, but of the four deployed forward one was incomplete, one was destroyed by mines, and the other two were demolished by enemy artillery. Working through the night, engineers were able to assemble a fifth bridge from the salvaged parts of the others, and it survived in use long enough to get more troops of the other companies over the Rapido.

Below San Angelo the 143rd Infantry Regiment fared little better, but did manage to get two footbridges across the river so that most of 1st Bn were able to go over. These efforts took most of the night. When dawn came, enemy observation of the sites allowed their artillery to register the

The First Battle: 12 January-8 February 1944

Heavy 4.2-in mortars from a Chemical Weapons Battalion attached to the US 36th Division, firing in support of the crossings of the Rapido near San Angelo. The 4.2-in rifled mortar was assigned to CW battalions because it was originally intended only for projecting smoke and gas shells. It was later employed as a general infantry support weapon, however, firing a variety of high explosive and chemical ordnance. (US National Archives)

bridges and both were destroyed, although it was possible for lone individuals to clamber across the broken debris. The 1/143rd then felt the effects of German counter-attacks as the enemy probed the tiny bridgehead. The Americans were contained in a pocket with their backs on the river. No heavy weapons had been brought over, and no further reinforcement was likely. Major Frazior, the battalion commander, requested permission to withdraw. It was refused; he was told to hold on and await reinforcement, but before he had received this curt reply from the divisional commander Frazior had pulled his men out. When enemy tanks came at his battalion he believed his position to be untenable, and decided that all of his men who could make it back across the river should do so.

Early the next morning the Fifth Army commander received news of the failure on the Rapido. Clark ordered Keyes to spare no effort to get tanks and tank-destroyers over the river to support the infantry. The pressure had to be kept up so that the enemy had either to reinforce or submit to a breakthrough. At all costs, the proposed Anzio landings had to be supported by continual attacks in the Liri valley. At around 1000 hours Gen Keyes visited Gen Walker's headquarters and ordered him to try again as soon as he could. This time, tank bridges were to be built immediately after the assault boats were launched, so that armour could be brought into the bridgehead. Walker explained that this was impossible; how could he do in daylight, with reduced forces, what he had not beern able to do under the cover of darkness? He had also given his own orders for a renewed attack to go in at 2100 hours that evening. General Keyes refused to accept this delay, and informed Walker that a fresh attack must be made by 1400 hours in the afternoon.

General Walker passed the revised instructions down to his regimental commanders. They, too, said that it could not be done. The situation down by the river was chaotic. The assault units had become dispersed and disorganised and morale was badly shaken. There were no serviceable boats on the river and the engineers had withdrawn. The perpetual smoke haze, generated to screen the crossing zone, was causing problems with the troop's orientation. Forward observers could not get a clear view of the site and counter-artillery fire could not be put down on German positions.

By contrast, enemy interference continued all day, with shells homing in on pre-registered targets.

Throughout the day these problems caused the attacks to be postponed despite constant urging by the divisional commander. The main cause of the delays was the non-arrival of storm boats at the crossing places. Eventually Gen Walker had had enough of these excuses, and ordered Col Martin to send the lead battalion of the 143rd Infantry across with whatever boats had arrived. At 1600 hours the 3/143rd began to cross the Rapido below the village of San Angelo under cover of a smoke screen. By 1830 hours they had managed to get all their rifle companies across, and were immediately followed by the 2nd Battalion. At the same time engineers worked feverishly in the gathering darkness to construct another footbridge.

The bridgehead expanded and the troops advanced about 500 yards from the river. Colonel Martin of the 143rd now urged the engineers to get larger bridges in place so that support weapons could be passed across. He requested that work begin immediately on a Bailey bridge capable of carrying tanks. This, however, was a major problem, for the 40-ton Bailey required transport vehicles to bring its steel sections up to the water's edge – and the moment heavy trucks moved off the road they foundered in the deep, sticky mud of the river banks. Engineers therefore had to manhandle the bridge sections forward, and it was a painfully slow and difficult task to get them to the assembly site. Although the engineers laboured long into the night, it soon became clear that no Bailey could be put over the river before daylight. The troops in the bridgehead would have to hold on without the aid of armour.

Meanwhile the 143rd Infantry's final battalion, 1/143rd, had also got across the river at its own crossing point and had carved out a 200-yard enclave. Major Frazior and his battalion were making a second attempt on the Rapido, but found the task just as traumatic as the first time. Within a short spell disaster had struck: Frazior was wounded, all of his rifle company commanders had become casualties, the footbridge connecting them to the near shore was destroyed, and all the boats on that section of the river were smashed. Throughout the night enemy attacks whittled away at the trapped battalion, reducing it to just 250 men by daybreak. Many of the troops had given way to despair

29

The First Battle: 12 January–8 February 1944

View across the Rapido and into the Liri valley from the slopes of Monte Trocchio, taken after the attempt by the 36th 'Texas' Division to cross the river; this gives a good impression of the exposure of the GIs to German observers on the Cassino feature, and their lack of cover from artillery fire. A few houses in the village of San Angelo can just be seen on the slight rise in the upper centre. The 141st Infantry Regiment made its assault on the right, upstream of the village, and the 143rd below San Angelo, to the left. (US National Archives)

and slipped back over the river to the friendly shore under cover of night.

Efforts continued in daylight to provide heavy bridges over the river, but losses among the skilled engineers and the extreme difficulty of having to physically carry every single item forward to the bridging sites caused work on the bridges to falter. By midmorning all work had stopped; many engineers had crept away to take cover from the withering enemy fire in foxholes well back from the river. With no hope of a Bailey bridge being established and with his isolated troops across the river exposed to armoured counter-attacks, Col Martin decided that the 143rd's hold on the far bank was untenable. He ordered his three battalions to withdraw.

The experiences of the 143rd south of San Angelo were mirrored by the 141st Infantry to the north of the village. Its crossing began at 2100 hours on the evening of 21 January. Most of its boats were defective and only one small part of Company F from 2nd Bn managed to get across in the first wave. This small party successfully cleared the enemy machine guns near the crossing places to allow the completion of two footbridges which allowed 3/141st to get over the river and establish itself. There was no sign of the men of 1st Bn who had formed the first bridgehead during the attack of the previous night. Together the two battalions advanced almost 1,000 yards from the Rapido until enemy fire caused them to halt and dig-in. Then 15.Panzer-Grenadier-Division struck back, putting down a

tremendous barrage of artillery and small arms fire into the American lodgement. Behind them, furious activity on the river banks heralded the start of bridge-building, but despite heroic efforts this, too, succumbed to the effective fire of alert enemy artillery. The footbridges were hit and washed away, the boats were wrecked and disappeared.

Daylight on 22 January revealed a hopeless situation. The two battalions of 141st were totally isolated, with no possibility of being reinforced and with little effective support fire at their disposal. The enemy now pressed in on the bridgehead relentlessly. First the field telephone links across the Rapido fell silent, then the radio messages ceased. Gradually the sound of small arms fire dwindled until everything went quiet. The crossing had failed.

General Walker's 36th Division alone lost 1,681 men during the three days of the Rapido crossing: 143 killed, 663 wounded and 875 missing – the great majority of these from among the roughly 5,200 officers and men of the six infantry battalions committed. To these must be added the casualties suffered by supporting units. In contrast, 15.Panzer-Grenadier-Division's casualties were negligible. The attack had been stopped dead at the water's edge, never once having caused the slightest alarm regarding the security of the Gustav Line. It was seen at the time by the Germans as being just a spoiling attack, one of many in the area to try to get the defenders off-balance. It was not until some appreciable time after the event that the German corps commander, Gen von Senger, realised that the Rapido crossings were in fact an element of a major American offensive by Fifth Army.

(Right) Wounded from the 141st Infantry streaming back towards Monte Trocchio after their disastrous attempts to cross the River Rapido. A smoke-screen in the background masks the area around 36th Division's crossing sites; but it was not enough to shield the area from enemy observers on the heights around Monte Cassino. See colour plate A1 opposite page 66. (US National Archives)

30

The First Battle: 12 January-8 February 1944

CHAPTER THREE

Anzio – Battle on Two Fronts: 22 January–8 February

Just after midnight on 22 January the invasion fleet dropped anchor off Cape Anzio and began to assemble its strike force. Packed into its ships were the 40,000 men and 5,200 vehicles of US VI Corps. Admiral Lowry's armada consisted of 289 craft, varying in size from great cruisers to small square-bowed LCVPs (Landing Craft Vehicles/Personnel). The black enemy shore a few miles away across the flat sea was just visible through the moonless night. The water was quiet and still. As the hours ticked away, assault craft were swung out from the landing ships and lowered to bob gently alongside. Scrambling nets were thrown over the ship's sides; last minute orders were given, and then the signal to load the assault boats was flashed from ship to ship. Heavily laden troops clambered precariously down the swaying nets, jumping awkwardly into the box-like hulls of the landing craft which rose and fell on the slight swell. Once filled with its thirty or so cramped, uneasy passengers each craft was gunned away from the looming side of its mother ship to circle in a precise pattern, waiting until the whole flotilla were ready. At the signal that loading was complete they peeled out of their circles and headed for shore in waves, line abreast. The guns of the escorting warships remained silent. The Anzio landings, planned to outflank the Gustav Line, began in stealth.

As the fragile landing craft carrying the lead battalions closed on the shore, just ten minutes before H-Hour, 0200 hours, an immense firework display lit up the sky and deafened observers with its eerie shrieking. Two British landing ships fitted with banks of rocket launchers had cut loose their salvos, and in a matter of seconds 798 five-inch rocket-propelled bombs slammed into the landing sites. The wild explosions plastered the enemy beaches, exploding minefields and destroying beach defences. The sudden, vicious eruption of flame and noise was intended to disorientate any possible enemy ambush force. Then came the naval bombardment: vast gouts of flame in the night, muzzle-blast battering the eardrums of the soldiers and sailors, and massive shells tearing through the sky with a sound like express trains, homing on to known and suspected German strongpoints. All the while the invasion force closed on the beaches; there was no answering fire – surprise was complete.

The first waves of infantry hit the shore and raced up the beaches. To everyone's amazement there was no enemy to greet them. The infantry pressed on over the beaches and inland: still there was no firing. The commanders in the warships peered expectantly through their field glasses, eager to locate any opposition to the landings. There was none; the enemy had been caught completely off guard. The news was quickly flashed back to the follow-up battalions. The whole invasion fleet now had one single goal: to get men and machines ashore as quickly as possible to take advantage of this extraordinary stroke of luck. Anzio was wide open to exploitation.

The commanders of the Anzio landings confer on board the headquarters ship HMS Bulolo *just prior to the invasion. From left to right: Rear Admiral Tom Troubridge USN, commander of Naval Task Force 'Peter', covering the British landings; Maj Gen John Lucas, commanding US VI Corps; and Maj Gen Penney, commander of the British 1st Infantry Division. HMS* Bulolo *had already carried out duties as Force Headquarters Ship during the 'Torch' landings in French North Africa and again for Operation 'Husky' in Sicily; she would later perform this role off 'Gold' Beach in Normandy during the 'Overlord' invasion on 6 June 1944. (Imperial War Museum)*

The invasion had been carried out in three distinct parts. On the left, British 1st Division had landed on beaches north of Anzio. Mines and shallow water caused some delays to its strict timetable, but by the end of the morning troops were two miles inland. Commandos landing with the infantry had moved out behind the town and cut the road to Albano, establishing roadblocks and defensive outposts.

In the centre of the landings, three battalions of American Rangers under the command of the redoubtable Col William O.Darby, together with Airborne troopers of 509th Parachute Infantry Bn, concentrated on Anzio itself. These special forces units were given the task of storming the harbour and then fanning out to take the town and the neighbouring seaside village of Nettuno, a mile away to the south. Darby landed with his men on the sandy beach right opposite the town's casino. They were opposed by just one German soldier, who was immediately shot dead. After an hour most of 1st and 4th Ranger Bns were ashore together with their mortars and support engineers. The town was quickly occupied and the Rangers deployed ready to meet any German counter-attack. Engineers set to work to make the port safe for the arrival of heavier landing craft and ships. It all seemed too easy.

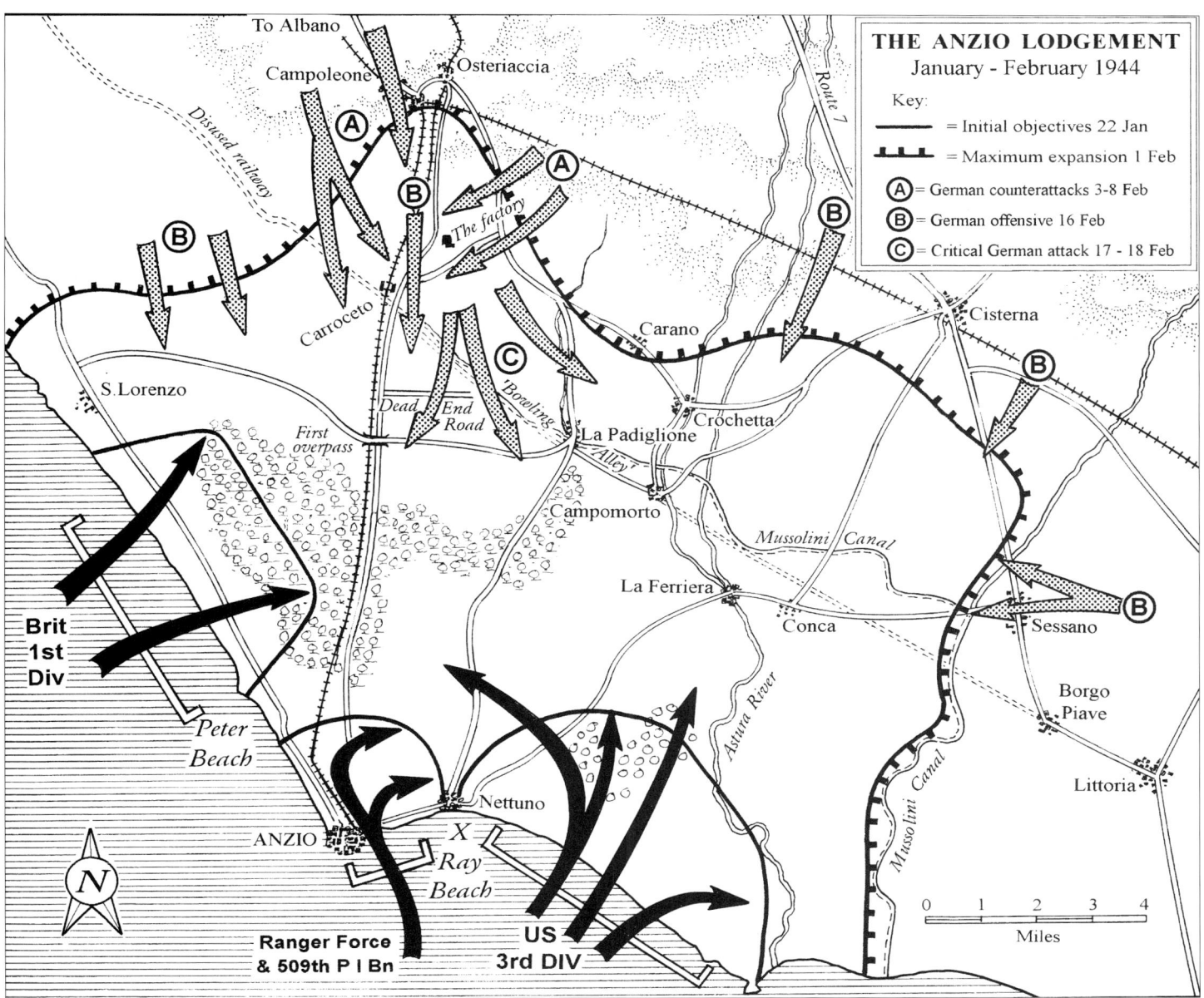

On the right of the landings US 3rd Division enjoyed a similar reception. Landing over the beaches south of Nettuno, Gen Lucian Truscott's division had to contend with little more that a few scattered minefields and the occasional shell fired from guns along the coast which came to life as dawn broke. The few German artillery pieces that did open up were quickly located and destroyed by the warships just off shore. By midday the division was three miles inland, had brought ashore all of its supporting artillery and tanks, and had demolished four bridges over the Mussolini Canal. With its right flank thus protected, it dug in to cover the follow-up troops and await the expected enemy counter-attack.

The area of the beachhead was now given over to the specialists to carve out a supply port. Engineers cleared minefields and bulldozed exit ramps from the beaches, while reception units and MPs organised the dispersal of growing streams of men and matériel that swarmed ashore. By the end of the day Gen Lucas had 36,000 men, 3,200 vehicles and 90 per cent of his initial supplies unloaded. Casualties had been extremely light: 13 killed, 97 wounded and 44 missing. The Luftwaffe had appeared over the landings during the day carrying out hit-and-run raids. One LCI (Landing Craft Infantry) was sunk and some damage was caused to the port, but apart from nuisance value the raids did little to interfere with the disembarkation. US VI Corps was ashore and ready for action.

★   ★   ★

German reaction to the landings was one of complete surprise, but the Commander-in-Chief Italy responded with his usual efficiency. Field Marshal Kesselring heard of the invasion just one hour after Allied troops had come ashore, and by 0500 hours information relayed to his headquarters had convinced him that he was faced with a full-scale operation rather than a diversionary raid. He quickly formed the opinion that Clark would probably move to seize the Alban Hills, and that if this action were successful then the German front on the Gustav Line would be untenable. Kesselring immediately ordered units from the incomplete and not yet activated 4.Fallschirmjäger-Division to move towards Anzio from its base north of Rome. Next he ordered those elements of the 'Hermann Göring' Division that had not already been sent south against British X Corps to join the paratroopers and block the roads leading from Anzio to the Alban Hills. (The replacement reception battalions of both the 'HG' Panzer-Grenadier regiments were instantly activated as third battalions of their regiments, and

Bren carriers and tanks from 46th Royal Tank Regiment moving off the beach north of Anzio. British 1st Division had an unopposed landing and was able to disembark almost the whole of 2 Infantry Brigade and 24 Guards Brigade over 'Peter' Beach during the first day, 22 January 1944. (Imperial War Museum)

(Right) *Troops of the US 3rd Infantry Division coming ashore at Anzio on 22 January. In the background a Landing Craft Infantry (LCI) burns after being hit by a German aircraft. The enemy air raid was the only real opposition faced by the landings on the first day. (US National Archives)*

the divisional battle school was transformed into an 'assault company' – typical of the speed and determination of which the best German divisions were still capable.) When he made his report to his masters at Oberkommando der Wehrmacht one hour later, he requested the release of further reinforcements. Hitler responded later in the day by ordering several units to the Anzio area, including 715.Division from southern France, 114.Jäger-Division from Yugoslavia, and from Germany miscellaneous units amounting to the equivalent of about another division.

Permission was also granted for Kesselring to activate a new division from several replacement (*Ersatz*) battalions that were being held in northern Italy. This 92.Division was formed and sent south, but did not join the fighting until much later. Made up of battalions of Germans, Austrians and ethnic Germans from occupied countries, 92.Division was stationed around Orbetello as a garrison and training unit. (The division, under the command of Gen Göritz, had a very short life. The Fourteenth Army Commander, Gen von Mackensen, was far from satisfied with its performance and later reported it to be unfit for intensive combat. The division was dissolved a few months later.)

To these units Field Marshal Kesselring added reserves of his own. At 0710 on 22 January he contacted Fourteenth Army Headquarters in northern Italy and ordered it to make forces available to counter the landings. Von Mackensen in turn arranged for 65. and 362.Divisions, each less one regiment, and elements of 16.SS Panzer-Grenadier-Division 'Reichsführer-SS' to make their way south to oppose the beachhead. To the consternation of Allied commanders, none of these units were engaged against US Fifth Army on the Gustav Line and so the first batch of German formations which moved towards the landings did not lessen German resistance at Cassino as hoped. However, at 0810 hours on the 22nd Kesselring reluctantly contacted Von Vietinghoff at Tenth Army HQ and instructed him to transfer all the troops he could spare.

Most immediate of the combat formations released by Von Vietinghoff was the headquarters of I Parachute Corps (which existed in name only at that date). General Schlemm and his staff were told to assume control of the troops opposing the landings and to organise and deploy reinforcements as they arrived. The corps staff became operational at 1700 hours and quickly took command of a variety of battalions which had struggled forward from the area of Rome. Defences were hastily improvised from any units available, including all anti-aircraft batteries in the area which could be used in a ground role, and the way to the Alban Hills was quickly blocked. Commander Tenth Army also moved 3.Panzer-Grenadier-Division less one regiment, 71.Division, and parts of the 'Herman Göring' Division who were opposing British X Corps on the Garigliano. Von Vietinghoff left the remainder of his front in the Cassino sector alone; but he also sent units to Anzio from his Adriatic front facing British Eighth Army, including 26.Panzer-Division and parts of 1.Fallschirmjäger-Division. Thus, by the end of the first day, German reaction had been both swift and substantial, but had not been at the expense of stripping the Cassino sector of significant numbers of units. By nightfall on 22 January they had recovered from their surprise; had established command and control over what Kesselring called a 'jumble of multifarious troops which streamed in from all directions'; and had set up a thin defensive line all around the Allied beachhead.

In striking contrast to the furiously energetic reaction by Kesselring and his commanders, Gen Lucas set about establishing his lodgement at Anzio in a thorough and methodical way. His orders were to seize and secure a beachhead and then advance on the Alban Hills, and that was exactly what he was doing. He had seized the beachhead that morning and was now about to ensure that it was secure. Throughout the day, and through the whole of the next two days, men and stores came ashore and were carefully established within the landing zone. On each of these days the beachhead expanded slightly to accommodate the rapidly enlarging American corps. British 1st Division moved a few miles forward to the River Moletta and strengthened the left flank, while Darby's Rangers, supported by 509th Parachute Infantry, took several more bridges over the Mussolini Canal. By dawn on 24 January the beachhead was seven miles deep and sixteen miles wide, carved out against negligible enemy resistance. There were as yet no preparations for a full scale attack inland; Lucas was still absorbed in the task of securing his beachhead as ordered.

During this lull, German units moved towards the Anzio area with great speed. Travelling mostly at night to avoid the attention of Allied fighters and bombers, the enemy troops moved into the cordon around Anzio with more speed than the Allied command had thought possible. To Kesselring's relief and surprise there was no attempted large-scale expansion of the beachhead, nor any determined move towards the strategically vital Alban Hills. The Allies had not conformed to the German High Command's expectations, and presented something of a puzzle. Kesselring knew that if the Americans attacked out of the lodgement before he could close the Anzio perimeter with a ring of steel, then they would in all probability reach the Alban Hills. Indeed, his chief-of-staff Gen Westphal was convinced that an attack at that time would be able to reach Rome. But Lucas did nothing beyond sending out reconnaissance patrols, thus confirming Kesselring's belief that, as usual, the Allies 'continued to show an amazing lack of imagination.'

By 25 February Gen von Mackensen had transferred his headquarters and arrived from northern Italy to take control of the Anzio cordon. He established his Fourteenth Army as the defenders of the perimeter and was ordered by Kesselring to start preparations for an offensive to pushing US VI Corps back into the sea. There were parts of eight German divisions now ringing the American corps, with elements of five more on the way. Von Mackensen organised his defence with 65.Division on the left opposing the British behind the River Moletta; 3.Panzer-Grenadier-Division defending Albano in the centre; and the 'Hermann Göring' Division units blocking the way to Cisterna on the right. Behind this perimeter other groups were organised ready to counter-attack any Allied breakthrough. By 28 January, Von Mackensen had formulated a plan for an attack to be launched against the Allied bridgehead on 1 February.

The time had now passed when Lucas could have moved with some certainty of making progress. The light resistance that had faced him on the morning of the landings had been replaced by very serious opposition indeed. Some of the enemy's best troops in Italy were now arriving to meet any threat that he might mount. Enemy reaction had been more focussed than that of the Allies. It seems inconceivable that so little was done to take advantage of the extraordinary good fortune that presented itself to the troops coming ashore: no German opposition and no enemy forces of any strength anywhere close by. So why didn't Lucas take advantage of this stroke of luck? The answer was in part due to the man and in part to his superiors.

Since the main purpose of the landings was to induce the Germans to withdraw Tenth Army from the Gustav Line, the obvious first objectives of VI Corps were to take Albano and the Alban Hills to cut Route 7, and also to push for Valmontone at the upper end of the Liri valley, which sat astride Route 6. Such gains would have severed the links between Von Vietinghoff's Tenth Army and Rome. Even the threat of them would probably have precipitated a withdrawal from the Cassino area. Indeed, when Von Vietinghoff was told to release troops to counter the Anzio landings he had telephoned Kesselring and advocated an immediate withdrawal from the Gustav Line, fearing that he would not now be strong enough to hold it (Kesselring, made of sterner stuff, had told him to stand fast).

If Gen Lucas had had to fight his way ashore and struggle to establish the beachhead – as had been expected in some quarters – he would not have been able to think of immediate offensive operations. But presented with an unopposed, almost peaceful disembarkation, he had got most of his troops and much of their equipment ashore on the first day. With superiority in numbers, what prevented him making some vigorous move in order to keep the initiative? He could at least have pushed inland immediately to seize the villages of Campoleone on the road to Albano, and Cisterna on the route to Valmontone. These two road junctions, vital for his eventual offensive moves, would also have acted as important cornerstones for a defensive line around his lodgement. Even by noon on D-Day he had enough troops ashore to make such a move possible. Yet any condemnation of Gen Lucas' inactivity must also take account of the equally inexplicable attitude of his two immediate superiors.

American tank landing ships (LSTs) unload vehicles in the inner harbour at Anzio. The buildings along the waterside have been damaged by long range German artillery, which kept up harassing fire during the whole life of the beachhead. The seemingly random nature of the shelling kept everyone in the lodgement on tenterhooks, not knowing where the next salvo might fall. (US National Archives)

(Right) *Cast-hull Sherman M4A1 tanks of 1st Armored Regiment from US 1st Armored Division move through the Anzio beachhead towards the front line. The most important element of US VI Corps' reserve throughout the Anzio fighting, Gen Harmon's division operated under unenviable conditions - to be shut up inside a cramped beachhead under constant artillery fire is about the worst situation a tank general could face. (US National Archives)*

When Gen Mark Clark visited Lucas on the first day he was very well satisfied with the landings, as was Alexander, who arrived there later on 22 January. All were concerned that the beachhead should be well established and supplied in order to support offensive action. Three days later they were all still of the same mind, with Clark cautioning Lucas to be alert for enemy counter-attacks. Alexander congratulated Lucas on his 'splendid piece of work' in establishing the lodgement, and Clark was impressed with his logistical arrangements. Only then did Clark urge Lucas to push out and take Campoleone and Cisterna; and he confided in his diary that he thought Lucas would have sufficient strength within the bridgehead to shift from defence to offence - within a week! With neither his Army nor his Army Group commander visibly anxious about his lack of progress inland, Lucas continued to busy himself with domestic improvements. The official American history of the campaign notes that he personally devoted his attention to the establishment of an anti-aircraft warning system, the construction of an airfield, and the clearance of supplies that jammed the beaches behind the first row of dunes. On 27 January, five days after the landings, Gen Lucas called his divisional commanders to a meeting to discuss plans for taking the offensive 'some time soon'.

The 'Red Bull' across the Rapido

To Gen Clark, the US 36th Division's debacle on the Rapido was just one failed attempt to get into the Liri valley; he was compelled to try again, to force an entrance through the Gustav Line in order to put sustained pressure on an enemy now distracted by the threat in his rear. He also needed to start his drive to link up with VI Corps' beachhead, to avoid its remaining isolated at the mercy of the gathering strength of German Fourteenth Army. The first of these objectives had been realised by the X Corps attack a few days before; the latter was not to be achieved for another four months.

Clark's army had stalled all along his front. McCreery's British X Corps was making little headway through the mountains on the left against fresh German reinforcements. Indeed, it was fortunate just to hold on to its gains in the face of determined German counter-attacks. On the right, Juin's CEF was fighting itself to a standstill against the fortified mountain positions of the Gustav Line. General Clark now decided that US II Corps would continue its attack across the Rapido, this time further upstream on the other side of Cassino where the river could be forded. General Keyes was ordered to send the US 34th Division over the river, up into the mountains, and then to wheel southwards to get behind Monte Cassino; the division would then sweep down on to Route 6 and into the Liri valley. At the same time, one of the division's regiments would move straight down the far bank of the Rapido and take the town of Cassino. The 34th Division had been kept back ready to exploit any breakthrough and to give weight to the drive to link up with Anzio; Clark was now forced to use it in an attempt to create the breakthrough itself.

Major General Charles Ryder, commanding the 34th 'Red Bull' Division, was, like Fred Walker of the 36th, a veteran of the AEF in the Great War. His division, too, was originally a National Guard formation, made up of troops from North and South Dakota, Iowa and Minnesota. It entered federal service in 1941 and was shipped to Northern Ireland early in 1942, being the first American division to arrive in the European theatre. Ryder had led his division during the 'Torch' landings and the subsequent fighting in North Africa. It joined US Fifth Army in Italy just after the Salerno landings, and was engaged on the Volturno. During the advance through the mountains which culminated in its arrival at Cassino it had suffered a great many casualties and had fought some very tough battles. Although designated a 'fresh division' for the attack at Cassino, it was in truth - again like the 'Texas' Division - a very tired outfit that was in need of a longer period of rest and replenishment.

The 'Red Bull' Division began its attack across the Rapido when 1st and 3rd Bns of the 133rd Infantry moved off at 2200 hours on 24 January. Their objective was the area around the disused Italian barracks two miles north of Cassino. The barracks were located on a slight rise of ground called Monte Villa, situated a few hundred yards from the river. The barracks consisted of a group of about twenty rectangular buildings in an open park; the whole camp had been damaged by shellfire and most of the buildings were in a ruinous state. German infantry had skilfully built concrete strongpoints within the ruins, camouflaging them so that they were almost impossible to locate amongst the debris. These positions, together with other pillboxes dug into the hills above the barracks, covered the approach to the river.

The task given to the 34th Division was almost an exact copy of 36th Division's attack of a few days before. It had to advance to the Rapido over open ground made marshy by flooding, and cross through scattered minefields and barbed wire entanglements, while being watched all the way by an entrenched enemy with superior observation. The only thing to its advantage was that instead of its troops having to take boats to get over the river, they could walk across.

The attack stalled almost immediately as the leading troops of 1/ and 3/133rd Infantry stumbled into uncleared minefields. Supporting Shermans from the 756th Tank Bn pressed forward to help, but soon began to skid and bog down in glutinous mud. Then the enemy artillery began to home in on the exposed American infantry and armour, disorganising the attack. The struggle continued throughout the night as the two battalions tried to press forward, but virtually no progress was made.

The next morning Gen Ryder ordered forward the 133rd Infantry's third battalion which he had been keeping back to exploit any breakthrough. At 0900 hours on 25 January an artillery barrage pounded the ground in front of the 100th Infantry Bn as it joined the line to the left of 1/

37

With the Germans having total observation over every square mile of the approaches to Cassino, all movement within sight of the enemy had to be curtailed. These GIs keep a low profile while on the slopes of Monte Trocchio during the planning of future operations in the Rapido valley. Monte Trocchio served as an observation post during the whole of the Cassino operations, enabling visiting senior officers and VIPs to view the area from relative safety. In the backround, towering above the whole battlefield, are the snow-capped heights of Monte Cairo. (US National Archives)

and 3/133rd in a concerted attack towards the river. This fresh battalion was composed entirely of Japanese-American *Nisei* - mostly from Hawaii, and taking as their motto 'Remember Pearl Harbor!'. They managed to get a few riflemen across the Rapido, but barbed wired stifled forward movement and machine guns forced the infantry to take cover. Over the next four hours all three battalions got men across and carved out small individual bridgeheads. Throughout the 25th more men gradually forced their way through into these isolated positions, and by the middle of the next night the 133rd Infantry had established a significant lodgement over the river. The divisional commander now urged Col Marshall to get his regiment to exploit towards the barracks and the high ground above them before daylight on the 26th. With an enlarged bridgehead Ryder could introduce a second regiment - the 168th Infantry - into the battle, and move down the valley to the left towards the town of Cassino.

Colonel Marshall's 133rd tried to move inland, but failed. The GIs could do little but take cover from the withering fire that was pouring down on them from the two high points behind the barracks. The German infantry holed up on these knolls, Points 56 and 213, had perfect observation and their weapons were registered on the static American targets. Every attempt to press inland, every movement backwards or forwards, was met with a hail of fire. 26 January came and went; the 133rd stayed put, and the 168th remained uncommitted.

There could be no forward movement until German resistance on Points 56 and 213 - especially 213 - was eliminated. Ryder decided it was time to introduce his last unit, the 135th Infantry. During the night of 26/27 January the regiment managed to put a part of its 1st Bn across the Rapido to the right of its stranded sister regiment, to form its own small bridgehead. Tanks supporting this effort once again bogged down, just as all other armour had done during the earlier attacks. The troops in this new bridgehead immediately suffered the same fate as those who had crossed before: flooded ditches, wire entanglements and minefields restricted manoeuvre, while enemy fire kept movement down to a minimum. In the early hours of 27 January things looked depressingly bad for the division.

General Ryder now ordered Col Mark Boatner's 168th Infantry into action. Instead of passing through the 133rd's turf it would carve out its own. Two battalions would attack abreast, each preceded by a rolling artillery barrage and a platoon of tanks, and make directly for Point 213. This would put Americans behind the barrack area, outflanking the defenders of Point 56.

The attack went in at daybreak on 27 January. Some tanks slipped from the narrow trackways up to the river laid by the engineers; some floundered in the mud; but two Shermans made it across the river by 0830 hours and were joined by two others at 0910. Their churning tracks tore up the ground to such an extent that tanks following behind became completely bogged down. None the less, these four tanks led the infantry forward, some sheltering in the lee of their steel bulk, others following behind in the lanes carved out by the Shermans. In the face of strong enemy fire several rifle companies persevered with the attack and managed to get over the river. Through sheer determination, the GIs of the 168th then made it across the open ground and on to the base of Point 213. In the process, all four of the tanks were lost.

After dark one company succeeded in getting to the top of the hill, but were pulled off at daybreak when their position became impossible. Withdrawal from contact under fire is one of the most murderously difficult of all movements, and enemy fire turned this disciplined retreat into something of a rout. Some troops lost control and fled back right across the river. Seeing this, other companies also became nervous; they too fell back across the Rapido, leav-

Bogged-down and knocked-out, this Sherman M4A2 from Company C, US 756th Tank Battalion lies abandoned on the floor of the Rapido valley after attempting to support the attack across the river by the 34th Infantry Division in late January. The previously flooded valley was still too boggy to carry 30-ton tanks; once off the road they stuck fast in the glutinous mud, at the mercy of enemy guns in the hills looking down on them. (US National Archives)

ing just two exposed companies on the enemy bank. These were felt to be too vulnerable, since the enemy now had full knowledge of their positions, so they too were ordered to pull out. The 168th Infantry and the whole of 34th Division were back to square one.

General Ryder tried again in the early hours of 29 January, this time intending to put in the 168th further to the north towards the village of Cairo. Every engineer of US II Corps had been assigned to the task of crossing the Rapido, with tracks down to the river being made into serviceable roads by laying strips of metal mesh to provide a firm grip for tanks. Engineers were held constantly at hand to keep crossing places serviceable. To add weight to the attack the 168th Regiment was given the support of two tank battalions and all available artillery. A prodigious barrage shot the 168th forward, and it moved off with all three infantry battalions in the line. By 0700 hours seven Shermans from the 760th Tank Bn were across the river, quickly followed by the infantry. By mid-morning on the 29th all three battalions were slowly advancing across the flat ground towards the hills. A few hours later the 756th Tank Bn was introduced into the action; by a stroke of good fortune it found a good approach route to the Rapido, and was able to put twenty-three tanks across by early afternoon. Their arrival in the bridgehead at last gave a much-needed impetus to the GIs' advance, as they blasted German strongpoints at very short range. The infantry responded, and by late afternoon had made it across the flat ground and into the hills. As darkness fell on 29 January they began moving on to the high ground; and by dawn the next day Points 56 and 213 were in American hands, although not completely secure from enemy infiltration and counter-attacks. The village of Cairo to the north had also been taken.

In five days of savage fighting the US 34th Division had made it across the Rapido and up into the hills overlooking the valley; but these small successes fell very far short of a breakthrough. The enemy still held the first key objective – the barracks – and the proposed advances across the Cassino massif and entry into the town had hardly started. All three of Ryder's regiments were starting to tire, but there was still a long way to go. Things elsewhere, however, were beginning to improve.

Monte Belvedere and the barracks
In ordering II Corps to continue with its attack over the Rapido, Gen Clark was applying continuous pressure on the Gustav Line. This pressure was also being focused on other sectors of the line to push the enemy off-balance. McCreery attacked once again with British X Corps against a reinforced German 94.Division and, in the mountains to the right of the 'Red Bull' Division's battle, Gen Juin's French Expeditionary Corps was again on the offensive. On 25 January, Juin directed his 3rd Algerian Division against Monte Belvedere, the 771-metre peak that overlooked the Americans from about five miles to the north of Cassino. In a mountain battle that lasted until 4 February, the French attacked over almost impassable ground and endured ferocious fighting to secure the peak. To help them Clark gave them the third regiment of US 36th Division, the 142nd Infantry, which had not been involved in the original attempt on the Rapido. This regiment attacked with its left flank overlooking US 34th Division and its right supporting the Algerians, and took Monte Manna after a brilliant advance over treacherous terrain. These successes gave heart to Fifth Army's commander, and he urged Gen Keyes to press on with his corps' attack on Cassino town and the high ground behind Monte Cassino.

On 1 February the 'Red Bulls' went after the Germans holed up in the barracks. With the 168th Infantry now on Point 213, the enemy in the derelict Italian camp had both their front and rear approaches to worry about. To further outflank the barracks Gen Ryder sent the 135th Infantry

M5A1 Stuart tank 'Dead Eye Dick' knocked out in the valley of the Rapido during the first battle for Cassino. The Stuart was a four-man light tank with a 37mm main gun. Completely outclassed as a battle tank by 1942, it served on until the end of the war with reconnaissance elements. Its crews relied for their lives on its speed and manoeuvrability. (US National Archives)

(Right) American artillery battery commander receiving information regarding a firing mission in support of US 34th Division. Allied fire control was superior to that of the German artillery. (US National Archives)

Regiment up into the hills and passed the unit through his other regiment on Point 213 to take Monte Castellone. At the same time the 142nd consolidated its gains on Monte Manna and gave protection to the 34th Division's right flank. Down on the valley floor, the 133rd Infantry attacked the barracks from their small lodgement. Fighting went on throughout the day and into the next before the Germans finally gave up the ruined camp. As the enemy withdrew Col Marshall tried to exploit his gains by sending a battalion, reinforced by some Shermans from the 756th Tank Bn, down the river bank towards Cassino town. Within a short time enemy machine gun and anti-tank fire forced them to an abrupt halt.

Despite this check on the road to Cassino, US II Corps was at last making significant progress. The 142nd Infantry handed Monte Manna over to the French and joined the 34th Division to beef up its attack. Over the next few days Gen Keyes began to wheel his four regiments to the south, and the corps' drive to break through into the Liri valley began. In the lead, the 135th Infantry moved from Monte Castellone along the ridge to the next peak of high ground, Point 706, while the 142nd came up behind. Next to these, the 168th Infantry pushed through the hills towards Point 593.

Along the Rapido, the 133rd resumed its attack into Cassino town, supported by armour. The GIs and a few tanks made it into the buildings on the northern edge of the town, but were unable to live with the volume of German fire brought down on them. The heavily-built stone courtyard-houses were painfully cleared of the enemy, only to be quickly retaken with great loss of life, and progress was measured in individual rooms and alleyways. It was impossible to keep even small parts of the town free of interference; the Germans infiltrated back into every building and outflanked any gains that the regiment made. They were supported by skilfully-handled self-propelled assault guns, which would dart out of their hides in the ruins to fire a few devastating rounds at short range before disappearing again. The few streets which the GIs had seized eventually became completely untenable, and the Americans withdrew.

The calvary of II Corps

Up on the mountains, progress was inexorable but deadly slow. Moving from one pile of rocks to another, from one boulder to the next, through gullies and over ravines, across a barren moonscape of scree and mud, the American infantry pressed forward. They moved in small groups, each mutually supportive to the others, the GIs clawing their way ahead like rats, avoiding any open ground or shell-torn tracks, measuring their advance in yards. Gradually the Germans gave ground in their inimitable way, resisting to the last, withdrawing a short distance and then counterattacking before the Americans became established. The fighting was unspeakably grim for all, but more telling on the attackers, who had to risk exposure - sniped at from every angle, blasted by shells and mortar bombs, torn apart by jagged splinters of steel and rock, their numbers steadily dwindled. Supply routes were marked out through the hills, but no wheeled transport could be got forward; everything necessary had to be carried by hand right up to the fighting line. Some mules were used, but often the only beasts of burden available were the fighting men themselves.

The weather was foul and exhausting: bitterly cold winds, intermittent rain, sleet, snow flurries and sharp frosts ground down the troops' natural resilience. Some men went for three weeks without a hot meal; and their clothing - ordinary temperate climate woollen uniforms, with only greatcoats for extra protection - was utterly inadequate. There was little usable cover; foxholes were out of the question - the barren rocks doomed from the start any attempt to get underground. Other than piling a few loose stones together to provide some shelter and concealment the infantry spent their nights and days on the open hillsides. All around, overlooking them from almost every angle, German-held heights seemed to watch their every move with vulture eyes. It was a tactical and human nightmare; and the steady streams of walking wounded staggering down the tracks began to be swollen by men who had simply had enough.

Artillery support for the troops on the mountainsides

was difficult to provide. The infantry were attacking across high ground parallel to the lines of guns, with the actual front line being just a jagged belt of 'no man's land' without specific boundaries. The GIs were in very close contact with the enemy, sometimes just yards apart. The artillery could pump shells on to known German strongpoints in their rear and place smoke on a few of the German-dominated peaks to give some cover, but could do little else. The fighting in the mountains was very much an infantryman's battle and he was usually left to fight it alone.

Still the attacks went on. Further gains were made when the 135th Infantry made a rapid move through an opening and advanced to a point near Monte Albaneta, just a mile away from the monastery on the top of Monte Cassino. Further down, another attack on the town, this time along the slopes that led up from the river, almost managed to get behind Cassino and reached a point just a few hundred yards from the monastery. These gains were made through desperate close-quarter fighting, wrenching ground from the Germans in grenade and small arms duels. Everywhere the resistance was furious, each German soldier clinging tenaciously to every rock. The US 151st Field Artillery fired 4,568 shells during this attack, but the rounds from the 105mm howitzers made little impact on the enemy's concrete bunkers.

★ ★ ★

By 4 February it was clear that the US 34th Division had exhausted itself; its numbers were seriously depleted and it needed rest. For the next three days it did as best it could to gather new strength while leaving the artillery and mortars to carry the fight to the enemy. General Keyes meanwhile planned yet another attack. He brought the remainder of the 36th Division over on to the mountains to the right of the 34th, and prepared for a two-division strike against the Cassino massif and the town. In support, Clark had urged McCreery and Juin to attack once again in their X Corps and CEF sectors on the same day. The whole of Fifth Army's front would come alive in one great push for the Liri valley. General McCreery's Tommies attacked during the night of 7 February; but Juin's North Africans could do nothing. The French Corps had fought itself to a standstill capturing and holding Monte Belvedere, and could not muster the strength to renew its offensive. (To put some human meaning into these words: by 3 February the three battalions of Col Roux's 4e Régiment de Tirailleurs Tunisiens had suffered 1,481 casualties, including every company officer – a rate of perhaps 70 per cent killed, wounded and missing. No one could fairly claim that Gen de Montsabert's 3rd Algerian Division had not already made a heart-breaking effort in drawing the enemy's eyes from the path of the 'Red Bull'.)

US II Corps began its move in the early hours of 8 February. The 133rd Infantry, backed by tanks and the massive firepower of 8-in howitzers firing in direct support, attacked Cassino town. Initial gains were made and the infantry penetrated 200 yards into the built-up area, but once again the shattered houses and the jumbled mountains of rubble spilling across the narrow streets slowed the progress of the tanks, while murderous fire from impregnable steel and concrete hides checked the infantry's attack. The house-by-house advance slowed to a halt, and then rocked back on its heels as the Germans counter-attacked.

A smokescreen put down on and around the medieval castle overlooking Cassino town (foreground) helps shield troops of the US 34th Division attacking across the Rapido towards the old Italian barracks a mile away to the north-right of this picture. Dominating the area is the monastery, which was, according to the enemy, free of any German soldiers. To the men on the ground below the fortress-like monastery seemed to be watching their every move. (US National Archives)

For no less than six days the 133rd Infantry clawed away at the enemy in the ruinous maze of Cassino town. The GIs used bazookas to blast their way into the buildings; anti-tank guns were dragged up to fire at point-blank range into emplacements, but made little impact. Each German soldier had to be driven out of his lair with grenade, Tommy gun or bayonet; and still the defenders refused to give ground.

Above on the bare mountainsides, the battalions of the 135th and 168th Infantry concentrated on the heights of Monte Cassino, the cornerstone of the defensive line. The GIs with the 'Red Bull' painted on their helmets pushed forward and got tantalisingly close, but were stifled by concentrated enemy fire. Great acts of heroism took place on the exposed ridges and in the narrow gullies, as individuals and small groups threw themselves into the attack, but the infantry were too exposed and the enemy too well entrenched for the exhausted Americans to be able to wrest the last few vital yards. On the right, Gen Walker committed the combined weight of his 36th Division against the same stubborn resistance, and the Texans' attack against Colle Maiola and Colle San Angelo met with similar results. Gains were made at great cost in lives, but the last few hundred yards seemed like miles. The ground, the weather and the enemy all conspired to frustrate II Corps's attempt at a breakthrough, and the attrition of its fighting strength finally forced Gen Keyes to call a halt to the offensive on 9 February.

The battle-weariness and low morale of the survivors, reported by many observers, reflected not just sheer exhaustion but also their reaction to a horrendous toll of casualties. Between 24 January and 12 February the US 34th Division as a whole recorded 2,351 killed, wounded and missing - a figure representing 49 per cent of the strength of the division's rifle companies. For the same twenty-day period the 3/133rd Infantry reported 249 dead, wounded and missing - 56 per cent of the battalion's rifle strength. The stark meaning of these figures is that, on average, every GI in the rifle companies who survived had lost about half of his buddies. But even these figures do not convey the level to which some units were ground away. In the 2/168th Infantry the three rifle companies - with an official establishment of 561 officers and men - ended the battle with a total strength of 85 all ranks. In the 36th Division the combined strength of both 1st and 3rd Bns, 141st Infantry - establishment, 1,742 officers and men - was reported on 12 February as 182 all ranks; and of these the remaining strength of the three rifle companies of the 3/141st totalled just 22 men. These were losses fully comparable to the experience of soldiers committed to major attacks on the Western Front in 1916-17 - which are often ignorantly regarded as slaughters unrepeatable in history.

General Keyes recognised that his corps was a spent force, and gave orders for the troops to dig in and hold what they had managed to seize. The first battle for the Cassino massif and the Gustav Line was over; it was time to pass the cup to the new troops who were now entering the shadows of the valley.

CHAPTER FOUR

Anzio – Build-Up, Check and Recoil: 28 January–4 February

By the fourth day of the Anzio landings Field Marshal Kesselring was convinced that the slow, methodical build-up of forces in the Allied beachhead, with little evidence of immediate aggressive intentions, meant that they would not risk an ambitious attack through the Alban Hills to Rome, but would only attempt to cut across the rear of German Tenth Army by making for Route 7 at Cisterna and Route 6 at Valmontone. The first Allied objective would have to be Cisterna; and it was there that he concentrated his main strength. He now knew that he was faced by cautious generals who would feel their way forward, rather than bold exponents of mobile warfare who were willing to take a gamble. Kesselring was confident that the troops which he was rapidly moving into the defensive line would be easily capable of suffocating the landings and, when they were properly organised, would be sufficiently strong to eliminate the beachhead completely.

By 28 January, six days after the landings, both Clark and Alexander were beginning to show some unease about the lack of movement from Anzio. Clark visited Gen Lucas and asked him when he was going to take Cisterna. He urged aggressive action at once, as further delay would allow the enemy to build up his forces to dangerous levels. By the 29th Lucas at last felt that he was strong enough to launch a full scale attack the following day, the ninth day of the invasion. He planned for two distinct advances: by British 1st Division towards Campoleone and then Albano, backed by tanks of US 1st Armored Division; and by US 3rd Division, with 504th Parachute Infantry (a detached regiment from the 82nd Airborne Division) and the Rangers under its control, towards Cisterna and then Valmontone.

While no major attacks had been ordered before this full-scale offensive, some initial movements had been taking place within the beachhead. Both of the Allied divisions had been probing the perimeter with limited advances and reconnaissance in force, gradually pushing back the enemy forces with which they came into contact. It was known that units of the 'Hermann Göring' Panzer-Division were established in front of Cisterna – there was no mistaking their white collar patches and divisional cuff titles – and that 3.Panzer-Grenadier-Division barred the way to Albano. Some stiff fighting had taken place during these encounters, leaving the two Allied divisional commanders in no doubt about the quality of the enemy units which lay in their path. Before launching his offensive, in order to concentrate his force on a narrow front to add weight to the attack, Lucas used the newly arrived US 45th Division to hold the beachhead flanks so that British 1st and US 3rd Divisions could release their full strength for the drive out of the perimeter.

The Allied offensive got underway on 30 January, just one day before Von Mackensen had intended to launch his counter-attack. The Germans were assembling thirty battalions of infantry for this move, supported by armour and artillery; six more battalions were held in reserve. The situation confronting Lucas was somewhat eased when German intelligence was deceived into expecting the possibility of further Allied landings in the region of Civitavecchia, and some troops were moved from the Anzio perimeter to counter this; but Von Mackensen still had a formidable force facing Anzio. That Lucas finally struck out when he did probably saved the whole beachhead.

The British attack opened just before midnight on 29

Sherman I tank of C Sqn, 46th Royal Tank Regt moving up from the Anzio beaches on the day after the landings, in support of 2nd Bn, North Staffordshire Regt from the British 1st Division. The tank shows the black 'liver bird' formation badge of 23 Armd Bde on its right differential housing; 46 RTR's Liverpool connection came from its having been formed from the Liverpool Welsh, a Territorial infantry battalion. The regiment had been part of the brigade during many battles in North Africa, including El Alamein and Tunisia, and in Sicily, but landed at Anzio as an independent unit. Note the big refuelling funnel among the gear on the front. Each night tank crews had to refuel from stacks of individual jerrycans. Their maintenance tasks meant that they got even less sleep than the infantry. (Imperial War Museum)

American infantry move up past a knocked-out Sherman during the battle to extend the beachhead. (US National Archives)

January with a preliminary move to capture the start line for the main advance; 24 Guards Brigade pushed forwards to capture the crossroads 2,000 yards south of the Campoleone railway overpass. Both of the leading battalions, 1st Scots Guards and 1st Irish Guards, ran into trouble. The Irish Guards were first stopped and then forced back by German tanks and had to be supported by a battalion of Shermans from US 1st Armored Division. The Scots Guards were delayed by an enemy roadblock and a minefield.

The main attack by 3 Brigade, commanded by Brig James, did not get going until 1510 hours on the afternoon of 30 January. Two battalions of infantry, 1st King's Shropshire Light Infantry and 1st Duke of Wellington's Regt, pressed forward against scattered opposition and gained the high ground just short of the overpass at Campoleone. The enemy's main defence line was along the railway, and accurate fire from this area stopped 3 Brigade moving any further forward. Tanks from 46th Royal Tank Regiment now came up to join in the attack on some enemy anti-tank guns beyond the railway embankment, but were unable to silence them. By this time the light was failing, and 1st Division's advance halted for the night.

General Harmon had planned for the lead regiment of his US 1st Armored Division to attack to the left of the British using the bed of the disused railway from Carroceto as a line of departure. He would then pass to the left of Campoleone and move on Albano from the flank, whilst the British infantry drove straight up the Anzio-Albano road. When they began their move, Harmon's tanks immediately ran into trouble from enemy resistance, minefields and mud. By the end of the day his Shermans were still struggling to take control of his start line.

This delay in getting the American armour forward – and pressure from Gen Clark when the army commander visited him that evening – prompted Gen Lucas to change his plan. He now decided that US 1st Armored Division would wait until the British had captured the road junction 1,000 yards north of Campoleone, then launch a column from 1st Armored Regiment through the British to attack up the Albano road. The rest of the division would follow as quickly as possible. On 31 January the British attacked with 2nd Sherwood Foresters supported by tanks from 46th RTR, but were unable to breach the enemy defences along the railway embankment. Try as they might they could not eliminate the well-entrenched anti-tank guns covering every approach. A minefield barred progress along the road. James halted his brigade's attack and called for tanks and artillery to soften up the enemy strongpoints. The Americans tried to get across the embankment to the left of the road with their tanks, but after some initial success in closing with the feature they were brought to a halt by the enemy guns.

Another attack was put in the next day, 1 February, when the US 1st Armored Regiment tried a frontal assault up the main road, but this too ground to a halt just short of the embankment. After a terrific artillery barrage the Sherwood Foresters made another attempt, only to be stopped once again by concentrated fire from beyond the embankment. Some progress was made by US 6th Armored Regiment along the disused railway bed, but this small gain was carved out at great cost and amounted to just 500 yards of new ground. By nightfall on 1 February it was clear that the enemy had established more than a covering screen across the Albano road: it appeared to be their main line of resistance. The left hand assault from the beachhead had been stopped dead with only the area around the station at Campoleone to show for its efforts. It was, none the less, a penetration of the enemy perimeter, and the attack had pushed a 2,000-yard salient into the junction of the two German divisions holding the area; there was now a considerable gap between the 65.Infanterie and 3.Panzer-Grenadier-Divisions. (See map on page 33.)

Meanwhile, on the right of the beachhead, Gen Lucian Truscott's US 3rd 'Marne' Division also began its attack on 30 January. The opening moves were made by the Rangers which had been placed under his command: Col Darby was ordered to send his 1st and 3rd Ranger Bns forward one hour before the main attack to infiltrate in the darkness across four miles of open fields and seize Cisterna by surprise. They were then to hold the town while the 4th Rangers and 3rd Bn, 15th Infantry from 3rd Division advanced straight down the Conca-Cisterna road to link up with them. Truscott planned to unleash his main attack at 0200 hours, a two-regiment advance with the objective of cutting Route 7 on either side of the town: the 7th Infantry would move forward on the left of the central road, while 15th Infantry advanced on the right. At the same time, 504th Parachute Infantry were to move aggressively down the Mussolini Canal to protect the division's right flank. (For all these moves, see map on page 33.)

The Rangers at Cisterna

At the appointed time Darby's Rangers moved out in two columns, creeping noiselessly forward towards Cisterna. At first progress was good and the long lines of silent men slipped between various German positions without rousing any sentries. Hugging the sides of a weaving ditch, the Rangers closed on their objective; but when the leading battalion came within 800 yards of Cisterna they walked into an ambush, and three German self-propelled guns opened fire on the strung-out column. Reacting swiftly, the Rangers knocked out the guns; but the noise of this engagement attracted the attention of more pockets of the enemy, and machine guns and mortars now started to home in on the exposed Americans.

The Germans had detected the Rangers' approach and had had sufficient time to organise a trap for the unsuspecting battalions. The 'Hermann Göring' Division had not had the chance to establish fixed defences but had made good use of what was available. The troops had emplaced machine guns and anti-tank weapons in every farmhouse along the road; many others scattered through the fields also housed heavy weapons. These strongpoints were co-ordinated to provide interlocking zones of fire. Strategically placed tanks and self-propelled guns also covered every approach, ready to counter any breakthrough. The Rangers now found themselves in the middle of this enemy battle zone.

They were crack troops, individually selected volunteers who were trained to a very high standard of fitness and battle skills; but they were essentially a light raiding force, organised in units only about half the size of standard line infantry battalions and armed only with the weapons which they could hand-carry. The criss-crossing German fire trapped the vulnerable Rangers in the open without cover. Men scrambled into ditches and made for the few scattered houses that there were, dodging enemy fire as they tried to establish some form of defence. With no front or rear, the enemy were all around them and attempts to find cover often brought them into yet closer contact with the Germans.

With customary efficiency, the men of the 'Hermann Göring' Panzer-Division now set about rolling up the American attack. Tanks came down Route 7 and spread out into the open fields, flushing out the Rangers and forcing them into small pockets. The Rangers fought back with bazookas and 'sticky' grenades, but it was a one-sided struggle. Although two Panzers were knocked out through brave individual actions, the remainder accomplished their task.

By noon the Rangers had all been rounded up or killed: of the 767 men from 1st and 3rd Ranger Bns who set out that morning, only six escaped. The vast majority of those who were missing had been captured by the enemy

Down the road back towards Conca, the 4th Ranger Bn and 3/15th Infantry made every effort to respond to the pleas for help coming over the radios from the two hard-pressed Ranger battalions, but were themselves held up near the village of Isola Bella. Trying to deploy off the road, the GIs made easy targets for the entrenched enemy 200 yards away. Two tank-destroyers and two half-tracks came up to try to give some cover, but immediately ran into a minefield and were destroyed. All day long the German defenders kept 4th Rangers at bay, resisting every move towards the village. Behind them, the 3/15th did manage to move off the road to the right in an attempt to support the isolated Rangers, but the battle was over long before they could cover the necessary ground. When this news reached him Col Manhart, CO of the 15th Infantry, recalled his 3rd Bn and told his men to veer to the left and try to gain the village of Isola Bella from the rear. This they did after a protracted fight in which tanks and tank-destroyers pounded the enemy-held houses to rubble. With the village in their hands, the Americans then turned south to move down the road and catch in the rear the enemy who were holding up the 4th Ranger Battalion.

These attacks on Cisterna had come up against Von Mackensen's main defensive line, which ran in front of the town and not to its rear, as had first been thought. Instead of thinly held outposts and a scattering of light forces forming a screen, the US 3rd Division's advance had run straight into a heavy concentration of first class German troops. The two flank attacks by Truscott's 7th Infantry Regiment and the other two battalions of the 15th encountered the same skilled and determined resistance as had the unfortunate Rangers. After some initial gains both were halted by the strong defensive line manned by the 'Hermann Göring' Division. Nor were these the only crack enemy units encountered: on the left, the 7th Infantry ran into paratroopers of the German 1.Fallschirmjäger-Division. On the right the flanking movement made by 504th Parachute Infantry had to withstand a counter-attack by the newly arrived 7th Luftwaffe Jäger Bn (though this was far from an elite unit, being a second-line battalion of air force conscripts half-trained for the infantry role). To add further strength to the line, the first units of 715.Division had also arrived and were immediately fed into the defences at Cisterna as they became available.

That evening Gen Clark visited VI Corps HQ and spoke with Lucas, receiving first hand the bad news about the advance. Clark was clearly unhappy with the way the attacks had been handled. He was disappointed to learn that half of the available armour of US 1st Armored Division had been committed to the protection of the left flank of the British advance; he ordered that this commitment be reversed, and that an all-out armoured attack be made from Campoleone the next day. Clark was also displeased to learn that US 3rd Division's advance on Cisterna had been spearheaded by the lightly-armed Rangers. 'This was a definite error of judgement', he told Lucas, 'for the Rangers do not have the support weapons to overcome the resistance indicated.' Using sharp language, he attempted to galvanise the corps commander into a more imaginative attack.

US Army wounded are brought back to a casualty clearing station near the Anzio front line. The rain, mud, overcrowding and shellfire produced conditions much like those of the old Western Front in 1915-18, and many weather-related casualties were suffered in addition to battle wounds. (US National Archives)

The 'Marne' Division checked

Truscott's efforts had gained a mile and a half of new ground towards Cisterna, but he still had two miles to go. During the night he arranged for a tidying up of the line: his men cleaned out pockets of the enemy that had been bypassed, brought up fresh stocks of ammunition and reinforced the forward troops, ready to continue the drive the next day. General Truscott had decided to dispense with his original plan to cut Route 7 above and below Cisterna, and now decided to launch his two regiments on frontal assaults directly at the town itself, using the roads from Isola Bella and Ponte Rotto as the axes of his attack.

The advance resumed on the morning of 31 January when 4th Ranger Bn continued its work of the previous day and pressed down the road towards Isola Bella to link up with 15th Infantry in the village. In the afternoon, preceded by an artillery barrage fired by all the guns of the division, the 15th tried once again. Its second battalion, fresh into the battle, passed through the positions of the 3/15th and made straight down the road for Cisterna. Behind it came the regiment's other two battalions, fanning out from the road to clear the fields and ditches on either side. The artillery support was lavish, as was the contribution from the tanks and tank-destroyers. The American troops fought with great spirit and determination, but so did the enemy, from entrenched positions and enjoying an equal measure of support from their Panzers, anti-tank guns and self-propelled assault guns. The result was stalemate after an advance of around a mile; there was still a mile to go to Cisterna.

The advance by the 7th Infantry along the road from Ponte Rotto got off to a slow start. Before its first battalion could reach the line of departure it was attacked by a force of fourteen tanks, some of them the monstrous 60-ton Tigers. (Armed with the lethal 88mm gun, and armoured so heavily as to be invulnerable at normal range, the Tiger was operated by heavy battalions at corps level; few were available in Italy, but some were temporarily attached to the 'Hermann Göring' Panzer-Division at Anzio, apparently from 3rd Company, Heavy Tank Bn 508.) For a while the enemy armour wrought havoc amongst the American infantry until support was brought up in the shape of Sherman tanks and M10 tank-destroyers. These stalked the enemy tanks, which were strung out along the road and had found it very difficult to deploy on the soft ground on either side. Two were quickly knocked out and three more succumbed during the ensuing struggle, as American field artillery joined in the short battle. It was too much for the Germans, and they withdrew

With the enemy counter-attack finally out of the way the 7th Infantry could get going again. At 1620 hours on 31 January, behind a concentration of fire laid down by three field artillery battalions, the advance resumed. Unfortunately, it only got a quarter of a mile beyond the village before darkness fell and the GIs had to dig in for the night. Other attacks were put in on the left side of the road towards the railway line before Cisterna, but these resulted in the same kind of desperate struggles as elsewhere on 3rd Division's front. Accurate enemy small arms fire criss-crossed the open fields, interlaced with armour piercing and high explosive shellfire from well established defensive positions. Small gains were made; farm houses changed hands at great human cost, only to be retaken by determined enemy infantry almost immediately. Troublesome German machine guns were overrun, only for the GIs to draw even more fire from others nearby. It was a nightmare advance that stumbled to a ragged halt as darkness descended over the battlefield. Day two of the battle to break out of the beachhead was rewarded by just a few yards of new territory. Cisterna appeared to be no nearer; VI Corps' frustrations continued. It was clear that more German units had arrived in the area; intelligence suggested that the bulk of 26. Panzer-Division's armour was now facing Lucas and his men.

On 1 February the attack resumed. Massed artillery plastered the area, troops moved forward, ground was gained, and then the enemy counter-attacked. The pattern was repeated along the whole of the 'Marne' Division's front. On the left the 7th Infantry met yet another new German unit when it was rebuffed by elements of 71.Division. By noon it was clear to Gen Truscott that his division was becoming exhausted; he could not now hope to take Cisterna from a German concentration which was well entrenched, resolute, and which appeared to be growing ever stronger. Each day new enemy units were entering the perimeter as they arrived, and Von Mackensen's forces now appeared to be numerically the stronger. The appear-

American infantry attack a German-held house with a bazooka 2.36-in anti-tank rocket launcher. Against the Panzers the bazooka was effective at a range of about 50 yards - in the hands of a very brave and skillful soldier. It was also useful in house-to-house fighting, though its fierce backblast made it dangerous to fire in a confined space. (US National Archives)

ance of 29.Panzer-Grenadier-Division from the Adriatic front - Kesselring's chief mobile reserve - was a clear indication that the enemy was gathering for a major counter-attack. Truscott knew that if such a counter-attack were to fall on his division as it struggled forward the result would be a disaster. He called a halt to the advance and gave the order for all troops to dig in immediately and brace themselves for whatever was hurled against them. Minefields were laid, wire barriers strung out and anti-tank guns sited to cover approaches. Behind this hasty rampart the Americans waited for the gathering storm to break.

On to the defensive
Truscott's shift to a defensive stance was agreed by both Lucas and Clark, and verbal orders were sent out to all units in the beachhead to prepare defensive positions to meet the expected German counter-attack. General Alexander was not comfortable with the situation and, at a meeting that morning, had urged for the advance to be continued until Campoleone and Cisterna were captured. He knew that the lodgement was too small to be safely held. The whole area was overlooked by high ground inland so that any part of the beachhead could be observed; the whole area was defenceless to long range enemy artillery fire, and virtually every sector of the perimeter was vulnerable to German assault. There was so little room for manoeuvre that a breakthrough anywhere would bring the enemy directly to the sea. Alexander felt that it was important to expand the beachhead as much as possible, but he too recognised the limits of prudent action now that the Germans were clearly massing for their counter-offensive.

Allied reinforcements and supplies continued to arrive through the port of Anzio and over the beaches. In an effort to match the German build-up around the perimeter, 168 Infantry Brigade from the British 56th Division landed in the beachhead to bolster the British effort; and on 2 February the US 1st Special Service Force was shipped in - a unique commando-style unit consisting of 1,800 picked American and Canadian troops. More anti-aircraft guns and artillery were also added to the arsenal of VI Corps.

Never the less, seen from the German perspective VI Corps' attack had in fact been a very near thing. Von Mackensen had been forced to commit the bulk of his forces to contain Lucas' advance, and German losses had been heavy. Most worrying to him was the armoured attack at Campoleone, where the Americans came close to breaking through the German line. US VI Corps' assault also finally convinced the commander of German Fourteenth Army to postpone his own attack, which had been timed for 1 February. Von Mackensen now doubted that he had sufficient strength to wipe out the Anzio lodgement, even though at that time he had a superiority in numbers of troops - 100,000 men, against 80,000 Allied troops. His main problem was a shortage of supplies, especially guns and ammunition. In the aftermath of the American attack Von Mackensen too now adopted a defensive attitude, with the goal of confining the Allies inside as small a lodgement as possible.

For the Allies the battle to break out of the beachhead had been a demoralising disappointment. Both the British 1st and US 3rd Divisions had gained only a few miles towards objectives that had been there for the taking in the first few hours of the landings. By contrast, the enemy had succeeded in assembling and rushing forward a reaction force of a wholly unexpected strength. Superb generalship by Kesselring had emasculated the power of the Anzio landing and contained its expansion; and he had achieved all this without denuding the forces facing US Fifth Army on the Gustav Line. After an astonishingly easy landing US VI Corps was now in great danger of becoming a liability. Its operations had not eased the situation at Cassino, nor had they posed an insurmountable threat to German strategy in Italy. Kesselring was confident that VI COrps could be contained and eventually eliminated. For the Allies, now on the defensive, Anzio would suck in increasing amounts of men, stores and shipping just to keep the lodgement supplied. Rather than landing a wildcat, as Churchill had envisaged, Alexander and Clark had beached a giant whale.

★ ★ ★

From a German point of view, the cordon that Fourteenth Army had placed around the Allied landings at Anzio was vulnerable in several places and strong in others. In the east, on the left of the German line, the Mussolini Canal acted as an anti-tank barrier for both sides. On the extreme right of the line to the west, where the perimeter curved around

German Army light flak crew covering the Anzio perimeter, spring 1944. The detachment are manning a 20mm Flakvierling quadruple cannon mount; with a practical rate of fire of 700-800 rounds per minute it was the most effective German light AA weapon, feared by low-flying Allied pilots. These cannon were used to great effect by the enemy during the first days of the landings when numbers of them were rushed into the perimeter and used against ground targets to counter the initial probes inland by US VI Corps troops. (Bundesarchiv)

the sea, the ground was fraught with danger for the Germans. This sector was vulnerable to heavy and accurate shellfire from Allied warships, and any movement or concentration during daylight brought instant retribution. It was in the centre that both sides concentrated the bulk of their forces, since the only two real axes for any advance into or out of Anzio were along the roads leading through Campoleone and Cisterna. General Lucas had based his break-out plans on these routes at the end of January; it was no surprise, then, that they also figured prominently in Von Mackensen's plans for his coming offensive.

Although he had no great enthusiasm for a frontal attack against the main strength of US VI Corps and would have preferred to outflank the Allied forces, Von Mackensen knew that he was vulnerable to the dreadfully destructive power of Allied naval gunfire if he strayed too close to the coast. To try to attack over the canals in the east would require complex bridging operations and slow down the initial assault. He therefore decided that his main offensive would have to be down the Albano-Anzio road. As a preliminary move he needed to control the network of roads around Aprilia, the village known to everyone in the beachhead as 'the Factory' (see map on page 33). Aprilia was at the base of the long Allied salient leading up to Campoleone sta-

tion which had been carved out by British 1st Division and American tanks during the first break-out battle.

In the early hours of 4 February, German troops struck both sides of the Campoleone salient simultaneously. From the west a regiment of 65.Division attacked, while from the east tanks of 3.Panzer-Grenadier-Division and infantry from 715.Division squeezed the other flank. Despite muddy conditions and fierce British resistance, the two enemy drives met on the main Albano-Anzio road, sealing the British forward troops in an isolated pocket around the Factory. The enemy now swung north to eliminate them. British 3 Brigade, with 24 Guards Brigade under command, were on their own; Lucas had withdrawn US 1st Armored Division into corps reserve.

The battle lasted throughout the day and was marked by stubborn resistance from the Guardsmen, the 'Dukes', the Foresters and KSLI. Under enemy pressure a bloody-minded determination to hold on to the disputed Factory area eventually caught fire into an offensive spirit as they gained the upper hand, and once again established contact with their comrades to the south. At a cost of 1,400 killed, wounded and missing, the Tommies had re-established the salient along the Albano road.

It was clear to Gen Lucas that although the Campoleone salient remained intact it would always be vulnerable to enemy flank attacks. The position was dangerously exposed and could not conform as part of a cohesive defensive line. The corps commander therefore gave orders for the forward troops to be withdrawn during the night, and for British 1st Division to establish a new line of defences. The British skilfully disengaged from the enemy and pulled out under the cover of darkness, withdrawing two and a half miles into new positions.

Von Mackensen's objective of eliminating the Campoleone salient had been achieved, but not at the expense of British 1st Division alone. The enemy had lost over 500 men killed and 300 taken prisoner, together with a good number of tanks and other heavy equipment. As a preliminary to the main offensive, the stubborn resistance put up by the British had taught the Germans that the defenders within the beachhead would be no pushover.

As this German attack was being developed on 4 February, Gen Lucas issued written orders to the beachhead commanders regarding defensive operations. All units were to dig in and hold where they were, but at Mark Clark's insistence a new beachhead final defence line was to be created several miles to their rear. This was to be the fallback line should the enemy penetrate existing defence lines, but there was to be no retreat beyond it: this line had to be held at all costs. It ran along the Moletta River, then across the central section of the lodgement about three miles behind the British front and five miles behind the American to the Mussolini Canal, and back down beside the waterway to the sea. The water features on both flanks were the easiest to defend; Lucas put one regiment from US 45th Division on the Moletta, and on the other side of the beachhead the sector along the canal was handed over to Gen Frederick's newly arrived 1st Special Service Force.

'Screaming Meemie' to the GIs, 'Moaning Minnie' to the Tommies: a German 15cm Nebelwerfer 41 rocket launcher in action in an Italian orchard. The Nebelwerfer's six launcher tubes mounted on a 3.7cm gun carriage could fire six 35kg (77lb) rocket-propelled mortar bombs in a ten-second salvo. Their nerve-shattering noise in flight and powerful blast effect on impact had a considerable effect on Allied morale. They did, however, leave a very noticeable smoke trail which enabled their firing positions to be pinpointed easily for counter-battery fire; their crews had to get in and out of action quickly. They also produced a fearful backblast when fired, which explains why the three crew members in the background are hastily making for the rear. (Bundesarchiv)

The remainder of the line was held as follows: the reinforced British 1st Division dug itself in from west of the Albano road to Carano, including the Factory; and US 3rd Division was responsible for the remainder of the central line across to the Mussolini Canal. The corps reserve was provided by US 1st Armored Division and the remainder of US 45th Division, strategically placed to counter any German breakthrough. These two reserve divisions were also set the task of organising the main part of the final defence line. With such preparations in place, VI Corps braced itself for the German onslaught.

CHAPTER FIVE

The Second Battle: 15–18 February

In the last days of January 1944 Gen Fridolin von Senger und Etterlin, commander of XIV Panzer Corps, whose troops were defending the Gustav Line against US Fifth Army, was beginning to feel that his hold on the line was slipping. The earlier attacks by British X Corps on his right across the Garigliano had compelled his superiors to release the two Panzer-Grenadier-Divisions that were German Army Group C's main reserves, in order to prevent what could have been a dangerous breakthrough; Von Senger had feared that the whole of the German line could have been rolled up from the south. The arrival of these two divisions and their deployment against McCreery's corps just as the British were pressing their attack quickly halted the offensive, and the Germans were able to stabilise that part of the line. The German 94.Division was then strengthened by various smaller units operating as local reserves and was able to regain its defensive stance. By the time the US II Corps had begun to press home its attack in the centre, the main threat against the German right had been removed. The 29. and part of 90.Panzer-Grenadier-Divisions could now be withdrawn and sent north against the Anzio landings. The remainder of 90.Panzer-Grenadier-Division became the new Army Group reserve behind the Cassino front, while still committed as back-up to 94. Division facing the British X Corps.

With Allied landings in his rear, Von Senger knew that he could no longer expect any more help from Army reserves; every available unit to the north of him was now fully committed in containing the Anzio landings and preparing for the counter-attack. XIV Panzer Corps would have to rely on its own resources to hold the line. By carefully withdrawing selected small units from various parts of his sector, Von Senger was able to create his own mobile reserves. Fresh troops had been promised him, but only as replacements for tired divisions that had to be pulled out of the line for rest. The 71.Division was on its way to relieve the exhausted men of Panzer-Grenadier Regiment 15 who were holding the centre of the Cassino line.

The first attempt on the Rapido caused Von Senger little concern, but the US 34th Division's attacks were another matter, as was the continued pressure that the French were applying up in the mountains on his left. The CEF had renewed their offensive and were attacking a section of the line held by the German 44. Division. This had originally been formed in Vienna in 1938, based on an expansion of the old 'Hoch und Deutschmeister' Viennese regiment of the Austrian army. During the early part of the war it took part in the Polish, French and Russian campaigns; but in winter 1942/43 the division was destroyed at Stalingrad. A new 44.Infanterie-Division was re-raised in Austria in 1943 and given the honorary title of 'Reichsgrenadier-Division Hoch und Deutschmeister'. The new 'H&D' was commanded by Lt Gen Dr Franz Bayer,

Major General Ernst-Günther Baade, one of the most colourful and idiosyncratic of German generals. He started the war as a squadron leader in Kavallerie - Regiment 3, and later held combat commands and staff appointments in Poland, France, North Africa, Russia, Sicily, Italy and North-West Europe. His defence of Cassino and the Hitler Line at the head of 90.Panzer-Grenadier Division earned him a high reputation amongst fellow officers. After finally commanding a Panzer Korps in Germany in 1945 he was to die of wounds on the last day of the war. The award on his right sleeve signifies the destruction of an enemy tank with a hand-held weapon - the Knight's Cross and Oakleaves were given to senior officers for command performance, but this was the kind of personal gallantry decoration which reassured a general's soldiers that he knew what his orders would mean for them. (Bundesarchiv)

who had previously commanded another Austrian division, 331.Infanterie, in Russia. The 'H&D' Division joined the Italian campaign in December 1943 and had fought defensively during the withdrawal to the Gustav Line, but in Gen von Senger's opinion it had not shown itself to be outstanding in battle.

General Juin's French forces were now applying sustained and determined pressure on the 'H&D' Division, and it was beginning to falter. Von Senger was able to stiffen its resolve by throwing in a completely fresh regiment from

Lieutenant General Bernard Freyberg VC, DSO, Commander New Zealand II Corps. Freyberg had won the first of his three DSOs when he swam ashore in the Dardanelles in 1915 to light beacons to deceive the Turks as to the landing beaches chosen for the Gallipoli campaign. He was later awarded the Victoria Cross for his 'splendid personal gallantry' as a battalion commander in November 1916. By the end of the Great War he had been wounded nine times, had been awarded two bars to his DSO, a CMG, and had risen to the rank of brigadier general. (Imperial War Museum)

71.Division, which had just arrived in the area to relieve Panzer-Grenadier Regiment 15. This held the line against elements of Juin's 3rd Algerian Division, but attacks further north threatened to produce a French breakthrough. To stem this attack, on 30 January Von Senger switched his only reserve - strong elements of 90.Panzer-Grenadier-Division - from British X Corp's front right across the Cassino massif to enter the line against Juin's North Africans. He knew that the decision was very risky; but with his masterly reading of the battlefield he could see that Clark's main offensive had switched from the lower Garigliano area to the mountains to the north of Cassino. He therefore committed his main reserve against the Allies' main effort. A characteristic example of Von Senger's good generalship, this move took the impetus out of Juin's attack.

Nevertheless, the losses endured by the Germans in these defensive battles were mounting considerably. By the end of January, XIV Panzer Corps was losing men at a rate of a battalion a day. The casualties sustained by XIV Corps between 11 and 20 January were 2,487, but rose between 21 and 31 January to 4,118. The corps commander was compelled to make up these losses by pressing men from support and supply units into the line as infantry - a very unsatisfactory practice, but one that was unavoidable. When Gen Keyes' US II Corps pressed in on Monte Cassino and seized the heights which almost overlooked the Liri valley, Von Senger 'mustered all the might of his authority' and requested that the whole Gustav Line be given up. He urged that Tenth Army should occupy a new line behind the Anzio bridgehead. Kesselring dismissed the suggestion, claiming that there was still a good deal of fight left in the defensive line and that it should be held at all costs. To help Von Senger, Kesselring switched a few parachute battalions of 1.Fallschirmjäger-Division from the Adriatic Front over to Cassino. 'Smiling Albert' was still optimistic, convinced that the Cassino sector could be held and that the Anzio bridgehead might be eliminated, or at least made untenable for the Allies.

XIV Panzer Corps was holding the Cassino position with a variety of units from a number of divisions. Few German formations were complete; each had given up battalions or regiments to other divisions to reinforce vulnerable points, or to help with countering the Anzio landings. The corps commander now brought all available units of Maj Gen Ernst-Günther Baade's 90.Panzer-Grenadier-Division into the Cassino sector and placed them and the existing Cassino defenders - some from 44. and 71.Divisions - under the unified command of Gen Baade. These troops were reinforced by two Parachute Rifle battalions and Parachute Machine Gun Battalion 1. It was these fresh units that US II Corps met during its last push on Monte Cassino at the beginning of February. It was not surprising that the tired Americans were brought to an abrupt halt.

In placing these units under one commander of the calibre of Ernst-Günther Baade, Gen von Senger was creating a formidable fighting team under a skilful and charismatic leader. Baade was a cavalry general; an international show-jumper before the war, in 1939 he had been a squadron leader in Kavallerie - Regiment 3 which Von Senger himself commanded. Baade was soon making a name for himself as 'an original character', and his idiosyncratic personality set him apart from most Wehrmacht senior officers. He often acted with remarkable daring, and his sense of humour was such that he sometimes went into action wearing a captured Scottish kilt. On one occasion, after a night raid, he radioed the British over their own net - 'Stop firing. On my way back. Baade.' But this clowning did not disguise the fact that Baade was also a very brave and independent leader of men, who had been decorated with the Knight's Cross with Oakleaves. He had fought in Poland, France, Russia, North Africa and Sicily before arriving in Italy in January 1944 as the new commander of the 90.Panzer-Grenadier-Division. (This had been re-formed on Corsica from the remnants of the old 90.Leichte Afrika-Division, a crack element of Rommel's desert army which had been lost in Tunisia.) In 1942 Baade had commanded Panzer-Grenadier - Regiment 115 with 15.Panzer-Division, and a 'battle group' of the Afrika Korps at El Alamein. He had shown solid command and staff talents during his career, successfully achieving a number of challenging missions - among them, command of the 'penal' 999.Leichte Afrika-Division during the May 1943 fighting in Tunisia, and a major role in the organisation of the surprisingly successful withdrawal from Sicily that August.

51

A pre-war picture of the Benedictine monastery on Monte Cassino showing the immense size and strength of the building. The great abbey was originally founded by St Benedict in AD 529, and it was on this site that he wrote his famous Rule, laying down the foundations of monastic life. During its long existence the abbey had been sacked and destroyed on three previous occasions, only to be rebuilt to even greater grandeur by successive generations. On 15 February 1944 it was to suffer its fourth, and greatest, violation. (Imperial War Museum)

General Baade's defence of the Cassino sector would earn him a high reputation, and Tenth Army's commander, Von Vietinghoff, regarded him and Gen Heidrich, commander of 1.Fallschirmjäger-Division, as being 'in a class by themselves'.

The creation of New Zealand II Corps

German casualties during the opening moves against the Gustav Line, heavy though they were, were only half those suffered by the Allies. All of the troops in Gen Clark's three corps were now tired and somewhat discouraged; they needed a rest, but there were few reinforcements available to replace the worn-out divisions in the line. Clark had been forced by events to commit his only American reserve, the US 45th 'Thunderbird' Division, to help confront the German threat at Anzio; and the British 5th Division was also being pulled out of McCreery's X Corps to help beef up the precarious beachhead. Fifteenth Army Group commander Gen Alexander had already realised that any hope of a breakthrough on the Cassino front would be dependent on the injection of fresh troops. He decided to further weaken Oliver Leese's British Eighth Army on the now static Adriatic front, and sent two new divisions across to help Mark Clark get things moving at Cassino. The first to arrive was the 2nd New Zealand Division, followed closely by the 4th Indian Division.

General Bernard Freyberg had commanded 2nd NZ Division since its formation just after the start of the war. He was a veteran of many battles; on the Western Front during the Great War he had won the Victoria Cross for supreme gallantry, and had risen to the rank of brigadier by the time he was thirty. Freyberg had the reputation of being a formidable character who inspired his men by leading from the front, never stood on his dignity, and paid genuine attention to their day-to-day needs.

The New Zealand Division had seen action in Greece, had fought German paratroopers in Crete (where Freyberg had been cruelly handicapped by the need to conceal his knowledge of 'Ultra' intelligence), took part in Auchinleck's Cyrenaica offensive in North Africa and was present at the relief of Tobruk. After a short period in Syria it rejoined Eighth Army in time for El Alamein, and during Rommel's retreat into Tunisia it performed the decisive flanking movement in the battle of the Mareth Line. In November 1943 it joined the fighting in Italy when it took part in the crossing of the River Sangro as part of Montgomery's Eighth Army.

The division was unique in a number of ways. General Freyberg was often able to influence high command decisions as to where and how it was used, since he reported not only to his corps commander but also directly to the New Zealand government. This often made things difficult for senior commanders when considering how to deploy the division and what casualties it might risk; none the less, its spirit was never brought into question. It was one of the best and strongest divisions in the whole of the Allied armies; its reputation was great and its heart immense.

General Freyberg began moving his division over the Apennines on 17 January. General Alexander had decided to create a new corps for Fifth Army with the sole intention of exploiting a breakthrough into the Liri valley when an opening was eventually made. When Freyberg arrived in the area he was given the task of creating and commanding this new corps - New Zealand II Corps - from scratch. His command of the New Zealand division was taken over by one of his brigadiers, Howard Kippenberger. His other formation was to be 4th Indian Division, commanded by Gen F.S.Tuker.

Alexander had originally envisaged that Freyberg's new corps would be ready to exploit US II Corps' breakthrough, but by 12 February it was clear that the Americans had been fought to the limit of their endurance and would have to be relieved. New Zealand 2nd Division was put into the line to hold the Rapido, while Tuker's 4th Indian would go up on to the mountains to take over from Keyes' exhausted US 34th and 36th Divisions. But Alexander was not content for these fresh troops to be whittled away while deployed in a holding capacity; he wanted them on the offensive. Freyberg was ordered to plan a new attack on the Cassino positions. The second battle of Cassino was about to take shape.

When Gen Tuker's 4th Indian Division arrived in the

west and moved on to the mountains to the north of Monte Cassino, it did so without him in command; he had been taken ill with a recurring complaint and his place had been assumed by Brig Harry Dimoline. To reach the positions occupied by US 34th Division the Indians had to make a seven-mile flanking march across the exposed Rapido valley, up a succession of tortuous tracks and across rubble-strewn hillsides, all under the watchful gaze of the Germans up on Monte Cassino. The route passed across many exposed sections devoid of cover, where enemy shells screamed in on the slow and the unwary. The Americans had carved out a separate enclave well ahead of the main battle line, exposed and vulnerable to both the enemy and the weather. The Indian troops were shocked by what they found there.

General Ryder's GIs were in a very poor state, having spent the last weeks in exposed positions, under constant German fire, with little shelter or respite. The weather had been appalling; wind, rain, sleet and snow had reduced their physical resistance to almost zero. Many of the troops had not moved for days, trapped by the enemy sniper fire that picked off anyone foolish enough to show himself. Some had to be lifted bodily from their piled-stone shelters and stretchered off the mountains. Everywhere there were corpses, both German and American, lying where they fell; it had been impossible to reach them under fire, and many wounded had died in agony on the bare mountainsides, in sight but beyond help. The dead could no more be buried in the rocks than the living could dig trenches. In these positions, overlooked from many sides, 4th Indian Division now took over the task of threatening the entrenched German defenders on Monte Cassino.

One of the finest divisions of the British Army in the Mediterranean, the 4th Indian had already had a long war since it left India in the autumn of 1939 for Egypt. It took part in most of the major offensives in North Africa as well as participating in the defeat of the Italians in Eritrea and the Vichy forces in Syria. After spells in Cyprus and Palestine, it attacked with Eighth Army at El Alamein. Later came the Mareth Line in Tunisia and the complete defeat of Axis forces in North Africa. The division came over to Italy in December 1943 and joined British Eighth Army to take part in the savage fighting around Ortona.

Each of the division's three infantry brigades consisted of one British and two Indian battalions. In support, its artillery was British while its service, ordnance and signals units were almost entirely Indian. The native troops who made up the division were all volunteers, recruited from the 'martial races' of the Indian subcontinent: Sikhs, Punjabis, Mahrattas, Rajputs and Gurkhas. They were proud and aggressive men who loved to fight as part of a disciplined army, and whose regimental identities and traditions stretched back a century and more. Their brave and ruthless approach to war was similar to that of the French colonial troops, but in contrast to the unruly nature and appearance of some units of Juin's CEF the Indians were disciplined, smart and well organised. Led by Gen Tuker, the division had a magnificent fighting reputation and was considered by some to be the most professional division in the Allied armies in Italy. Francis Tuker was himself an exceptional commander, an able tactician with a fine military mind. His forthright manner made him a difficult subordinate to deal with, but his talents more than outweighed his outspoken character.

Freyberg's plan for a renewed attack on the Cassino defences was, for the most part, just a continuation of the attacks already carried out by US II Corps. He intended that 4th Indian Division should move on to and behind Monte Cassino and down into the Liri valley, while 2nd NZ Division would simultaneously make yet another Allied attack across the Rapido, this time in the vicinity of Cassino railway station, so as to release armour to advance along Route 6.

Although on his sickbed, Gen Tuker was quick to express his views on the attack. A head-on assault on the monastery on the summit of Monte Cassino was doomed to

Lieutenant Colonel Hal Reese, US 36th Division (right), with three German soldiers on Monte Castellone; all the latter wear the mountain troops' special anorak. After a particularly savage period of fighting the Germans requested a truce so that they could recover their dead. This was agreed by Gen Walker, the divisional commander, and was arranged for the period 0800-1100 hours on 14 February - the day before the bombing of the monastery. At the appointed time Lt Col Reese went forward to supervise the truce and had this meeting with the German sergeant who was organising the retrieval of the bodies. When news of this meeting reached Berlin, Hitler was furious; he hated truces and demanded an explanation. General Baade covered for his men, saying that the truce had been requested by the Americans to recover the remains of hundreds of men that they had lost during the battle. (US National Archives)

failure because of the strong defences. The start line for such an attack was exposed to such an extent that the leading troops would have to run the gauntlet of fire from a succession of overlooking peaks. The Americans had tried this approach again and again earlier in the month, and all their efforts had been stopped dead with horrific casualties. Tuker favoured a wider sweep through the mountains, with Juin's corps also attacking on his right. His views were listened to, but rejected. His division would attack as planned. Alexander and Clark had been given a warning, probably through intercepted 'Ultra' messages, that the Germans were about to launch a major counter-attack against the Anzio bridgehead, and it was imperative that pressure be reapplied to the Cassino sector in order to worry the enemy into diverting troops away from the north. Alexander was pushing Clark to attack a soon as possible; Clark in turn pushed Freyberg, and Freyberg pushed Dimoline. The 4th Indian Division was to get into position to launch its assault on Monte Cassino with the least possible delay.

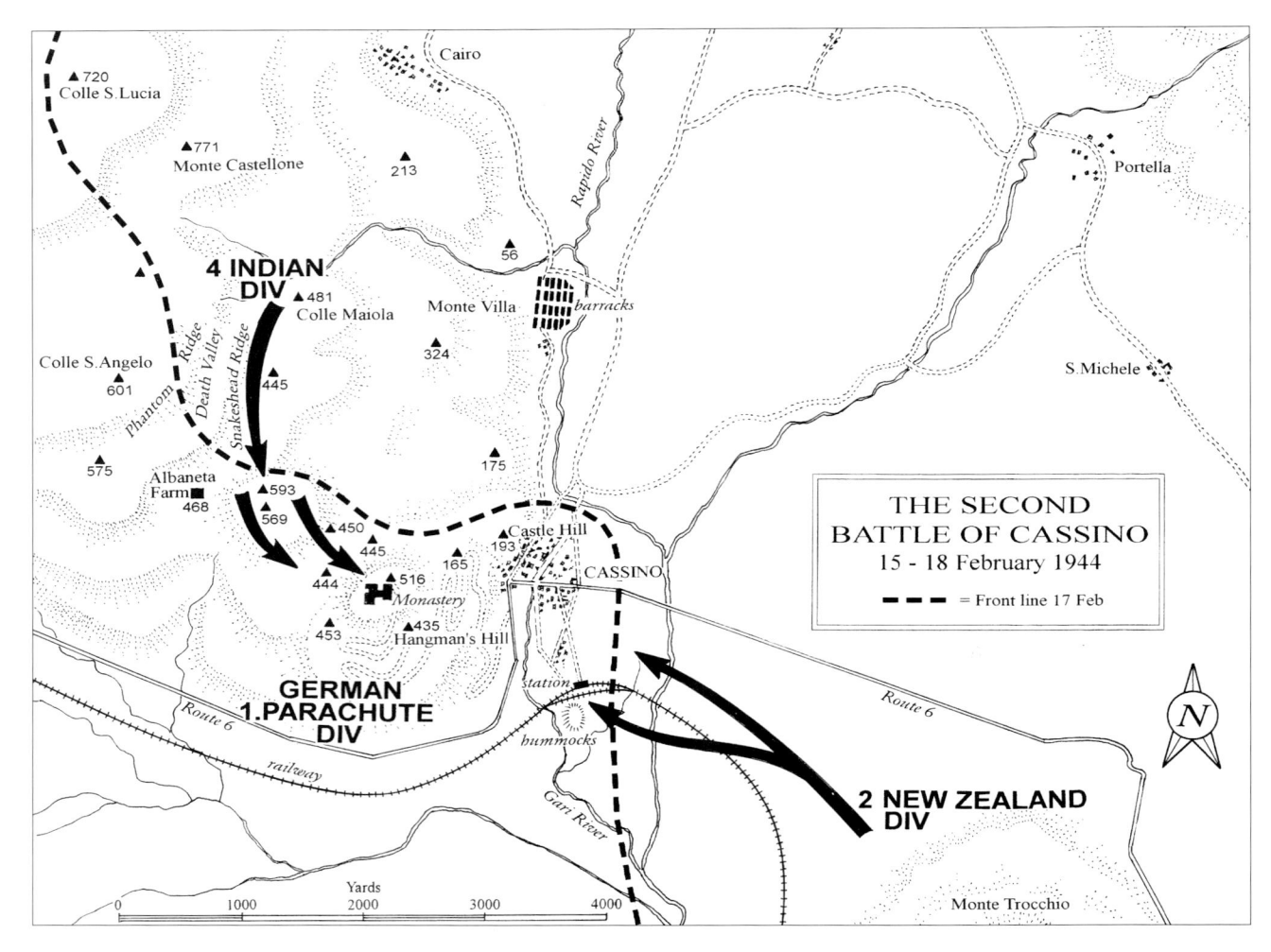

General Freyberg was aware of the difficulties facing the Indians; but he believed that the Americans' failure to secure a foothold on Monastery Hill had been due to their exhaustion by that stage of the fighting. He felt that tiredness had robbed them of final victory by a narrow margin. The fresh troops of New Zealand II Corps, and more especially the men of 4th Indian Division with their experience of mountain warfare, were just the troops required to go that extra few hundred yards and reach the summit of Monte Cassino. There was another good reason for Freyberg to hope for a breakthrough: he had been promised overwhelming air support to help blast his corps forward.

The key to the success of the offensive was Monte Cassino, known to the Allies as 'Monastery Hill' from the brooding bulk of the medieval Benedictine monastery (also sometimes called the Abbey) that sat squarely on the summit. Although the monastery was alleged to be completely free of German troops (and they were in fact forbidden by senior command to even enter its gates), few of the soldiers fighting and dying on the mountains below it believed that Nazis could be true to their word. The Germans had originally proclaimed a 300-metre 'neutrality zone' around the monastery, but this instruction was soon forgotten when the fighting drew near. They set up an arms dump in a cave, and built a concrete bunker, machine gun posts and several observation points all well within the zone. The corps commander had even told his men to make defences right up to the wall of the monastery if necessary. In deciding to pivot his Gustav Line on Monte Cassino, Von Senger had brought the building within his fortress zone. It would be a miracle if the monastery could escape damage while the world went crazy all around it. As the fighting intensified on the nearby mountains and the Americans closed on the isolated monastery, shells and mortar bombs from both sides began to hit the building.

The great monastery dominated the mountains to the north-east, overlooked the town below, and sat sentinel over the whole of the entrance to the Liri valley. From wherever they were in the forward area, the men of the Fifth Army could see the building and feel its eyes on them. The enemy was known to have gun positions and observation posts right up against its walls. If the Germans did not actually have observers in the confines of the religious building, everyone who came under accurate artillery fire as they approached within miles of Monastery Hill believed that they did. The GIs in the forward positions were certainly convinced of it, and were aggrieved that orders forbade the taking of direct action against the building. Soldiers could fight all around the building, they could die against the walls of the monastery itself, but they could not shell or mark its venerable precincts. It seemed to them to be an intolerable frustration.

There was no doubt in anyone's mind that Monastery Hill commanded every approach to the Liri valley and formed the anchor point of the whole of the central sector of the Gustav Line. For Fifth Army to advance past the Cassino massif and link up with the Anzio landings, Monte Cassino had to be isolated, taken and cleared of all German forces. General Tuker had been given the task of assaulting Monastery Hill; and the intelligence he had been given about the construction of the monastery reinforced his belief that the building was a German strongpoint. The monastery building was ostensibly a religious house, but it was also a fortress. It had previously been destroyed three times in its long history, and the rebuilding and restoration work done in the 16th and 17th centuries ensured that it could withstand a great deal of bombardment. The monastery was over 200 yards long; its walls were up to 150 feet high, built of solid masonry, ten feet thick at their base. Its one entrance was narrow and lined with stone blocks 30 feet long. There were loopholes and small windows along its sides, and battlements on the top of its walls. Tuker felt that any army engineers given the task of reducing it would be hard put to do so with the means at their disposal.

The commander of 4th Indian Division was also unhappy that his orders were to attack the summit head-on from the adjoining peaks. The ground his men would have to cover was precipitous, rock-strewn and overlooked by the enemy. There was no cover to be had on the bare mountainsides, and the last few hundred yards of open ground up to the summit would demand an advance straight into the guns of the German defenders. While the monastery loomed menacingly over Tuker's men, its black eyes apparently - surely - watching their every move, the task of taking Monte Cassino seemed impossible. Tuker decided that the monastery and the top of Monte Cassino would have to be 'taken out'.

The decision to bomb the monastery
General Tuker expressed his misgivings about his orders in a report to Freyberg, reiterating his preference for a wide outflanking movement to get behind Monastery Hill rather than a head-on assault. If, however, he had to carry out the attack as ordered, then he requested that the monastery be bombed with 'blockbuster' bombs so as to penetrate its thick walls.

Allied policy was quite clear on such a request. Whilst the Allies accepted that they had a special responsibility to respect historical monuments and religious buildings, such self-restraint had to be consistent with vital military needs. General Clark himself had reinforced this message when addressing his troop commanders in October 1943, urging them to take every precaution to protect church property, but if military necessity should dictate otherwise, 'there should be no hesitation in taking whatever action the situation warrants'.

The bombing of an important religious building of international renown was not a decision to be taken lightly. Freyberg telephoned Fifth Army Headquarters and spoke with Gen Gruenther, Clark's chief-of-staff - Clark was away at the time visiting the Anzio beachhead. Freyberg requested bombing missions to support the Indian attack, and more especially to destroy the monastery. Gruenther could not authorise such air missions and promised to take the matter up with Clark, although he knew that his boss was not in favour of the destruction of the monastery. Unable to reach Clark immediately, Gruenther called Gen Alexander's chief-of-staff, Gen John Harding, and outlined the situation to him, saying that a decision to bomb the monastery would put Clark in a delicate situation. Both men then discussed the matter individually with their superiors. Clark's view was that the bombing was unnecessary and that such destruction would achieve little military gain. This view was backed up by Gen Keyes of US II Corps, who thought that the bombing of the monastery would 'probably enhance its value as a military obstacle, because the Germans would feel free to use it as a barricade.' Alexander, on the other hand, felt that although it was to be regretted, if Freyberg believed that the bombing was a military necessity then he had every faith in Freyberg's judgement. He added, 'If there is any reasonable probability that the building is being used for military purposes, I believe that its destruction is warranted.' The monastery's fate was sealed.

There was at the time, and still is today, a strong body of opinion holding that the monastery was indeed being used by the Germans for military purposes. The US official history of the Italian campaign cites many instances of enemy soldiers being seen there, observation posts being established in the building, and sniper fire coming from the monastery. An Italian civilian reported that 80 soldiers and 30 machine guns had been seen in the building. Just before the bombing Gen Ira Eaker, commander of Mediterranean Air Command, flew over Monte Cassino with Gen Devers in a small aircraft. Both generals believed they saw at least one military radio aerial and German soldiers moving in and out of the building. Such reports convinced Gen Sir Henry Maitland Wilson, Commander-in-Chief Mediterranean, that 'military necessity' existed, and he approved the bombing of the monastery. German commanders interviewed after the war categorically deny that there were ever any German troops in the monastery. To their mind the monastery remained inviolate until the Allies bombed the place.

Once the go-ahead for the bombing of the monastery had been given, air force planners seized on the opportunity to demonstrate the power of air bombardment in the tactical support of ground forces. Both heavy and medium bombers were to be used in a concentrated mass to give support to ground troops in the seizing of a single objective; this had never been done before and the raid was something of an experiment. Previously ground support had been given only by medium bombers from the tactical air forces; now the plan was to use the heaviest bombers from the strategic air commands. If Freyberg wanted the monastery taken out, then the air forces were going to absolutely annihilate it.

When Brig Dimoline, temporarily in command of 4th Indian Division, had been given his orders for the attack it was intended that the division would make its assault on

A 194mm railway gun of the Italian Co-Belligerent Forces, one of three operated by 269 Battery, Italian 1st Armoured Artillery Regt, firing in support of the action at Cassino. With a range of 16.5km (over 10 miles) they were a useful addition to the Allied arsenal. There were three batteries in the regiment, but two had been captured by the Germans during their take-over of Italy in 1943 and were located in the north of the country. (Imperial War Museum)

(Right) *The monastery after the air raid, showing the total destruction wreaked by the effects of high explosive 'blockbuster' bombs; the raid by 229 heavy and medium bombers lasted throughout the morning of 15 February. The maze of ruined walls formed perfect defensive positions for the German paratroopers, who immediately moved into the rubble to defend the fortress mountain. (Imperial War Museum)*

Monastery Hill from Point 593, a rocky prominence dominating a ridge known to the Americans as 'Snakeshead'. This high point was only 1,000 yards from the rear entrance to the monastery, and was connected to Monte Cassino by a narrow spur. The lead brigade of the division, 7 Indian Brigade commanded by Brig O.Lovett, was supposed to assault the hill from this secure base; but when it arrived to take over from the 'Red Bull' Division it found that Point 593 was still in German hands - the GIs had actually been on Point 593, but they had been knocked off it by an enemy counter-attack. They now held only a precarious foothold on the reverse slope; the remainder of the feature was securely in German hands. Before any attempt could be made on Monastery Hill, Point 593 would have to be taken.

The relief of the Americans by 7 Indian Brigade was a nightmare. The 200 or so infantrymen from US 34th Division who held the forward positions were totally exhausted and needed help to get off the ridge. No movement was possible in daylight and so carrying parties had to be held back until darkness. The actual change-over took several days to effect. During this period, before they could get themselves established, the brigade was forced to help US 36th Division, which was holding the heights to the right, to fight off a German counter-attack aimed at Monte Castellone. These diversions all helped confuse the relief and the start of 4th Indian Division's attack kept having to be postponed. Eventually, the night of 14/15 February was selected for the clearing of Point 593, with the following night being given by Brig Lovett as the earliest time his attack could go in on Monastery Hill.

To Freyberg these delays were unacceptable, and he continually pressurised Dimoline to get his men moving. The bombing of the monastery, once it had been ordered, could not be delayed. If the New Zealand Corps did not use the bombers on offer on the day that they were available, they would be used elsewhere, most notably at Anzio. On 14 February Freyberg learned that a break in the weather conditions dictated that the bombing missions must begin at 0930 hours on the 15th. If they were postponed further, there would not be another opportunity for several days.

Whether the Indian Division was ready or not, the raid was going in. In fact the Indian Division was not ready; further complications had forced Lovett to postpone his attack for yet another 24 hours. The assault on Monastery Hill would not now take place until the night of 16/17 February, the night after preliminary moves to clear Point 593 and almost two days after the bombing of the monastery. The bombing raid and the 4th Indian Division's attack no longer bore a semblance of air/ground force co-ordination.

Fifth Army intelligence knew that the abbot of the Cassino monastery and his monks were still inside the building, even though all of its treasures and important religious artefacts had been removed to the Vatican for safe-keeping (with, it should be added, the help of one Lt Col Schlegel of the 'Hermann Göring' Division). Also inside were civilian refugees using the monastery as a safe haven. These innocent people now had to be warned of their grave danger and urged to leave the precincts immediately. The day before the raid, aircraft dropped leaflets over Monastery Hill addressed to 'Our Italian Friends'. They warned that the battle was closing in on Monte Cassino and the sacred building would no longer be free from harm. Weapons would soon be aimed against the monastery itself; and all of them should leave the area at once. The message brought panic to the civilians and great consternation to the brothers. Abbot Bishop Gregorio Diamare made contact with the Germans later that evening and arranged for the paths leading down to Route 6 to be opened for the refugees from midnight until 0600 hours on the night of the 15/16th. Unknown to all concerned, this was to be fifteen hours after the bombing had been planned to commence.

The morning of 15 February was bright and sunny. For the infantry of the 4th Indian Division crouched in their stone *sangars* it was a time to keep low and evade the attention of enemy snipers while preparations were made for the coming attack. At 0930 hours a persistent drone was heard which slowly grew in intensity. As the troops looked up they could see the first formation of US Fifteenth Army Air Force B17 bombers passing high overhead, glinting silver in a clear blue sky. Then, without any warning, the whine of bombs and crash of thunder blotted out every other sound. A few hundred yards away huge black explosions blossomed, tearing the hillsides apart, and the ancient monastery began to disintegrate in a pall of smoke and flying debris. Splinters of rock and huge boulders tumbled down the mountains, showering the more exposed of the Indian troops. Men pressed themselves into the rock face to escape the blast from wayward bombs that crashed down far from their intended target. All around casualties began to mount, but there was no escape; the exposed infantry had to steel their nerves and wait for the terror to subside. There was little respite; after the first wave came another, and then another. Throughout the morning successive groups of aircraft homed in on the battered grey monastery sitting vulnerably on the mountain top. After the 142 heavy 'Flying Fortresses' came the mediums: 87 B25 Mitchell and B26 Marauder bombers of Twelfth Air Force. In the afternoon, 27 more medium bombers returned to pound the carcass of the monastery once more, churning up the ruins as they lay under a huge dust haze. Tuker's wish had been granted; the monastery of Monte Cassino had been 'taken out'.

As the dust settled the toll was counted: scores of Germans were dead and injured, together with over forty of the Indian Division and, most pathetically of all, many civilian refugees who had still been cowering in the imagined sanctuary of the church. The abbot was saved together with many of his monks. German propagandists manipulated the bombing as an act of mindless barbarism, exploiting the frail abbot in photographs and eliciting from him in a radio interview the view that were absolutely no German soldiers in the building. Some senior Allied commanders also saw the bombing as a senseless act of destruction with little military value. Indeed, to this day argument over the necessity for the bombing still rumbles on. However, to the men on the mountainsides around Cassino in the cold February of 1944, the bombing had removed the malevolent, silent eyes that had watched their every move and brought fear and death to many. No longer would artillery observers take great pains to avoid hitting the monastery, nor mortar batteries try to lob bombs on to the German strongpoints without grazing the sacred walls. The monastery had gone and with it the restrictions. All-out war could now descend on the enemy lurking on Monte Cassino; the full weight of Allied firepower could be brought to bear on the most important hill in the Gustav Line. To the men in the mountains, the bombing was most definitely a military necessity, and most of the survivors still think so today.

The Royal Sussex at Point 593
The destructive power of large aerial bombs dropped into a confined area is enormous. Any of the enemy who survive such an assault are usually dazed, disorganised and shocked. The practice of using bombers to strike a tactical target in support of ground forces can only work well when the attacking infantry follow up the raid with an immediate assault. On 15 February 1944 the top of Monte Cassino was reduced to a rubble-strewn moonscape with the German defenders shattered and disorientated. Their nightmare continued when the guns of the New Zealand Corps and US II Corps pounded the area with high explosive, neutralising any attempt at reorganisation. The Indian Division should have attacked immediately; but it didn't.

As the winter's day faded and darkness descended across the bleak hillsides, Dimoline's division finally moved. One company, C Coy of 1st Bn, Royal Sussex Regiment – just three officers and sixty-three men – slipped silently from their refuges and advanced against the enemy outposts some seventy yards away. A hundred yards further on was Point 593, the preliminary objective before the assault on Monastery Hill. The greatest raid ever laid on to support a ground attack was being followed by an assault of less that seventy infantrymen.

The task given to C Coy, 1st Royal Sussex was a daunting one. In the darkness they advanced, two platoons abreast, over a battleground of loose rocks, huge boulders and gorse thickets. Their attempted silent approach on the enemy positions was soon foiled by the rattle of stones displaced by heavy boots. After an advance of no more than fifty yards the leading troops were caught by bursts of accurate machine gun fire. The men dropped flat on the ground,

(Left) Lower right, an empty Gurkha sangar built into the side of 'Hangman's Hill', lying alongside the winding road that leads up to the monastery. It was impossible to dig any sort of cover in the stony ground and so shelter had to be created by piling loose rocks together to form two-man hides. (US National Archives)

(Right) Lieutenant General Fridolin von Senger und Etterlin (second left), Commander German XIV Panzer Corps, helps the shocked 88-year-old Abbot Bishop Gregorio Diamare into a German staff car to be taken to a place of safety after his harrowing experiences during the bombing of his monastery. (Imperial War Museum)

seeking any sort of cover for protection. Officers and NCOs urged them forward, seeking ways to outflank the enemy guns, but the steep ground, seamed with crevices and edged by precipitous drops, baffled all bravery and initiative. The Tommies tried and tried again throughout the night, but found no way forward to close the few yards to the top. From their prone positions they could only lob grenades and pepper the well entrenched machine gun posts with small arms fire until their ammunition ran out. More grenades were passed forward, more ammunition was dragged up to the leading men, but these were quickly expended in the furious firefight. Movement forward was impossible, and as the night slowly began to pale C Coy, or what was left of it, was withdrawn back into the relative safety of the battalion's positions. Two officers and thirty-three men of the original sixty-six who had set out were killed or wounded during the fifty-yard advance.

Freyberg urged Dimoline to get his division straight across the open ground and on to Monte Cassino; further delays could not be tolerated. The corps commander was not convinced that the capture of Point 593 was an absolute pre-requisite for an assault on Monastery Hill, but both Dimoline and his brigadier were adamant that it was. Freyberg demurred, but insisted that an attack on Monte Cassino itself could not be deferred beyond the next night. Dimoline passed the message on to the 7 Brigade commander, Brig Lovett, who was told to try again. The 1st Royal Sussex was ordered to undertake another attack on Point 593.

On the night of 16/17 February the battalion made their second attemp on Point 593, this time in full strength, with the depleted C Coy held in reserve. Three companies were to advance over the same ground as the night before, but with one attempting a diversionary attack while the other two companies stormed Point 593. The attack did not get going until midnight; the mule trains bringing ammunition up to the battalion were delayed. The 1st Royal Sussex was given no supporting artillery fire, nor was there much in the way of mortar fire, so close were the two sides. The shelling that did come over was aimed at the heights just a few hundred yards away, placed to ensure that the enemy overlooking the Sussex spur did not interfere with the assault. Some of this fire fell on to Snakeshead Ridge and among the Sussex infantry; so low was the trajectory of the shells from the gun positions back on the plains before the Rapido that they failed to clear the high ridge where the battalion waited. Being shelled by one's own side was not an auspicious start to the attack.

The storming of Point 593 met with the same success as the previous attempt the night before. After fifty yards the enemy opened up with machine gun fire. The diversionary effort on the left ran foul of the precipitous terrain, this company being confronted with vertical drops at every turn. The infantrymen were confined solely to the top of the ridge; try as they might, they could not move around the flank. The main effort managed to get among some of the enemy machine gun posts and brave men forced their way on to the slopes of Point 593, only to be caught by resolute German defenders. The battle developed into hand-to-hand combat, point blank firefights and grenade-throwing duels. The reserve company was committed to try to carry the position, but was sucked into the melee without gain. The advance degenerated into disorganised individual struggles in the icy darkness, the only outcomes being death, capture or flight. Victory was never an option; the Germans were too well established. The impetus of the attack slowed to a halt; eventually the battalion was withdrawn into its original positions. This time the cost was ten officers and 130 men.

Two days had now passed since the bombing, and the Indian Division was still stuck on its start line. The enemy's offensive spirit and fortified positions on the peaks around the Cassino massif were proving impossible to break. Well entrenched, determined, supplied through soundly established lines to the rear, the German infantry were almost impervious to artillery fire, well able to absorb the punishment dished out by Allied guns miles away down on the Rapido plain. Frontal attacks against their fortified emplacements appeared to be suicidal while each peak of high ground supported its neighbour. But as long as Generals Freyberg, Clark and Alexander were set on seizing the shortest and most direct route to get into the Liri valley, the troops of NZ II Corps had no other option than to keep battering away at the most heavily fortified sector of that line.

When Freyberg heard of the 4th Indian Division's failure to make any progress at the second attempt, orders went out to both of his divisions to attack again on 17 February. He instructed Brig Dimoline to abandon the idea of taking Point 593 before launching his push on Monastery Hill. The Indian Division was directed to assault Monte Cassino in strength with a series of simultaneous attacks on a number of high points that led up to the monastery, rather than moving along the ridge taking them one by one. Brigadier Lovett of 7 Brigade was told to draw up a plan to seize Points 593, 569, 444 and 445 and open the way for the rest of the division to get onto Monastery Hill. It was to be a five-battalion attack, under Lovett's command, using two of his own battalions to provide a firm base, while a battalion from each of the division's three brigades made the assault. With his original efforts in mind, Lovett planned once again to attack Point 593 two hours before the start of the main attack, but this time the remainder of the assault was not dependent upon its capture. If he got on to the strongpoint, all well and good; but if his men could not take the peak, then the other battalions would have to attack their objectives across the face of the German machine guns entrenched on Point 593, regardless of the consequences.

The New Zealanders at the station
Meanwhile, down in the valley, 2nd NZ Division, now under the command of Brig Kippenberger, had been holding the line of the Rapido opposite San Angelo since 6 February, waiting for its chance to be introduced into the battle. Freyberg's plan of attack had been to carry out a pincer movement to encircle Cassino town and open up the entrance into the Liri valley: 4th Indian Division attacking on to and around Monastery Hill, while 2nd NZ Division crossed the Rapido in the vicinity of Cassino railway station and got on to that section of Route 6 which wound its way around the base of the mountain. Freyberg's armour – Combat Command B from US 1st Armored Division, supported by 4 NZ Armoured Brigade – could then drive down the road into the open valley beyond.

The New Zealand Division had been planning its attack for many days, waiting for the Indians to get amongst the enemy up in the mountains. When Brig Kippenberger was given the order to start his assault he was more than ready. However, just as the 4th Indian Division's great attack began with a company of infantry because of local difficulties, so the New Zealanders' initial attack would be confined by the nature of its front to the efforts of just one battalion. The main problem was the sodden state of the ground.

The whole valley of the Rapido had been inundated with flood water by the Germans, and this still lay several inches deep in places. Clearly – as had been seen during the US 34th Division's attempt to get tanks across the valley in the last week of January – the ground was too soft for armour. There was, however, one possible solution. Running along the valley was a raised railway embankment which led up to Cassino station, and this was wide enough to carry tanks. The enemy had also realised the tactical significance of this approach and had, through a series of demolitions, cratered the route in twelve places, each of which would have to be bridged before tanks could cross over. This embankment was the only passable route forward and was therefore chosen as the NZ Division's axis of attack. Its comparative narrowness meant, however, that there was no room to deploy more than one battalion in the attack.

The notorious Point 593 on the leading edge of Snakeshead Ridge. The stark, rock-strewn landscape shows the type of ground across which successive waves of American, British, Indian and Polish troops had to attack during their abortive attempts to take this commanding German strongpoint. The picture was taken on 19 May, just after the Poles had captured the abbey, from the German side of the ridge between the Allied positions and Monte Cassino. (Imperial War Museum)

The assault on Cassino station began at 2130 hours on 17 February, when 28th (Maori) Bn from NZ 5 Brigade pushed out along the embankment route from the shelter of Monte Trocchio with two companies in the lead. Every available weapon was brought to bear on the Germans to keep them bottled up and give an impression that the attack was going in on a broad front. B Company's objective was to capture the station buildings and engine sheds and then seize the road that led into the town; A Coy planned to take the yards around the station and capture a small enemy-held rise to the south of the station known as the 'Hummocks'. Closely behind the Maoris came the engineers, ready to deal with the demolitions and to bridge the two waterways that barred the route for tanks.

The move forward made steady progress despite enemy machine gun and mortar fire. As the two companies approached the area of the station they became embroiled in extensive minefields and barbed wire entanglements. German counter-fire became heavier and more accurate the closer they got to their objectives. Such setbacks did not dampen the fighting spirit of the battalion; brilliantly led by junior officers, they pressed on, and B Coy stormed the station and engine sheds around midnight. A Company were unable to secure possession of the Hummocks, however. Nevertheless, by the early hours of the morning of the 18th the two companies had established themselves in the station area and awaited the welcome arrival of reinforcements in the shape of tanks and anti-tank guns.

Back on the railway embankment, the sappers had been working feverishly throughout the night to complete their tasks, despite heavy shelling and mortaring. Mines were lifted, boobytraps made safe, craters filled in and gaps closed. The two crossings over the Rapido and an adjoining canal were successfully bridged; gradually the completed roadway edged closer to the station. As daylight approached there remained just one large gap to be bridged. The engineers tried hard, but were beaten by just minutes. Daylight brought with it the attention of the myriad of German observation points overlooking the valley. There could be no more work on the causeway until darkness returned.

This left the Maoris very exposed; without anti-tank guns they would be sitting ducks if the Germans counter-attacked with tanks. Brigadier Hartnell, commander of 5 Brigade, asked Kippenberger for permission to withdraw the battalion. The general refused; he felt it was just possible that the enemy would not counter-attack with tanks or, if they did, that his artillery could beat them off. It was a risk, but it had to be tried. With the enclave around the station providing a start line, operations the next night could well lead to the elusive breakthrough of the Cassino position. The Maoris were now told to hold on to their gains without the aid of armour or anti-tank guns. The rest of the division, waiting expectantly for the order to move up, also stood by, as did the 180 American tanks behind Monte Trocchio. Everyone was waiting for darkness to return; but nightfall was twelve long hours away.

★ ★ ★

Up in the mountains, 4th Indian Division also waited for the return of the merciful blanket of darkness. Its night had been less successful than that of the 'Kiwis', despite the introduction of three fresh battalions into the fight. The attack had begun with 4/6th Rajputana Rifles attempting Point 593, but within an hour of its departure it was pinned down in the same area by the same withering German counter-fire. The infantry tried every conceivable route to the top, weaving between boulders and scrambling across gullies to get to the summit, but all failed - bar one. A small party did make it on to Point 593, but all were lost, killed or wounded by the enemy. The rest of the night developed as had the previous two: great acts of bravery, brilliant leadership by officers and NCOs, resolute efforts to gain ground, shrieking ricochets, dark figures pressing themselves against boulders under the icy light of parachute flares

Men of 1/4th Bn, Essex Regt pause in a ravine on 27 February, along the road leading from the Rapido valley up to Cairo village. The battalion was part of 5 Bde, 4th Indian Division, held in reserve during the second battle for Cassino. In the background is Monte Cairo. (Imperial War Museum)

– and eventual stalemate in the face of an entrenched and determined enemy with apparently limitless firepower.

While the Rajputs battled it out on the rear slopes of 593, Lovett's other two assault units attacked. Two battalions, 1/2nd and 1/9th Gurkha Rifles, came down the eastern slopes of Snakeshead Ridge on a direct route to Monastery Hill, 1/2nd heading for Point 444, 1/9th aiming at Point 450. The Gurkhas were recruited in Nepal, a country set high in the Himalayas, and were probably the fittest and most expert mountain troops in the whole Allied armies. The advance across the rocky slopes was well within their capabilities; however, it was not the terrain that threatened to defeat them.

As foreseen by Brig Lovett, the Gurkhas' attacks immediately came under concerted crossfire from Point 593 and the peaks beyond. The 1/9th Gurkhas veered to the right to counter this fire, but could make little real headway and quickly became pinned down on the bare mountainside beneath Point 593. Over on their left, 1/2nd Gurkhas slipped down into the ravine at the base of Monastery Hill and tried to assault up the mountain by the most direct route, harried all the way by fire from 593 and other strongpoints. At the base of the ravine the leading troops ran into an area of gorse scrub that was mined and boobytrapped. Showered by grenades thrown down on them from above, and blown apart by mines under their feet, the leading infantry suffered horrendous casualties. Follow-up companies tried to press on up to the monastery, but were halted by lines of machine guns on top of the hill firing continuously through the darkness. The Gurkhas got to within 400 yards of the top, but failed in a last desperate attempt.

As daylight broke, the survivors of the three attacking Indian battalions were all back on Snakeshead Ridge with little to show for their efforts except an enhanced reputation for heroic determination, and a growing list of casualties. The Rajputs had lost 196 officers and men; 1/2nd Gurkhas had suffered 149 casualties including their CO; and 1/9th Gurkhas had lost 96 from their ranks. No ground had been gained.

Troops of the New Zealand 28th (Maori) Bn watch the bombing of Cassino monastery from their positions well back from the River Rapido. This battalion carried out the first attack on Cassino town made by the 2nd NZ Division two days later, on 17 February, and briefly captured the railway station. (US National Archives)

Down on the valley floor, the companies of 28th (Maori) Bn tensed themselves in expectation of the inevitable German counter-attack against their positions. The battalion was very exposed, and Gen Kippenberger knew it. Everything depended on the Maoris' holding on to the station area for the whole of the day. Without any serious means of dealing with an armoured attack, this was a very tall order. Kippenberger went forward to speak with the Maoris' CO, Lt Col Russell Young. He found the battalion in confident spirits; the forward companies had established a good defensive enclave, using the solid stone buildings as a base and well dug-in forward positions to cover all approaches. What they lacked in weight of fire they made up for in commitment. To cover them, Kippenberger arranged for a smokescreen to be laid to shield the Maoris from German observation from the overlooking heights of Monte Cassino. He feared that no one would be left alive at the end of the day if the troops had no concealment.

For 2nd NZ Division, 18 February was a very long day. For the Maori battalion it was particularly so, although the agonising wait was felt equally by the rest of the division and its support arms. By noon the exposed outpost was still being mortared, as it had been since the previous night, but the effectiveness of its well-built cover prevented major casualties. By 1500 hours in the afternoon everyone was beginning to feel hopeful; the smokescreen was consistent and thick, although its acrid fumes caused some discomfort. The troops in their foxholes had been fed and resupplied, and the enveloping darkness was just three hours away. All this changed just forty-five minutes later, when 5 Brigade HQ received a report that tank tracks had been heard.

The German defenders in Cassino took every advantage of the smokescreen laid down by the NZ Division. Unseen, they were able to advance close to the exposed battalion and surprise it with an infantry attack on both sides of the station, supported by tanks. The Maoris tried to hold them back using hand-held PIATs, but an infantryman carrying this unwieldy rocket projector had to stalk a tank to within at most a hundred yards to have a realistic hope of knocking it out. The German infantry and the tank machine gunners were well aware of the need to sweep the ground to keep tank-killer teams at a distance, and inevitably the Maoris carrying these vulnerable weapons became very early victims of the armoured counter-attack. Within just a few minutes the Germans were amongst the New Zealanders, breaking up their defensive line and spreading confusion through the enclave. There was a very short struggle as the tanks ploughed into the exposed defenders. Those of the Maoris who were not killed, injured or taken withdrew along the embankment.

By late afternoon on 18 February the 2nd NZ Division was back on its start line. The Maori battalion's losses were 128 killed and wounded. The second battle of Cassino was over; it had gained nothing.

CHAPTER SIX

Counter-Attack and Stalemate: 4 February–14 March

Preparing for his counter-offensive to wipe out the Anzio beachhead, Gen von Mackensen ordered a series of small scale assaults to be made against the whole of US VI Corps. After his first preliminary attack against British 3 Brigade in the Campoleone salient on 4 February he wanted to conceal the point where he was going to launch his major blow, and so applied pressure all along the perimeter. These attacks often took the form of tactical thrusts in order to seize important road junctions and other features which needed to be in German hands at the start of the offensive. The US 3rd Division suffered a series of these local attacks. Other probes were made simply to confuse and disrupt the beachhead, such as the one against the 157th Infantry from US 45th Division on the night of 6/7 February, when it was subjected to a German attempt across the River Moletta; but this threatened crossing was easily dispersed by artillery fire.

In front of British 1st Division, where Gen Penney had all three of his brigades in the line to defend his sector, the enemy's continuing desire to take the area around the Factory and Carroceto gave rise to a more concentrated assault. Attacks began on 7 February and continued over the next few days. On 9 February the Factory fell to the enemy, and Panzer-Grenadiers from Battle Group Gräser pressed on towards Carroceto and the overpass (see map on page 33). The next day the station at Carroceto changed hands three times during a particularly severe period of close-quarter fighting. Penney called for help to stem the German tide, and the 180th Infantry from US 45th 'Thunderbird' Division – former National Guardsmen from the South-Western states – came forward to join the fight. By the night of 10/11 February both sides had fought themselves to a standstill.

German Fourteenth Army had taken its objectives and pushed US VI Corps back from the road network around Aprilia as intended. Four days of bitter fighting had, however, left its mark, for each day the Germans had to throw in more and more reserves to keep up their momentum. By the end of this phase Von Mackensen had committed the equivalent of six full regiments to the battle. Allied artillery fire, backed by air bombardment and naval gunfire, had taken a heavy toll of the exposed German infantry, crowded as they were into such a confined area. Fourteenth Army now paused to gather strength and replenish its losses. But the Allies did not.

It was important that VI Corps regain the Factory area and Carroceto, but the exhausted British 1st Division was in no fit state to do so. The division was eased out of the line and its positions taken over by the 179th and 180th Infantry from Gen Eagles' US 45th Division. At 0630 hours on 11 February the 179th Infantry attacked with tank support behind a fifteen-minute artillery concentration. The assault

Captured Panzer-Grenadier from the 'Hermann Göring' Panzer Division; he wears a camouflaged field jacket characteristic of Luftwaffe ground troops, with the Luftwaffe version of the national badge on his chest. (US National Archives)

on the Factory came from two directions, one up the Albano road through the underpass, the other along a lateral road from the south-east. Both brought fire on to the buildings of the Factory and got within striking distance, but eventually withdrew around midday to replenish their ammunition. Artillery fire continued to pour down on the German defenders. A second attack in the afternoon was pressed home by tanks and infantry and penetrated among the ruined houses of Aprilia; some of the enemy infantry and tanks pulled out, only to counter-attack later. Hand-to-hand combat raged all afternoon until the Americans were once again forced to retire. The Germans still held the Factory.

The 179th and their supporting Shermans attacked again in the early hours of the next day. A hastily laid enemy minefield, put down during the night, caused the tank

A German tank crew repairing the track of a PzKw IV in an Italian orchard near Nettuno, March 1944. The first production PzKw IV was completed in 1937 and in successive marks, with up-graded guns and armour, it continued to be built until 1945. By 1944 it was seriously outdated, however, and needed an external armour 'kit' including these hooked-on side skirts. (Bundesarchiv)

Von Mackensen's counter-offensive

The first wave of the assault was to include six divisions. On the left, 1 Parachute Corps with 4.Fallschirmjäger and 65.Infanterie-Divisions would attack down the west side of the Anzio-Albano road; LXXVI Panzer Corps with the Lehr-Regiment, 3.Panzer-Grenadier, 114.Jäger and 715.Infanterie-Divisions, would make the main thrust just east of the Albano road. The second wave, in reserve to exploit the breakthrough, consisted of 29.Panzer-Grenadier and 26.Panzer-Divisions.

The main Allied line across the beachhead began with the newly arrived and complete British 56th Division holding the left flank close to the sea; next came US 45th Division astride the Albano-Annzio road; adjacent to this was US 3rd Division, with the Special Service Force holding the Mussolini Canal line back to the sea on the right flank. The mauled British 1st Division had been pulled out of the line into corps reserve, although its artillery remained in support of 56th Division. Further reserves in the shape of two regiments of the US 1st Armored Division remained behind the final defensive line.

In an attempt to disguise the actual point of his major blow, Von Mackensen ordered a continuation of small scale assaults along the entire front. The opening moves began on the morning of 16 February with the 'Hermann Göring' Division launching a feint attack near Cisterna against US 3rd Division. This was eventually repulsed, mainly by accurate artillery fire, although the 'HG' did gain about 1,000 yards near Ponte Rotto. German Fourteenth Army's main attack along the Albano road began with 1 Parachute Corps striking the right hand side of British 56th Division's sector. The German 65.Division together with 4. Fallschirmjäger-Division (who were fighting for the first time as a complete division) hit 167 Brigade's part of the British line with such strength that it began to yield. In the centre of the German attack, following a heavy artillery preparation, 3.Panzer-Grenadier and 715.Divisions attacked either side of the main road, striking the two American infantry regiments holding the line. Both of these units, the 157th and 179th Infantry, took the shock of the assault with some penetration of their lines. On the main road itself the Lehr-Regiment attacked straight down the route to Anzio.

The German assault was ferocious; artillery and self-propelled guns pounded known targets and laid down a great deal of fire on counter-battery positions. The Allied artillery none the less continued to demonstrate its superiority over the enemy guns, pouring accurate and decisive concentrations into the advancing infantry. The ground off the roads was too soft to support the weight of much armour, so that the impetus of the German attack began to fade as the infantry moved ahead of their road-bound tanks. In the face of such a determined offensive, however, it was inevitable that the Allied line would be penetrated in many places. On the left, British 167 Brigade was pushed back about a mile; a gap began to open up between the mutually supporting US 157th and 179th Infantry Regiments; but everywhere the line held.

attack to falter. The lead battalion regrouped and tried once more, eventually fighting its way into the Factory for a second time. Again the enemy counter-attacked and threw them out, forcing the Americans to retire 500 yards. It was here they stayed until relieved. The Factory was just too difficult an objective to crack without extra help.

The commander of German Fourteenth Army was not yet ready start his counter-offensive, since the Allied attacks at the end of January and his own limited attacks of the past seven days had reduced his available strength. Political considerations also influenced his planning when Hitler decreed that US VI Corps must be swept into the sea at all costs. The Führer felt that if this landing could be annihilated then the Allied powers might be more hesitant about launching their cross-Channel attempt against North-West Europe. The propaganda value of a decisive Allied defeat at Anzio would be immense. General von Mackensen had best not fumble the opportunity.

After consulting with Kesselring, Von Mackensen set 16 February as the start date for his main assault. Hitler gave close attention to the planning of the offensive, even going to the extent of calling Von Mackensen back to report to him and brief him personally. The plan was agreed in outline but, typically, Hitler insisted on interfering over details of which he had only a superficial understanding. He wished to see the initial attack go in on a narrow front behind a rolling artillery barrage 'reminiscent of those used in the First War.' He also wanted the main effort to be led by the Infanterie - Lehr - Regiment, which he valued most highly. The Lehr - Regiment was a well-equipped demonstration unit made up of officers and men with excellent individual records; but despite its fine human material its role had been entirely on the home front, and it had never before operated as a complete unit in battle. Both Kesselring and Von Mackensen were unhappy about these two points, but they were forced to comply. Kesselring was hoping to attack on a broader front which would pin down a greater number of Allied troops and, depending on events, would allow him to choose the point through which to apply his main thrust. As for the deployment of the Lehr - Regiment, Kesselring thought that such an offensive should be led by an experienced formation such as 29.Panzer-Grenadier or 26.Panzer-Division. Events were to prove him right; once again, as so often before and afterwards, on all fronts, the Allies had reason to thank God for ex-Corporal Hitler's gross military limitations.

(continued on page 77)

COLOUR PLATES A-B

A1: Automatic rifleman, 141st Infantry Regiment, US 36th Infantry Division; Rapido River, 20-22 January 1944
The 36th 'Texas' Division was originally formed from National Guard volunteers. Its commander, Maj Gen Fred Walker, was a patriarchal figure who was regarded with some affection by his soldiers; he had two of his sons on his staff, the elder as G-3 Operations Officer and the younger as an aide-de-camp. The division had had a difficult time since its first action during the Salerno landings; it fought a succession of severe winter battles and suffered considerable casualties in the mountains during the advance to the Gustav Line, and by January 1944 it was beginning to feel itself a 'hard luck' division. Large drafts of replacements had arrived to fill the gaps, but the infantry were still 500 men under strength when they attacked across the Rapido.

After immediate treatment by a company medical orderly this lightly wounded GI is handing over his weapon and ammunition to his squad before walking out of the line. As the 'BAR man' he carries the M1918A2 Browning Automatic Rifle, a .30cal fully automatic weapon; he has dumped its bipod to lessen its weight. His web belt has six pouches carrying twelve 20-round magazines. The BAR was a reliable weapon, but gave the squad much less firepower than the German infantry section's belt-fed MG42 light machine gun. His M1 steel helmet is smeared with river mud for camouflage. Like many GIs in winter 1943/44 he has acquired the blanket-lined winter combat jacket and bib-fronted trousers which are normally associated with US Army tank crews. The 'tanker jacket', with its knitted collar, cuffs and waistband, was much sought-after; the trousers were rather cumbersome for infantry use. The medic has used the BAR man's own field dressing from the small pouch on his belt to bandage his wounded hand, and has rigged him a sling. The tied-on label notes what treatment he has already received, for the guidance of staff at the aid post in the rear. Like the rest of this uniform, the strip of white bandage tied round his left upper arm is taken from a photo of a group of walking wounded; it may be a local sign to MPs that he has permission to leave the line.

A2: Rifle grenadier, 100th Infantry Battalion, US 34th Infantry Division; Cassino town, first week of February 1944
The 100th Bn was composed of some 1,500 Nisei - Americans of Japanese descent, mainly former Hawaii National Guardsmen. In September 1943 the unit replaced the 2/133rd Inf Regt in the 34th 'Red Bull' Division (that battalion remaining in Algeria on HQ security duty). The enlistment of Japanese-Americans was controversial; but both this unit and the 442nd Regimental Combat Team (which would also be sent to the 34th Division, just after the Anzio break-out) would earn a high reputation in battle. The 34th Division, raised mainly in Minnesota and the Dakotas, would see more than 500 days of combat by VE-Day. It was one of the first divisions to order the painting of its shoulder insignia on the steel helmet, and photos also show widespread use of the red buffalo skull patch on combat clothing. This private first class wears the standard 1941 pattern 'Parsons' field jacket, made of windproof cotton with a flannel lining. It was not very protective, and quickly faded in use to a rather too visibly pale shade of 'olive drab'. For extra protection he has a pair of greenish herringbone twill (HBT) fatigue trousers over his wool trousers, confined by the standard issue canvas leggings over russet leather service shoes. His web equipment includes the rifle cartridge belt with ten pockets each holding one eight-round clip for his M1 Garand .30cal semi-automatic rifle; shoulder suspenders for the upper component of the M1928 pack, with his bayonet attached to it behind his left shoulder; a first aid pouch, and a canteen.

At least one rifleman in each infantry squad of ten to twelve men carried a muzzle launcher attachment for MkIIA1 fragmentation grenades. During the street fighting in Cassino this man's job is to fire grenades into upper windows. **(Inset)** Shoulder insignia of 34th and 36th Divisions.

B1: Machine gunner, Fallschirm-Maschinengewehr-Bataillon 1, 1.Fallschirmjäger-Division; Monte Cassino, February 1944
Germany organised her parachute troops as part of the air force; like the 'Hermann Göring' armoured division, they wore Luftwaffe uniforms and insignia. General Heidrich's 1.Parachute Rifle Division was introduced into the fighting around Cassino in piecemeal fashion, units being sent into the line as they arrived from early February onwards; the division also had to provide various regiments and battalions for both the Anzio and Adriatic fronts. One of the first to go into action on the slopes of 'Monastery Hill' was Parachute Machine Gun Bn 1, which formed part of Kesselring's 'fire brigade' - Kampfgruppe Schultz - alongside Para Rifle Regt 1 (FJR 1) and 3rd Bn, Para Rifle Regt 3 (III/FJR 3).

This 'Number 1' in a machine gun team carries the lethal, fast-firing 7.92mm MG42 (all German light machine guns were known to Allied troops by the generic name of 'Spandau', after one of the main producing factories). To keep the linked ammunition belt out of the dirt - which could cause stoppages - a 50-round section is rolled in a metal 'drum' attached to the left side of the receiver. The brown Luftwaffe belt and braces support a Walther P38 automatic pistol for self-defence, a black leather pouch for machine gun spare parts and, at the rear, his water canteen and 'bread bag'. Fighting in a defensive position in the rubble, he need carry no other kit. A photo of this unit shows paratroopers with their grey/blue-painted steel helmets covered with large-mesh camouflage nets. Over the blue Luftwaffe 'flyer's blouse', displaying his yellow collar patches of rank, this man wears the first camouflaged version of the paratrooper's distinctive jumpsmock, in a printed 'splinter' pattern and bearing the Luftwaffe design of national eagle-and-swastika badge on the right breast. There is a snap-fastened knife pocket in the knee seam of his loose-fitting field grey jump-trousers, which are tucked into centre-lacing second pattern black jump-boots.

B2: Parachute rifleman, 1.Fallschirmjäger-Division; Monte Cassino, April 1944
The 1.Parachute Rifle Division was formed early in 1943 from surviving elements of 7.Air Division, which had taken very heavy casualties in Crete in 1941 and had then been sent to the Leningrad sector of the Russian Front. The high cost of the Crete operation in men and aircraft dissuaded the Germans from any further large-scale airborne assaults, and thereafter paratroopers were sent into the line simply as crack light infantry. By autumn 1942 the division had to be withdrawn to southern France for rebuilding. The new GOC, Maj Gen Richard Heidrich, was an exceptional commander who demanded a lot from his men but earned their complete loyalty; he generated an esprit de corps second to none, which was often noted by Allied troops when they managed to take any of his paratroopers prisoner. By the time they arrived at Cassino they had been blooded on Sicily and in delaying actions during the retreat up Italy. Still volunteers and still jump-qualified, the Fallschirmjäger were a true elite.

Here, during the lull between the Third and Fourth Battles, a young replacement for one of the Parachute Rifle battalions carries spare MG barrels and 300-round ammunition boxes up to a position on the slopes of 'Monastery Hill'. With the warmer weather he has been issued the Luftwaffe's pale khaki tropical uniform. Although a khaki version was available his headgear is the standard M1943 all-arms field cap in Luftwaffe blue, badged with the Luftwaffe eagle and national cockade. His 'bone sack', worn here with the hem snap-fastened into short legs, is of a later model with a softer-edged printed pattern; slung on his belt, his helmet still has a cover in the original sharp-edged 'splinter'. This is also used for the cartridge bandoleer unique to the paratroopers, one end just visible in front of his left hip; it is a broad doubled strip of cloth passing round the neck, with five snap-fastened pockets at each end which open from either side. His weapon is the Wehrmacht's standard issue 7.92mm Mauser Kar98k bolt-action rifle; its bayonet is strapped to his entrenching tool to stop it flapping, and he has an M1924 'stick' grenade thrust into his belt.

COLOUR PLATES C-D

C1: Senior NCO, III Btl/ Gebirgsjäger-Regiment 85, 5.Gebirgs-Division; Monna Casale, 12 January 1944
Veterans of mountain battles in Greece and of the invasion of Crete in 1941, the regiments of 'Papa' Ringel's 5.Mountain Division - like so many German units originally trained and equipped for specialist roles - had been fighting as ordinary infantry for many months by winter 1943/44, with little but their elite title and weak assets to distinguish them from any other division. Formed in 1940 with Bavarian and Austrian personnel and trained in mountain skills, this light formation lacked self-propelled artillery and was weak in motor transport, tending to rely on horsepower. Before being transferred to Italy the Gebirgsjäger had seen eighteen months' hard service on the northern sector of the Russian Front from June 1942.

This senior NCO is about to fire a flare to illuminate the night attack of the Algerian 7e RTA on the 'Jumelles' features guarding Monna Casale. He wears a wool toque under his standard issue M1935 steel helmet; a mountain anorak, reversible from field grey to white; field grey mountain trousers, short puttees and heavily cleated brown leather mountain boots. His belt and Y-braces support two canvas triple magazine pouches for his 9mm MP40 machine pistol and, at the rear, his canteen and 'bread bag'. D-rings on the back of the braces support behind his shoulders a web A-frame 'assault pack' to which are attached his messtins, rolled tent quarter/poncho, and gasmask canister. Over all he has slung the large flare cartridge pouch for his M1928 signal pistol.

C2: Junior NCO, Pioniere-Abteilung 194, 94.Infanterie-Division; Colle San Martino, early May 1944
On the eve of the Fourth Battle this division held positions north of Route 7 between Santa Crocce and the Colle San Martino, at the extreme right of the German line facing the US 85th Infantry Division. As always, the German field defences were prepared with energy and skill; this assault engineer is laying anti-tank Tellermines. The original 94.Infanterie-Division was raised from reservists in Saxony and the Sudetenland in 1939. In November 1942 it was surrounded with the Sixth Army at Stalingrad, where it was destroyed, but not before the headquarters and some other troops escaped. These provided a core around which the division was reformed at Lorient, France, in April 1943. In August it was sent to Italy in the coastal defence role, but was eventually drawn into the fighting on the Winter Line and later the Gustav Line.

This Obergefreiter is a Russian Front veteran; in his buttonhole he wears the ribbons of the Eastern Front winter 1941/42 medal and the Iron Cross 2nd Class, on his left pocket a Wound Badge, and on his left sleeve his chevrons of rank. His helmet, field-painted in camouflage colours, is the flared-rim M1943. His M1942 lightweight summer uniform in reed green fabric has a subdued Army breast eagle and collar patches, and the field grey shoulder straps from his wool uniform piped in the black of the engineer branch. Canvas anklets and laced ankle boots have now replaced the old 'dice-shaker' high marching boots. After the German defeat in North Africa the combination of black leather belt with tropical web braces was not uncommon. He has a holstered pistol and a fighting knife for self-defence and carries the standard entrenching tool. The canvas engineer's packs slung at each hip, with a third invisible on his back, would accomodate a total of 11kg (24lb) of explosive charges and also his personal equipment - gasmask, messtins, tent quarter, etc. - with rifle ammunition in the small end pockets.

D1: Bren gun 'Number 1', 3rd Bn Coldstream Guards, British 201 Guards Brigade; Monte Camino, November-December 1943
This independent brigade landed on the Salerno beaches in September 1943 and fought with British X Corps during the long slog up to the Gustav Line. The preliminary assaults on the Winter Line mountain defences in November were carried out under appalling conditions. The infantry had to attack well-prepared defences at an altitude of 3,000 feet, in bitter cold and torrential rain. The Guardsmen clung to their exposed positions for days on end, repelling numerous counter-attacks, only to be called off the mountain when their situation was judged untenable. A renewed attempt on 1 December took ten days to capture Monte Camino, with heavy casualties.

The British ten-man infantry section at full strength had a 'Bren group' of two men led by a lance-corporal, and a 'rifle group' of six led by a corporal armed with a sub-machine gun. All tactics revolved around the 'base of fire' provided by the .303in Bren light machine gun - a well-designed, very accurate, but rather slow-firing weapon. This Bren gunner has the spare parts/tools wallet slung on his right hip. Photos show Guardsmen bundled in all their cold weather clothing: the knitted 'cap, comforter' worn under the MkII steel helmet, and both the leather jerkin and greatcoat worn over the wool battledress. The 1937 pattern web equipment was designed around belt and braces supporting the large 'universal' ammunition pouches (each here carrying two 30-round Bren magazines), canteen, and (invisible here) the bayonet and entrenching tool. Hooked to the pouches by L-straps, the haversack carried rations, messtins, washing gear, sweater and groundsheet; the rolled anti-gas cape is tied to the back of the belt below it. Many Tommies also carried a General Service pick or shovel, since the entrenching tool was too small for serious digging-in.

D2: Bren gun 'Number 2', 6th Bn Black Watch, British 4th Infantry Division; Liri valley, mid-May 1944
This unit led the advance of 12 Inf Bde towards the Cassino-Pignataro road in the early stages of Operation 'Diadem'. On 14 May it was hampered by early morning mist, and its supporting Sherman tanks of the Lothian & Border Horse also kept blundering off course. The CO of 6th Black Watch, Lt Col Madden, settled on a novel idea to keep the battle group together: he reverted to the ancient practice of forming a hollow square, with the tanks in the middle. This archaic formation made remarkable progress. When enemy fire became too heavy the infantry went to ground and the tanks fired over them until the opposition was silenced, then the infantry got up again and the advance continued, until the objective was reached and the Germans were forced back off the road.

During a sunny spell this Jock has stowed his blouse and marches in the collarless 'shirt, angora' and the trousers of his 1940 pattern wool serge battledress, confined by web anklets above his hobnailed 'ammunition boots.' In the distinctive map pocket on the left thigh he seems to carry either a tobacco tin or the emergency ration tin. His distinctive regimental headgear is the Balmoral bonnet worn with the Black Watch's red feather 'hackle' but without a cap badge. His slung helmet has string and netting for the attachment of camouflage. His web equipment is basically the same as for D1, but as the assistant Bren gunner he also has a pair of 'utility' pouches slung high on the chest, each containing two more Bren magazines. A fifth is carried in one of his 'universal' belt pouches, and in the other 50 rounds for his own .303in Short Magazine Lee Enfield Rifle No.1 MkIII. Over his left shoulder he carries the Bren holdall with a spare barrel and the cleaning kit. Behind this protrudes the haft of his entrenching tool strapped horizontally below the belt. In the open throat of his shirt can be seen his green and red fibre identity tags; the former will be left with the corpse if he becomes a casualty, while the latter is handed in as a record of his death.

(Inset left): The Roman 'III' worn by 3rd Coldstream on both upper sleeves of the battledress blouse, below the arc-shaped white-on-red 'Coldstream Guards' shoulder title. Guardsmen wore no red arm-of-service strip on the sleeves of greatcoats or blouses.

(Inset right): 4th Infantry Division's shoulder insignia at this date was the red 'quadrant'. Below it on the upper sleeves of the blouse 6th Black Watch wore a strip of French 1914-18 Croix de Guerre ribbon, a privilege awarded to the battalion during the Great War.

PLATE A

A1: BAR gunner, 141st Inf Regt, US 36th Division; River Rapido, January 1944

A2: Rifle grenadier, 100th Inf Bn, US 34th Division; Cassino town, February 1944

PLATE B

B1: MG 42 gunner, Parachute MG Bn 1, 1st Parachute Rifle Division; Monte Cassino, February 1944

B2: Rifleman, 1st Parachute Rifle Division; Monte Cassino, April 1944

PLATE C

C1: Senior NCO, Mountain Rifle Regt 85, 5th Mountain Division; Monna Casale, January 1944

C2: Junior NCO, Assault Engineer Bn 194, 94th Infantry Division; Colle San Martino, May 1944

PLATE D

D1: Bren gunner, 3rd Bn Coldstream Guards, 201 Guards Brigade; Monte Camino, November–December 1943

D2: Assistant Bren gunner, 6th Bn Black Watch, 4th Infantry Division; Liri valley, May 1944

70

PLATE E

E1: Lt Col Bredin DSO, MC,
6th Bn Royal Inniskilling Fusiliers,
78th Division; Monte Cairo,
March–April 1944

E2: Capt Wakeford VC, 2/4th Bn Hampshire Regt,
4th Division; Rapido bridgehead, May 1944

71

PLATE F

F1: Section commander, 4/16th Punjab Regt, 4th Indian Division; Snakeshead Ridge, February–March 19

F2: Platoon commander, 1/2nd Gurkha Rifles, 4th Indian Division; Monastery Hill, February 1944

PLATE G

G1: Rifleman, 28th (Maori) Bn,
2nd New Zealand Division; Cassino town,
February 1944

NEW ZEALAND

CANADA

G2: Medical orderly, PPCLI, 1st Canadian Division;
Hitler Line, May 1944

PLATE H

H1: Section commander, 17th Tabor, 3rd Group of Moroccan Tabors, CEF; Monna Casale, January 1944

H2: Pte Nowicki, PIAT man, 16th Rifle Bn, Polish 5th 'Kresowa' Division; Monastery Hill, 17 May 1944

COLOUR PLATES E-G

E1: Lieutenant-Colonel 'Bala' Bredin DSO, MC, 6th Bn Royal Inniskilling Fusiliers, British 78th Infantry Division; Monte Cairo, March–April 1944
At this time 78th Division were holding a line from Cassino station in the south, through the town and north as far as the slopes of Monte Cairo, where 38 (Irish) Bde were deployed. The brigade - consisting of 6th Royal Inniskilling Fusiliers, 1st Royal Irish Fusiliers and 2nd London Irish Rifles - was very close-knit and jealous of its Irish identity. Colonel Bredin, originally commissioned in the Royal Ulster Rifles and later trained as a paratrooper, was second-in-command of 1st Royal Irish Fusiliers when he was posted to take over the 6th 'Skins' in March. A popular and much-decorated officer, he was seriously wounded in both legs on 17 May during the capture of the village of Piumerola in the Liri valley from men of Pz-Gren Regt 361, 90.Pz-Gren Division. Returning to the division later in the Italian campaign he took command of 2nd London Irish Rifles; he had thus held command or been second-in-command of all three battalions of the Irish Brigade.

His headgear is a caubeen - the bonnet traditionally worn by pipers of Irish regiments - which was locally made from captured grey-green Italian greatcoat material (a fashion started by 2nd 'Skins' in 5th Division which spread rapidly). It bears the large piper's 'castle' cap badge worn by officers and WOs of the Inniskillings, with the regiment's grey feather hackle. His 1938 pattern battledress is worn in officer's fashion with the collar pressed open over a shirt and tie; photos show the battalion's officers wearing metal badges of rank on the shoulder straps. On both sleeves he wears the 78th Division sign of a yellow battleaxe on black, over the infantry red arm-of-service strip, over the Irish Brigade's green shamrock bearing the Inniskillings' red triangle. His parachute wings are invisible here, at the top of his right sleeve. His ribbons are those of the DSO, MC, prewar General Service Medal and Africa Star.

E2: Captain R.Wakeford (VC), 2/4th Bn Hampshire Regiment, British 4th Infantry Division; Rapido bridgehead, 13 May 1944
This battalion had a chequered history. As part of the original 128 (Hampshire) Bde it saw action in Tunisia, most famously at Hunt's Gap; but it was then converted into 20 & 21 Beach Group Defence Units. After Salerno its CO, Lt Col Fowler-Esson, lobbied tirelessly and the battalion was eventually reconstituted, but it was four months before it returned to the line in 28 Bde of 4th Division. Early in the Liri valley battle 28 Bde saw very hard fighting in a small bridgehead across the Rapido. On 13 May Capt Wakeford led his B Company, 2/4th Hampshires onto their objective, killing a number of the enemy with an automatic pistol and taking some 20 prisoners while accompanied only by his orderly; later he led a further attack with Thompson guns and grenades on enemy-held buildings. On the evening of 14 May the battalion advanced towards the Piopetta River; withering fire cost them a hundred men in two minutes, but the CO led them across the river and up the slope beyond. Already wounded in the face and both arms, Capt Wakeford kept B Coy moving and under perfect control, and led a party which silenced enemy machine guns. Wounded again in both legs by mortar fire, he continued until the objective had been seized and consolidated. It was seven hours before stretcher-bearers could reach him. For his gallantry, leadership and disregard of his own injuries Capt Wakeford was awarded the Victoria Cross.

When the 2/4th Hampshires joined 28 Bde they adopted 4th Division practice of wearing the division's red 'quadrant' sign and a regimental device - in their case, the yellow-on-black shoulder title 'The Hampshire Regt.'; the red loop outside the captain's three rank 'pips' on the shoulder straps identified B Company. We illustrate Capt Wakeford's automatic pistol as a .45in Colt M1911A1.

F1: Section commander, 4th Bn, 16th Punjab Regiment, 4th Indian Division; Snakeshead Ridge, February–March 1944
This battalion formed - with 1st Royal Sussex and 1/2nd Gurkha Rifles - 7 Brigade of 4th Indian Division. During the Second Battle in mid-February the 4/16th Punjabis were not committed to the division's costly attacks on enemy positions on the saddle leading to Monastery Hill, instead digging in to provide covering fire. During the Third Battle they were held in reserve. Yet between 15 February and 23 March the battalion still suffered 250 battle casualties to heavy and accurate fire directed by nearby enemy observers. By day they occupied precarious positions among the rocks in appalling rain, sleet, snow and cold; by night they struggled up and down slopes of shale or knee-deep mud to bring up supplies and evacuate the wounded.

The 4/16th Punjabis were a mixed battalion recruited from several of the Indian 'martial races': Punjabi Mussulmans, Jat Sikhs and Dogras. This corporal (naik) is a Sikh, his uncut hair and beard confined under the characteristic paggri; photos show this turban worn instead of a steel helmet by groups and individuals within such units. His badges of rank are the only visible insignia. Over his battledress he wears an improvised sheepskin jerkin. The .45in Thompson gun, here the M1A1 model, remained the most popular junior leader's weapon in Eighth Army despite the growing availability of the 9mm Sten gun.

F2: Platoon commander, 1st Bn, 2nd King Edward's Own Gurkha Rifles, 4th Indian Division; Monastery Hill, 18 February 1944
During the Second Battle units from 7 Bde were given the task of launching New Zealand II Corps' attack on Monastery Hill after the bombing of the monastery; the first objective was the notorious peak of Point 593, held by paratroopers from 1.Fallschirmjäger Regiment. On two successive nights 1st Royal Sussex were beaten off, suffering 174 casualties. On the third night 1/2nd Gurkha Rifles joined the battle with a direct assault towards Point 445, by-passing Point 593. When they reached the bottom of a ravine which led up to the summit they ran into a hidden scrub-covered minefield which decimated the battalion. Machine gun fire then poured into their ranks and grenades were lobbed down the slopes onto their heads. The attack quickly broke up, and in this one short action 1/2nd Gurkhas suffered 149 casualties. It must be remembered that nearly all losses in infantry battalions were suffered among the roughly 25 officers and 400 men of the rifle companies, and a few days of continuous fighting could often cost them anything between 20 and 50 per cent casualties.

Indian-made battledress was of a coarser, slightly greener material than British but was of the same design. Viceroy's Commissioned Officers like this jemadar (second lieutenant) were supposed to wear strips of red/yellow/red ribbon beneath their stars of rank, but sources show this combination of insignia worn by 2nd Gurkhas VCOs in Italy: no ribbon, red-backed black rank stars, black metal '2G' titles, and a black lanyard. This commissioned former Rifleman wears the medal ribbons of the Military Medal for gallantry, 1936-37 India General Service Medal and Africa Star. His officer's web set is of regulation British pattern, here worn with the pistol holster and cartridge pouch on the left and binocular and compass pouches on the right. All ranks of the Gurkhas usually carried the kukri in a scabbard behind the hip. During the Cassino fighting units might be cut off for days within close range of enemy positions, under constant shellfire and repeated counter-attacks; ammunition, food and water sometimes had to be air-dropped and mostly fell into enemy hands. During the Third Battle 1/9th Gurkhas from 5 Bde were cut off on the slopes of Hangman's Hill for eight terrible days and nights; but they still regarded air-dropped American rations with some suspicion in case they contained beef, forbidden by their religion.
(Inset): The sign of 4th Indian Division; photos show that this was normally removed from the shoulders as a security measure.

G1: Private, 28th (Maori) Battalion, 2nd New Zealand Division; south-east outskirts of Cassino, 17 February 1944
General Freyberg's 2nd NZ Division had fought a long, hard war since arriving in Britain in 1940. Sent to the Middle East, it saw action in the Western Desert, Greece and Crete, at El Alamein, the Mareth Line and in Tunisia. In Italy it

COLOUR PLATES G-H

fought with Eighth Army on the River Sangro before coming over the Appenines to join US Fifth Army. During the Second Battle the attack of 28th (Maori) Bn from 5 NZ Inf Bde on the railway station on 17-18 February was one of the few successes of the NZ II Corps operation, albeit a short-lived one. Two companies took the station itself but, still under heavy fire from the 'Hummocks' to the south, were unable to hold it next day when Inf Regt 211 from 71.Infanterie-Division counter-attacked with tank support. The Maori companies committed to this action lost about 50 per cent casualties.

New Zealand battledress differed from British in having a buttoned tab at the throat rather than hooks and eyes. The national title was worn at the base of the shoulder straps by all ranks and units. This Maori, in full regulation fighting order, is picking up a box of twelve No.36 fragmentation grenades, the box marked with the four-second timing of the fuzes fitted to the detonators also carried in the box. For an assault he will probably carry two grenades in one of his 'universal' pouches, together with 50 rounds of rifle ammunition issued in a disposable cotton bandoleer, and extra bandoleers may be worn slung. The second pouch will carry two magazines for the section's Bren gun; in all the ten-man section can carry about 780 rounds for the Bren in their equipment. In the German infantry section the MG team alone could carry 900 rounds. In practice all infantrymen on both sides tended to be burdened with additional ammunition for the section and platoon heavy weapons, which was expended at a ferocious rate.

G2: Medical orderly, Princess Patricia's Canadian Light Infantry, 1st Canadian Infantry Division; Hitler Line, 23 May 1944

This division had waited three and a half years to go into battle as a complete formation since arriving in Britain in December 1939. After providing troops for the Spitzbergen expedition in 1941 and the very costly Dieppe raid of 1942, it left for the Mediterranean in June 1943. After fighting in Sicily it crossed to the 'toe' of Italy on 3 September, advancing up the Adriatic coast with Eighth Army, and taking heavy casualties in the savage seven-day street battle for Ortona over Christmas 1943. In April 1944 it was brought over to the Cassino front for Operation 'Diadem'. During the assault on the Hitler Line the 'Princess Pats' were on the extreme right of 2 Inf Bde's attack towards the Pontecorvo-Aquino road, and suffered heavy losses to strongly emplaced paratroopers of 1.Fallschirmjäger-Division withdrawn from Monte Cassino. Concreted-in Panther tank turrets also inflicted severe losses on the Canadians' supporting tanks from the North Irish Horse - ten of the original eighteen Churchills assigned to the brigade were knocked out in short order, and one Panther turret is said to have destroyed thirteen tanks on its own before being knocked out with an armour-piercing shell. The attack was pressed home, however, and ended in success.

A photo of two of the battalion's medical orderlies with a jeep-ambulance shows both - unusually - with full beards, which are normally the privilege of pioneer sergeants alone in armies following the British tradition. This soldier wears the regimental cap badge on a khaki beret, and Canadian-made khaki drill bush shirt and khaki denim trousers. The white-on-red regimental title 'P.P.C.L.I.' is sewn to the sleeve above 1st Division's plain red patch.

(Inset): New Zealand and Canadian national shoulder titles, the latter worn on battledress by most units during 1939-45.

H1: Section commander, 18e Goum, 17e Tabor, 3e Groupement de Tabors Marocains, Corps Expeditionnaire Francais; Monna Casale, second week of January 1944

These Berber irregulars made their first impact in Italy when the 3e and 4e GTM fought alongside the Moroccan and Algerian Divisions in the French Expeditionary Corps' successful January attacks on the line held by Ringel's 5.Mountain Division. Later the consolidated Tabors of Gen Augustin Guillaume's 'Mountain Corps' did very well in the third week of May, making a lightning advance over the Petrella massif in the Aurunci Mountains on the left of the CEF's drive to the Hitler Line. For this operation 3e GTM with 2e Régiment de Tirailleurs Marocains formed the 'Bondis Group'.

All observers remarked on their high mobility on foot over difficult terrain, with only mules to carry supplies. They also showed aggressive energy, skill in small unit tactics, and initiative in exploiting success. They were, however, soldiers in an archaic tradition; they did not take to modern European military disciplines, and needed careful leadership by officers who understood their culture. Each Tabor (battalion) had an establishment of only about 65 French officers and senior NCOs to 895 goumiers (a much smaller European cadre than the Tirailleurs battalions, which had about 325 Frenchmen to 700 North Africans). The official British history said of the goumier that he 'valued life cheaply and regarded the killing of enemies as an honourable and agreeable duty to be undertaken with zest'. It was widely believed - though vehemently denied by the French - that the goumiers sodomised and castrated German prisoners; a veteran protested that they were far more interested in selling them for cash to units which had none of their own to show. They certainly looted and raped mercilessly in Italian villages.

Some Goums were given pre-war Armée d'Afrique uniforms including these very loose seroual trousers; woollen socks and footless tariouines stockings were worn with naala (sing., nail) sandals as often as with French M1917 boots. Before some uniformity was introduced for the 1944-45 campaign in France each company tended to wear its own random pattern of the heavy, hooded djellaba, striped in browns, greys, black and off-white. An ecusson of pale blue bearing the Tabor number in dark blue was sometimes seen on the left arm; this haoun or corporal wears his yellow braid chevrons above it. The M1917A1 helmet (worn over a low turban) and M1917/18 web equipment are US World War I surplus, with M1936 suspenders added, and the French ANP31 gasmask satchel is slung as a haversack; some French M1916 leather equipment was also seen. Photos show the French 8mm 'straight-pull' bolt action M1908/15 Berthier rifle, with a three-round magazine, still in use that winter, although US 1903 or 1917 rifles soon became general issue to the CEF.

H2: Private Ferdynand Nowicki, 16th Rifle Bn, 6th 'Lwowska' Rifle Brigade, Polish 5th 'Kresowa' Division; Monte Cassino, 17 May 1944

The Polish II Corps commanded by Lt Gen Anders had not seen action before arriving on the Cassino front, although most of its men already had a grim story to tell. It was largely made up of Polish soldiers taken into captivity in the USSR after the fall and division of Poland in 1939. Their release was negotiated in August 1942, and Gen Anders led a great exodus to the British- occupied Middle East via Iraq. There 1st Carpathian Inf Bde, raised from refugees who had made their own way to the West in 1939/40, was already in North Africa with British Eighth Army. Equipped, organised and trained according to British practice and establishments, these soldiers formed the basis of the 3rd 'Carpathian' and 5th 'Kresowa' Infantry Divisions.

'Ferdic' Nowicki was a young private in the 3rd Coy of 16.Lwowski Batalion Strzelcow, 6.Lwowska Brygada Strzelcow, 5.Kresowej Dywizji Piechoty at the final battle for Monte Cassino. Previously he had been armed with a Thompson sub-machine gun, but shortly before the attack he was ordered to take over as Number 1 on the platoon's PIAT - Projector, Infantry, Anti- Tank - with his comrade Stanislaw Rosinski as the Number 2 carrying ammunition. (The PIAT fired a rocket projectile with an accurate range of about 100 yards; it took considerable strength and nerve to fire it effectively, but the 3lb hollow charge was devastating against bunkers as well as tanks.) As his unit fought its way on to the Colle San'Angelo on the night of 17/18 May, Ferdic was wounded in the head, wrist and leg by shell splinters; he still carries metal from the battle. After the war Ferdic and Stan settled in England, where they remain 56 years later, still comrades. In 1999 they were instrumental in having a plaque erected in Poland to the 16th Bn's part in the capture of Monte Cassino.

Ferdic remembers all the uniform details shown, including the 'Poland' national title and 5th Division bison patch worn above that of the 6th Brigade, but cannot recall what type of revolver he was issued as a personal weapon when assigned to carry the PIAT.

(continued from page 64)

German prisoners captured at Anzio. One soldier (centre) wears an over-suit locally made up in Italian camouflage material - these were popular among Wehrmacht troops; from his short-peaked Bergmütze and heavily cleated boots he seems to be from a mountain unit. Several men (e.g. left background) wear some kind of skullcap; they perhaps belong to one of the several Eastern Legion units, recruited in occupied areas of the USSR, which were sent to Italy in 1943. (US National Archives)

The German formations attacking on this first day of the battle were surprised by the tough resistance that the Allied units were able to put up. The weight of Allied artillery fire and the activity of Allied aircraft was particularly daunting. The US Twelfth Tactical Air Force and the British Desert Air Force dropped 174 tons of bombs on the battlefield during the day, returning during the night to drop even more. The four lead German divisions fought well in spite of the devastating return fire. There was, however, one notable exception: Hitler's great faith in the Infanterie-Lehr-Regiment did not prove to be well founded.

Attacking straight down the Anzio road, this supposedly crack unit broke under intense Allied artillery fire. Although they had long trained others in the arts of war, most of its men and many of its officers had never been in combat before. They arrived in the line immediately before the battle and had not had time to acclimatise themselves to the conditions of life at the front - which in the freezing, muddy Italian winter were particularly unwelcoming. Thrown into their first action along the most important and exposed axis of the attack, they had a shocking introduction to battle in a sector which should have been entrusted only to the most experienced shock troops. It was obvious that the Allies would cover this route with the utmost firepower available; and both the US and British artillery branches had long since earned a reputation for murderous efficiency against the German armies. The Lehr-Regiment walked into a storm of steel almost immediately it stepped off from its start line and began taking severe casualties at once, especially among its officers. Before long this untried regiment broke and fled, robbing the offensive of much of its momentum along its important central artery.

At the end of the day both sides reviewed the situation. For Von Mackensen the battle seemed to be progressing well. Despite relatively high losses his attack was gaining ground and there was still enough fight in his two attacking corps to make further gains the next day. He also still had his strong armoured second wave to introduce into the action when the time was right for exploitation. As for Gen Lucas, he had not been forced to retire to his final beachhead line, nor had he needed to commit his main reserve, the US 1st Armored Division.

As the early winter darkness fell on 16 February, Von Mackensen urged his commanders to allow the Allies no respite during the night. He expected strong assault parties to harass the British and Americans, supported by tanks where possible, to exert pressure and probe for openings which could be exploited during daylight. That night one such attack by the 715.Division overran a battalion and prised open the gap between the US 157th and 179th Infantry.

Through this gap the next morning a composite strike force supported by sixty tanks attacked the 2/179th, forcing the battalion back more than a mile, almost to the final beachhead line. This attack was followed up by an air raid by about forty-five German aircraft which strafed and bombed the new American positions. Again, German infantry and tanks pounded the gap, exploited the confusion and widened the penetration. General Eagles, commander of the US 45th Division, gave the 179th Regiment's CO permission to pull back his other two battalions 1,000 yards to tie in his flanks. This withdrawal was made in full daylight; the enemy took advantage of the fluid nature of the situation, and hammered the two retreating battalions all the way. By midday, Fourteenth Army had driven a wedge two miles wide and over a mile deep into the defences of the 'Thunderbird' Division.

The situation in front of the 45th Division had become critical. The weight of the German attack was becoming overwhelming, for during the late morning Von Mackensen had introduced his reserves from his first wave into the battle. There were now fourteen battalions of infantry and tanks attacking through the gap. Commander Fourteenth Army was looking for the moment to send his second wave through the breach to finally eliminate the beachhead. Behind the US 45th Division the final defence line was barely held and vulnerable. Lucas decided to move up the

German dead lying in a drainage ditch beside the Mussolini Canal after their failed counter-offensive; one, killed during attacks on the lines of the US 3rd Division, wears the cuff title of the 'Hermann Göring' Panzer Division. (US National Archives)

British 1st Division to hold the final line to the rear of British 56th and US 45th Divisions. He also sent more artillery, tanks and 90mm anti-aircraft guns to the aid of Gen Eagles' division, and raided his corps reserve to make available a tank battalion from US 1st Armored Division. He then called up the air forces and asked for every available bomber to attack German concentrations.

Throughout the afternoon of the 17th the battle raged with unabating fury. Each German commander knew that a breakthrough must be close; each Allied commander knew that he had to hold. Everyone tried for just one last effort. The Americans refused to let go, although their line was stretched to the limit and close to collapse. Combining with this fierce determination by the infantry was the superb support of the artillery, whose expenditure of ammunition was prodigious. To this was added the fire of tanks, tank-destroyers, anti-aircraft guns and mortars, enabling a curtain of fire to stifle most enemy attacks. By nightfall the line still held.

That evening Von Mackensen deliberated on the progress of the battle. During the day he had had to commit the reserves of his attacking divisions without effecting a complete penetration of the Allied line. His losses were becoming serious. The question was, could they continue attacking for a third day? If he used his follow-up divisions too soon in an attempt to engineer the breakthrough then they might not have the strength remaining to destroy the beachhead. Should he cancel the offensive altogether and regroup to try again with a different plan; or would one more push shatter the equally exhausted defenders in front of him? He decided to throw the dice again, and asked his commanders to fight on through the night. In their rear 29.Panzer-Grenadier and 26.Panzer-Divisions moved into position ready to attack at 0400 hours on 18 February. The second wave was going in.

The fresh German divisions attacked just before dawn; smashing into the already depleted US 179th Infantry, they drove a great bulge in the front and pushed it back into the final defensive line. Throughout the morning, seemingly endless streams of German infantry and armour came at the Americans. Some attacks were broken up well before they were launched through the effective use of artillery. At around 1100 hours Capt William McKay, flying a Cub observation plane, observed a large force of about 2,500 enemy soldiers supported by tanks moving down the Albano road south of Carroceto. He radioed the sighting back to the artillery, and within twelve minutes a massed force of 224 British and American guns zeroed in on the marching enemy infantry. The ground through which the Germans were moving erupted into an inferno of fire and shrapnel, disorganising the advance and scattering the men and tanks. During the next hour McKay in his Piper Cub brought down this incredible weight of fire on four other concentrations of German infantry massing for the attack. Yet still they came on.

By noon the US 179th Infantry were almost finished, their commander close to collapse from overwork and lack of sleep. General Lucas replaced him with Col Darby, commander of the now greatly diminished Ranger force. When he took over the regiment in the early afternoon he was horrified by what he found. The 3rd Bn was shattered and had to be withdrawn to reorganise; the exhausted 2nd Bn was down to less than half its strength, and only the 1st Bn was capable of any organised resistance. Colonel Darby requested permission for the regiment to withdraw from the line and seek shelter in the Padiglione woods to the rear. Permission was refused: Gen Eagles was adamant that the final beachhead line would be held at all costs.

The enemy came again at the 45th Division during the afternoon, but for some reason shifted the focus of their assault to the left and had the misfortune to strike the 180th Infantry – a regiment which was still relatively intact, and gave as good as it received. Throughout the remainder of the day, through hours of ferocious fighting, the 'Thunderbird' Division held the remainder of the line. By nightfall it was obvious that the enemy had failed in his attempt to break through.

Kesselring and Von Mackensen agreed that the offensive to destroy the Allied beachhead could not now achieve its goal. Further attacks were put in the next day, 19 February, to try to consolidate the gains already made, but these were not successful. In the afternoon Gen Lucas launched a counter-attack backed by tanks and succeeded in pushing the demoralised Germans back a mile from the final defensive line. A last effort was made by the enemy on 20 February without causing any difficulty to the defenders. After this date Von Mackensen went over to the defensive save for sporadic nuisance attacks and raids.

General von Mackensen had committed his freshest and strongest troops to his offensive, combined with two crack armoured units to exploit the breakthrough, but had failed to make the penetration required. Before another attempt could begin he needed to pause for a period of rest and reorganisation. The Germans had suffered heavily during the five-day attack, losing 5,389 men killed, wounded or missing. Most of the damage had been done by the Allied artillery – Von Mackensen estimated that 75 per cent of all wounds were caused by shellfire. Captured Germans commented on the 'terrific' and 'continuous' artillery fire. The official American history of the battle claims that the artillery 'caused heavy casualties, shattered nerves, destroyed morale and brought some enemy units to the verge of panic.' At the peak of the attack, for every shell the enemy artillery fired, the US and British gunners of VI Corps threw back fifteen to twenty.

On the Allied side the human cost had also been substantial. During the period 16-20 February battle casualties amounted to 3,496 killed, wounded and missing. Non-battle casualties in the appalling winter weather, caused mainly by exposure, exhaustion and trench foot, also reached 1,637. It was a heavy price to pay, but when the smoke of battle had settled the beachhead seemed to be just a little more secure.

In addition to the great loss of life on both sides, there was one more casualty of the battle: on 22 February, one month after the landings began, Gen Lucas was relieved of the command of US VI Corps. It had been clear for some time that both Clark and Alexander were unhappy with

In the ruins of Nettuno, Gen Alexander meets with Lt Gen Truscott to discuss the situation in the beachhead. Lucian Truscott - wearing a shined-up helmet and a flying jacket with the patch of his new command - took over US VI Corps after the departure of Maj Gen Lucas in late February 1944. (Imperial War Museum)

what was happening in the beachhead, and a lack of 'drive and enthusiasm' was detected. In Alexander's words: 'The VI Corps commander lacked initiative and the staff was depressed'. Clark agreed that a change in command would be advisable, but under no circumstances would he wish to hurt Lucas. A figleaf was devised: Lucas would ostensibly be replaced by two joint deputy commanders, one American and one British, each helping to direct the national component parts of the beachhead, and soon after Lucas had left the American commander would take over VI Corps. Thus it was that Gen Lucian Truscott left his US 3rd Division and Gen Vivian Evelegh temporarily moved from his British 6th Armoured Division. General Lucas was moved to US Fifth Army HQ as Clark's deputy. Three weeks later he was recalled to the USA to take over US Fourth Army.

The performance of the VI Corps commander has often been called into question. On the one hand many people, including Gen Clark, said that he was right not to make for the Alban Hills immediately after the landings, as he would in all probability been been counter-attacked from the flanks and possibly thrown back into the sea. This may very well have been true; but one of the possible outcomes proposed by the planners was that just the threat of taking the Alban Hills and cutting the communications of Tenth Army would have precipitated a German withdrawal

Rising above the town, Castle Hill (centre) was 193 metres high, and looked formidable from close quarters - 600 feet of solid rock with a medieval fortress perched on its summit; but the hill was itself dwarfed by the dominating high ground on three sides. The castle was sited to bar access to a ravine which ran up to the monastery and formed a natural route to the top of Monte Cassino. The German paratroopers made enormous efforts to deny the Allies possession of the feature, and later to deny its garrison any chance of mounting a surprise attack up the ravine. (US National Archives)

from the south. Indeed, on hearing the news of the landings Von Vietinghoff requested permission to do just that. At the very least, Lucas should have taken Albano and Cisterna on the first day when the two towns were wide open. Without these in his possession, no advance inland would ever have been possible. One wonders what a German commander would have done in the same situation - with two complete divisions at large in the rear of his enemy, with another on the way to support him, and nothing in front to stop him.

Stalemate, 19 February–14 March
The end of the second battle for Cassino on 18 February did not, in the short term, prompt a major rethink of the tactics being employed to engineer a break in the Gustav Line; nor was the strategy of trying to get into the Liri valley past its strongest point called into serious question. Mounting dissatisfaction with the progress of the war in Italy was expressed in both Washington and London. Generals Alexander and Clark were under considerable pressure to get things moving. In response to this urging from the highest level, their only plan was to order Freyberg to try again. Clark seemed to have little regard for the effectiveness of the NZ Corps and its commander; yet he increasingly left Freyberg to run his own battle.

The simultaneous deterioration in the situation at Anzio took most of Clark's attention, and at the end of the second week of February it is clear that his mind was focussed on the vulnerable position of US VI Corps. It was now obvious that far from being a bold, decisive strike behind enemy lines to outflank German Tenth Army, the Anzio lodgement was a failure, sucking in men and matériel at an alarming rate in order simply to hold on to the beachhead. There could be no escape from the confines of the Anzio perimeter until the isolated garrison had been reinforced and resupplied substantially enough to give it the punch to break through the German cordon. In short, it was a liability. If the five-plus divisions stranded at Anzio had been available to Clark at Cassino, a breakthough into the Liri valley would by this time have been a certainty.

Clark's three other corps facing the enemy across the Gustav Line were all stagnant. The exhausting and demoralising winter weather, the mountain battlefield, the prepared enemy positions, and the tiredness of the British X Corps and French CEF infantry had resulted in stalemate on the two flanks of the front. US II Corps was in no fit state to do anything but hold defensive positions while it rebuilt its resources; and Freyberg's corps, although relatively fresh, with twelve infantry battalions and an armoured brigade still uncommitted, had been dribbled into the battle in small packets due to the restrictive nature of the terrain. The competence of Allied generalship was coming into serious question.

On the German side, Von Senger was somewhat surprised by the unimaginative direction of the second battle

Almost constant rain had turned the battlefield into a quagmire. This picture, taken on 25 February, demonstrates why the third battle was continually postponed over several weeks while Gen Freyberg waited for three rain-free days before launching his attack. The driver of this bogged-down light truck from 4th Indian Division inspects the bottom of his engine to make sure it has not sustained a cracked sump. It is a Morris 4x2 Light Utility Truck, derived from the basic chassis of a pre-war family saloon car; under these conditions its value off-road was severely limited. (US National Archives)

for Cassino. The plan had been so similar to the first one that it held few surprises for him. The NZ Corps had attacked in the same places that the Americans had tried, with the same results. Point 593 and the surrounding peaks were all excellent defensive positions which had been improved daily since the US 34th Division had tried to capture them. While he had some misgivings about the integrity of his line should the Allies attack in strength against his flanks - particularly the sector facing the French - he knew that Cassino town and Monte Cassino were as tight as he could make them. He had concentrated the best of his troops and the heaviest of his weapons to protect Monastery Hill, knowing that it was the cornerstone of his defence. He was surprised that Alexander and Clark continued to sacrifice their infantry against this bastion for so little return.

After the failure of the NZ Corps' attack Alexander and Clark were agreed that Freyberg should make another attempt to take the Cassino feature, though each knew that the elusive breakthrough was unlikely now to take place. But Freyberg had to try again simply to avoid the front becoming completely stagnant. Pressure must be maintained to prevent German Tenth Army shifting any forces northwards against the Anzio bridgehead. It was a simple case of doing something rather than doing nothing; but there had to be a better strategy than this. And there was.

On 21 February, Alexander's chief-of-staff Gen John Harding drew up an appreciation of the situation in Italy. This argued that the existing front would most likely be stabilised by the enemy, because Clark did not have enough troops to be sure of breaking the main German line of defence. To crack the Gustav Line to the extent that it would collapse completely would need a local superiority of at least three to one in infantry and the maximum concentration of artillery and armour possible. The front now occupied by US Fifth Army would have to undergo a complete reorganisation, with a view to employing almost the entire strength of Fifteenth Army Group against the Gustav Line. New divisions were now arriving in Italy to enable at least part of this expansion to take place, but the remainder of the force required would have to be gleaned from elsewhere in the Italian theatre. British Eighth Army, at least in part, would have to come over the Apennines from its Adriatic front and get involved in the battle for the gates of the Liri valley; but such moves would take at least two months to complete.

In the meantime NZ Corps were ordered to attack once again, even though everyone in authority knew that the outcome would probably be dismal. General Alexander was coming to realise that the only way into the Liri valley would be to mount an overwhelming assault along the whole of the line. All he could hope for from Freyberg's new attack was a bridgehead over the Rapido and the capture of Cassino town to act as a base for further offensive action when the time was right.

The plan for NZ II Corps' second attempt on the Cassino feature varied from its first in that part of the 4th Indian Division was to come down off the mountains to attack along the axis of the Rapido. The 2nd NZ Division would once more assault the town, this time through the lodgement won by US 34th Division, along the road from the north. The Indian Division would also attack from the north but along the foothills parallel to the road. Both divisions together would roll up the German defences in the town, capture Castle Hill, sweep along the lower eastern slopes of Monte Cassino, and gain a footing on the twisting road that led up to the ruined monastery. From ledges cut in the rock to carry the road around the hairpin bends, a final assault would be launched on the summit of Monastery Hill. To help exploit any breakthrough, another of Eighth Army's divisions - the 78th - was to join NZ II Corps, ready to push into the Liri valley with the supporting tanks of NZ 4th Armoured Brigade.

To kick off the attack, the town of Cassino would receive the same treatment that was meted out to the monastery during the corps' first battle: the whole area would be devastated by both heavy and medium bombers. Those of the enemy who remained holed up in the stone houses and concrete bunkers of Cassino would be blasted into oblivion or buried in the ruins. The operation was set to commence on 24 February; but before it could begin Freyberg insisted that there be three days of clear weather to allow the sodden ground to dry out, so that his tanks would at least have some chance to deploy off the roads without sinking to their bellies in the mud.

Given all the other dire circumstances and predictions attending the New Zealanders' battles at Cassino, however, it seems unsurprising that the weather should now have joined in a conspiracy to frustrate their plan. The rain, sleet and snow of this most depressing of Italian winters continued unabated. The start of the battle was postponed as 24 February came and went in a swirl of rain clouds. Delay followed delay; days stretched into weeks. The NZ Corps continued to wait for a change in the weather; London and Washington continued to loose patience with the conduct of the war in Italy; Alexander's staff continued planning their big offensive, and Clark continued with his build-up at Anzio; but on the Cassino front, nothing happened. Nothing, that is, except for an cruel stroke of bad luck for the 2nd NZ Division: on 2 March, after attending a corps conference, the able and well-respected divisional commander Maj Gen Howard Kippenberger stepped on a German *Schu* mine while visiting Monte Trocchio and blew his foot off - the other was badly mangled and had to be amputated. His place was taken by Brigadier Parkinson.

On 29 February changes were made to the disposition of the German troops in front on the New Zealanders that would have a profound effect on the future conduct of the fighting. On that day, Gen Ernst-Günther Baade's 90.Panzer-Grenadier-Division handed over Monte Cassino to Gen Richard Heidrich's 1. Fallschirmjäger-Division. The Panzer-Grenadiers had given a good account of themselves in the line; but Heidrich's paratroopers were now about to create for themselves an almost mythical reputation for tenacious resistance.

Major (later Lieutenant) General Richard Heidrich had served as a volunteer in the Great War, rising to become regimental adjutant. He later attended a staff course at the War Academy, and was involved in the formation of the original parachute infantry in 1936. After a period back with the army, during which he rose to regimental command, he rejoined the Luftwaffe paratroopers as commander of Parachute Rifle Regiment 3, part of 7.Luft - (Air) Division, and went on to see action both in Crete and on the Russian Front, where his regiment was particularly associated with the battle of Leningrad. When 7.Luft-Division returned to the West after being decimated in Russia it was redesignated 1.Fallschirmjäger-Division, and Heidrich took command. His division fought well in withdrawal actions in Sicily and through southern Italy, building a reputation as an elite unit.

Richard Heidrich was an exceptional combat commander who demanded and received the utmost loyalty from his men. He had instilled in them a ruthless energy in the attack and a stubborn tenacity in defence. No problem seemed too great for his paratroopers to surmount. Before they went into action, his last instructions to them were: 'Keep together - and don't forget the dead, and those you left at home.' His division were by now seasoned fighters whose impressively high morale, noted by all observers, was built not upon Nazi indoctrination but upon well-founded self-confidence and complete trust in their remarkable commander.

★ ★ ★

On the Anzio front, things remained grim. The conditions of daily survival reminded older observers of the Western Front in 1915-18. Within the limited beachhead units were cramped together too closely, under constant threat of enemy fire, and the infantry had to dig in deep. Entrenchments developed most of the features of the old Ypres salient - thick wire entanglements, daylight movement possible only through communication trenches, icy rain lashing down on ground which was quickly churned into soupy mud. The Allied units suffered a constant trickle of casualties from random shell and mortar fire and in confusing night patrol actions - a trickle which over a few weeks could change a majority of the faces in a company or even a battalion.

After the failure of the German offensive on 20 February, the new VI Corps commander Gen Truscott began to regroup and rotate his dispositions in order to shorten his line and give his exhausted troops some rest. The Germans continued to harass the beachhead with small scale attacks and raids, but both sides knew that they had fought themselves to a standstill.

Field Marshal Kesselring was not, however, content to let matters rest, and immediately charged Von Mackensen with the task of planning further offensive action against VI Corps's lodgement. Knowing that another frontal attack along the Albano road would be futile, the commander of Fourteenth Army turned his attention to the 'shoulders' of the beachhead. Over the next eight days he rested and replenished his divisions; he then moved a strike force across to Cisterna, planning an attack against US 3rd Division's sector together with a diversionary assault against British 56th Division on the other flank.

The main attack against Gen O'Daniel's 3rd Division began on the night of 28/29 February when a violent German artillery barrage hit the division's front line. American artillery responded in kind, sending back twenty shells for each one received. At first light the next morning the German 715. and 362.Divisions moved against the Americans; they made little headway, except for some gains in the line opposite the US 509th Parachute Infantry Battalion. This penetration was eventually stopped by concentrated shellfire. Elsewhere the fighting went on all morning; in the afternoon the weather cleared sufficiently for American fighter-bombers to strafe the rear areas of the German attacking forces.

The 26.Panzer-Division now joined in the battle with

its Mark IV and Mark V Panther tanks, striking down the Cisterna-Campomorto road. Other tanks from the Panzer Regiment 'Hermann Göring' struck down the road to Isola Bella. Both advances were stopped by well-sited anti-tank guns and tank-destroyer battalions. German infantry veered towards the Mussolini Canal, moving down the eastern flanks of the beachhead, where they were unfortunate enough to run headlong into the entrenched positions of the newly promoted Brig Gen Frederick's formidable 1st Special Service Force. At the end of the first day of this operation the enemy had hardly dented the American outer defence line. The attacks had been powerful and well directed, but the telling strength of well established defences, accurate artillery fire and overwhelming air support had taken the sting out of the assault. The next day the Germans tried again, following closely the tactics of the previous day, but with less force available to them; the weather was on their side, however, as heavy rain kept American aircraft grounded. Some gains were made, but the German grasp on this new ground was tenuous and easily reversed by determined counter-attacks. The next day the skies cleared, and American aircraft appeared over Anzio in massive strength - not just the tactical squadrons, but no less than 241 B24 Liberators and 100 B17 Fortresses from the strategic bomber fleet, escorted by 176 fighters. The 'heav-

On the left is Lt Gen Richard Heidrich, commander of 1.Fallschirmjäger (Parachute Rifle) Division. On the right is Gen Valin Feurstein, commanding LI Mountain Corps, who had taken over the sector of the line responsible for Cassino, and Heidrich's paratroopers with it. Centre is Gen Wolfram von Richthofen, commanding the German air forces in Italy. (Imperial War Museum)

ies' bombed the German rear areas of Cisterna, Valletri and Carroceto while an equally impressive force of medium and fighter-bombers concentrated their efforts on enemy tanks, gun emplacements and assembly areas. There was very limited ground combat that day; the same was true on 3 March, when the German attacks became more isolated and sporadic. It soon became clear that this German initiative, too, had failed, and Kesselring called a halt to the attacks. He recognised the bitter truth that the Anzio lodgement could no longer be eliminated with the troops he had at his disposal in Italy. Nothing remained but to keep US VI Corps penned up in its cramped beachhead; Fourteenth Army now went over to the defensive.

For Gen Truscott and his tired troops the rebuff of the enemy offensive was a clear victory. The Anzio enclave was now relatively safe from annihilation, and Alexander had briefed his corps commander that the beachhead would be reinforced by the addition of US 34th and 36th Divisions to ensure that it would be strong enough to effect a break-out

Series of pictures showing a patrol from the 1st Special Service Force attacking an enemy position near the Mussolini Canal on the right of the Anzio beachhead. The SSF was a 'commando' unit of hand-picked American and Canadian troops trained to undertake long-range sabotage operations. At Anzio the Force - with a nominal establishment of six 'battalions' but actually only about 1,850 strong - spent three months holding a sector of the perimeter equal to that of a division. The man in the centre (above) can be seen to carry a M1941 Johnson light machine gun, a weapon unique to the SSF in Europe; the 'Y'-shaped light marking on the rear of the left hand man's helmet is probably a taped temporary recognition sign for a junior leader. (US National Archives)

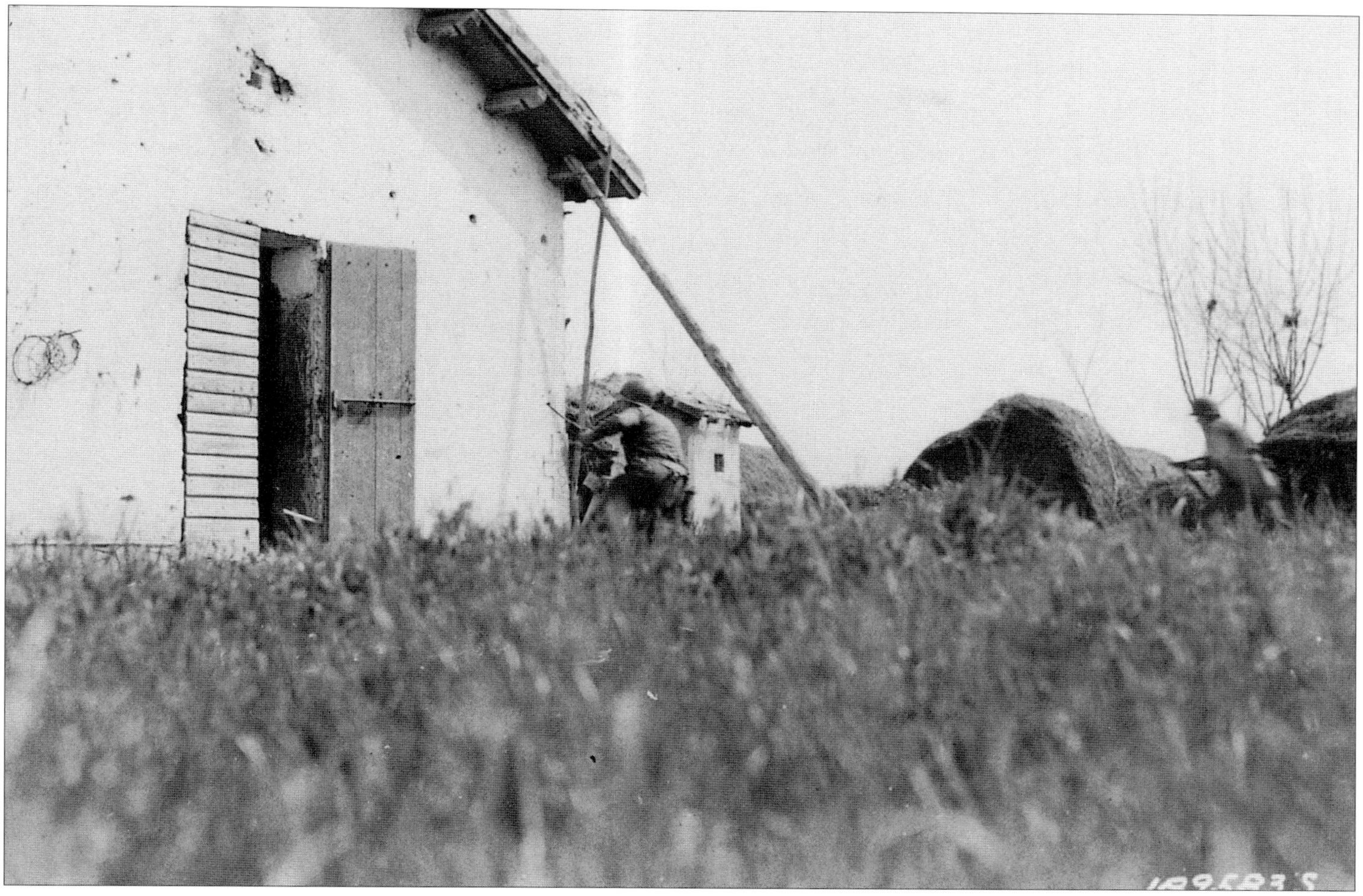

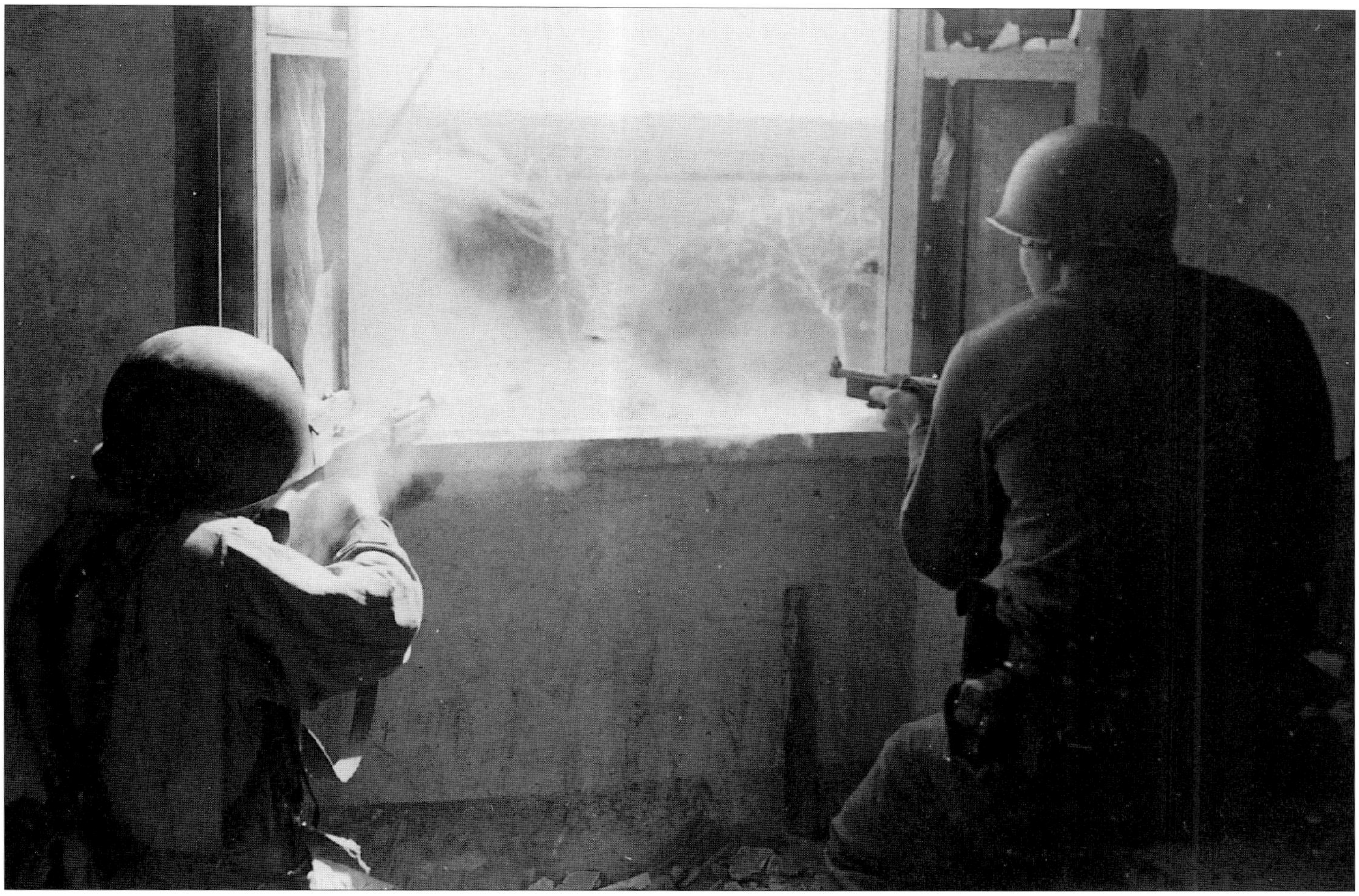

Gen Mark Clark (right), visiting HQ British 5th Division, meets two of its senior officers: Brigadier Lorne MacLaine Campbell VC, commanding 13 Bde (left), and Maj Gen Gregson Ellis, the divisional commander (centre). Brigadier Campbell had won his Victoria Cross when in command of 7th Bn, Argyll & Sutherland Highlanders at Wadi Akarit in Tunisia on 6 April 1943. (Imperial War Museum)

when the time was right. In the meantime, British 5th Division was to be landed to replace the tired 56th Division, and further fresh troops would soon arrive – two crack British battalions, Nos 9 and 40 (Royal Marine) Commandos, landed on 2 March.

Anzio now settled down into a stalemate. The Germans were not powerful enough to eliminate the landings, and VI Corps was not strong enough to break out. Both sides knew that all they could do was to harass each other through raids, patrols and remote artillery fire. Von Mackensen could not release much of his containing force to be used elsewhere lest VI Corps take advantage of his weakness. Tenth Army could not disengage any more troops from the Cassino sector lest it too weakened its defences enough to give Clark an opportunity. Kesselring knew that the Allies would gather strength for a spring offensive; Alexander knew that no new German formations were entering the Italian theatre. It would now be prudent for all sectors to hold the line, gather strength, and plan for the new offensive that was clearly going to take place when the weather improved.

This was in fact what happened, with one notable exception: the New Zealand Corps was still under orders to make its second assault on Monte Cassino.

CHAPTER SEVEN

The Third Battle: 15–23 March

After nearly three weeks of frustrated anticipation as they waited for the weather, on 14 March the word went out to the assaulting battalions of New Zealand II Corps that the bombing of Cassino town would take place the next day, heralding the start of Gen Freyberg's second attempt to break into the Liri valley. The third battle of Cassino was about to begin, despite the fact that most of the senior commanders in Fifteenth Army Group believed that it was doomed to failure. Alexander now saw the attack as being the means of carving out a bridgehead over the Rapido to allow the deployment of 'an overwhelmingly superior force' to advance through the Liri valley. This 'superior force' did not yet exist, nor would it be available for almost another two months. Even supposing that the bridgehead were gained, it would still have to be held for at least eight weeks under the eyes and guns of the enemy on Monte Cassino.

In his plan of attack, Freyberg relied heavily on the power of aerial bombing to obliterate the German defenders who had burrowed and concreted their way into the old stone houses of Cassino town. Major General John K. Cannon, commander of the Mediterranean Allied Tactical Air Forces, was confident that the town and its defences would be eliminated by the weight of explosives about to be dropped on them, thus blasting a path forward for the ground troops. His superior, Lt Gen Ira Eaker, was of a differing opinion. He suspected that the severity of the bombing would lead to the complete destruction of every building, and that the ruins might present formidable obstacles to the advancing infantry and armour. Tank movement would be heavily circumscribed, if not impossible, without extensive engineering work. Freyberg countered this objection by replying that if the ruins prevented him using tanks then they would also prevent the Germans using them. In any case, there were bulldozers available to clear any necessary paths. This might be true if the enemy were bombed out of existence and such work could progress without interference; but if the Germans were still clinging on in Cassino, the outcome might be alarmingly different.

At 0830 hours on the morning of 15 March the bombing of Cassino town began. Every serviceable heavy day bomber from Mediterranean Allied Strategic Air Force and almost all of the medium bombers of Mediterranean Allied Tactical Air Forces were put into the air to obliterate German resistance in the town. During the morning 114 B17 Flying Fortresses, 164 B24 Liberators, 105 B26 Maurauders and 72 B25 Mitchells dropped 992 tons of high explosive. The bombing lasted until around noon, and the results looked impressive, with the air forces claiming that 47 per cent of the bombs fell within one mile of the centre of the town. The whereabouts of some of the other 53 per cent were not hard to find: they fell on the innocent villages of Venafro, Pozilli and Montaquila, all miles from Cassino;

The scatter of equipment left outside the sangar *strongly suggests that this group of men from 1/4th Bn, Essex Regt, 4th Indian Division have been persuaded to pose for this picture by an Army photographer. (Combat troops and their officers often resented orders to co-operate in such pantomimes, especially if they had just come out of the line.) The location seems to be north of the town, beside the Rapido valley. The infantryman nearest the camera is holding the standard British .303in SMLE rifle, and the man beside him a .45in Thompson sub-machine gun. (Imperial War Museum)*

on the HQ of Eighth Army's commander, Gen Leese; on a Moroccan military hospital; on New Zealand 6 Brigade HQ, where fifteen personnel were killed; on Allied artillery positions, and on the rear supply train of the 4th Indian Division. A total of 96 Allied soldiers were killed, and 140 civilians; the German dead in Cassino town numbered about 300 men. But Cassino had erupted into a vast cloud of black smoke shot through with yellow flame; the roaring explosions rent the place asunder, obliterating the buildings just as the air force commanders had promised.

At noon, immediately after the last of the bombers had droned away into the distance, the Allied artillery programme commenced. For the next eight hours 890 weapons, ranging from 3-inch guns to 240mm howitzers, placed almost 200,000 shells on their appointed targets. The bulk of this weight of fire was provided by the magnificent gunners of the field artillery regiments, as 312 British 25-pounders fired an average of 380 rounds apiece.

Allied bombers lay waste to Cassino town on 15 March at the start of the long-delayed third battle. Liberators, Fortresses, Mitchells and Marauders dropped nearly a thousand tons of high explosive on the town and its approaches; as Gen Ira Eaker of the USAAF had predicted, the result was to make the town more defensible than ever. (US National Archives)

Prior to the bombing the New Zealand troops had been withdrawn a 'safe' distance back, leaving an empty 'no man's land' on the northern edge of the town. General Freyberg's plan called for a speedy reoccupation of the area immediately after the air raid and for attacking troops to rush the built-up area and throw themselves on to their objectives. He intended that they take the town and Castle Hill as the first step to bringing the 4th Indian Division through on the right, to capture the eastern slopes of Monastery Hill. In doing so the Indians would take over Castle Hill while the New Zealanders continued their move through Cassino to capture the railway station and that part of Route 6 that ran around the base of Monte Cassino. The plan was dependent on the German defenders being blasted out of their lairs by the bombing and shelling, or at least being weakened beyond the capability of offering much resistance.

When the lead battalion of 6 NZ Brigade finally moved out from its start line to launch its attack, it was met with streams of small arms and mortar fire together with salvos of *Nebelwerfer* rockets. It soon became all too clear that the enemy had not been destroyed or left impotent by the bombardment, but was alive and vengeful in the ruins of Cassino.

Hauptmann Foltin in the ruins

The German garrison in the town before the bombing was provided by the 2nd Bn, Parachute Rifle Regiment 3 commanded by Capt Foltin. The battalion had suffered heavy losses during the air raid, but when it was over about half of the paratroopers struggled free from the rubble and resolutely stood to arms. There were still enough of them to move through the ruins and re-establish themselves in the remains of their strongpoints and bunkers, many of which were still intact. Others resumed their sniping positions overlooking the routes into the town. Weapons were dug out of the rubble and prepared for use. The paratroopers of II/FJR 3 had been forced to endure unimaginable torment; all wartime memoirs agree that the experience of heavy, prolonged bombing and shelling in static positions was almost more than the human body and mind could withstand. But these were not ordinary soldiers; their pride in themselves and their unit gave them a tenacity and confidence well above the norm. They were the best German infantry on the Italian front, and they knew it.

At noon, when the bombing ceased and the artillery barrage opened up, the New Zealanders attacked. Leading the assault was 25th Bn, moving down the axis of the main road from the north in two columns, one file on the road,

Immediately after the bombing: the town of Cassino is reduced to a jumbled pile of ruins. Huge craters block the roads and rubble fills the streets, making them impassable to tanks. The only way into the town was on foot, and the whole area was full of German paratroopers who had survived the bombardment. (Imperial War Museum)

the other along the shallow river bed of the Rapido. Ahead of the infantry lurched the tanks of 19th NZ Armoured Regiment; more Shermans moved along the parallel road to the left. Almost immediately the armour ran into trouble. The roads had been heavily damaged by explosions and were made virtually impassable by huge craters; some of these could be spanned with bridging tanks, but others were too large. Tank crews had to leave their vehicles to help patch the ground with picks and shovels, while engineers bulldozed debris into the larger holes so that the advance could continue. Enemy snipers interfered with the repairs, picking off the New Zealanders with accurate rifle fire as they worked. A few more yards were gained, but the craters and heaps of rubble stretched right forward into the town. The progress of the tanks was distressingly slow.

The infantry left their protective armour behind and moved ahead. By the time they had reached the outskirts of Cassino adjacent to Castle Hill things were beginning to get much worse. The town began to come to life as Capt Foltin organised his surviving paratroopers to counter the attack. To add weight to his numbers, service personnel from the division were being moved from their support role into the town to take up arms and close the gaps in the defensive ring. The NZ 25th Bn pressed on into the town, but could not reach their initial objective, the line of Route 6 as it ran into Cassino. A company was detached to move out to the right and assault Castle Hill, while the remaining three companies struggled forward into the heart of the town.

It was a battle of small arms and machine gun fire. With no heavy weapons forward, the infantry had to prise out each of the well entrenched German defenders individually. Progress was painfully slow, as the snipers and machine gun posts were gradually located and attacked. Enemy posts would suddenly burst into life behind the leading troops as they pressed forward. 'Mopping up' in the ruined maze of narrow streets and courtyard houses was confusing and deadly dangerous, as individual German paratroopers would disappear from in front only to reappear with a lethal burst of fire from the rear. Movement through the rubble-choked streets, often completely obliterated where houses had been pummelled into shapeless mounds of brick and stone, was a nerve-wracking business demanding patience and constant vigilance.

The hideous experience of the bombing had enraged the paratroopers, and the survivors vented their anger on the New Zealanders; no quarter was asked or given. The Germans used the baffling jumble of ruins expertly. Every time an infantryman rose to begin his next dash forward, enemy fire zipped and ricocheted around him. For the less fortunate a chance exposure would lead to a sniper's bullet punching through his back or skull. The enemy's strongpoints were almost invisible in the crazy heaps of rubble, revealing themselves only when they cut down a few more of the khaki-clad figures inching through the labyrinth. Before one could be captured the attacking infantry would have to run the gauntlet of other posts nearby, with enemy fire enfilading their approach in mutual support. The ferocity of the fighting went well beyond any idea of 'fair play'; even the medics and stretcher-bearers were targets for the snipers. The battle to take Cassino town was a nightmare.

Castle Hill

While the bulk of 25th Bn tackled the enemy in the town, D Company attacked Castle Hill, the strongpoint that dominated Cassino. From the start the plan went awry, as B Coy were unable to clear the area at the base of the hill from which D were supposed to launch their assault. The company commander, Maj Hewitt, therefore decided to pursue a plan of his own. Coming off the road short of the town, he moved his men up on to the slopes to his right and managed to reach a ravine that ran up to the castle ruins from the other side. Sending a platoon round each face of the hill, he moved the rest of his company against the castle itself. The right hand platoon reached the south-west corner and began to climb a ridge that led up to Point 165. Here they surprised the enemy lookouts and took the summit. A further push captured an enemy pillbox and took more than twenty prisoners. This now put the platoon higher than the castle ruins and able to look down on their defenders. They tried to descend the ridge leading to the battered medieval keep that surmounted Castle Hill, at the same time as the remainder of D Coy attacked the ruins. This two-pronged assault drove the German defenders back into the inner courtyard of the castle where they took refuge in the keep. Bottled up in this isolated sanctuary, the defenders soon lost their nerve when grenades and Bren gun fire tore through every opening in the medieval masonry. Within a short time they had surrendered, and the New Zealanders took possession of this important height. Now 5 Brigade of 4th Indian Division could be called forward to take over Castle Hill and press on to the slopes of Monastery Hill.

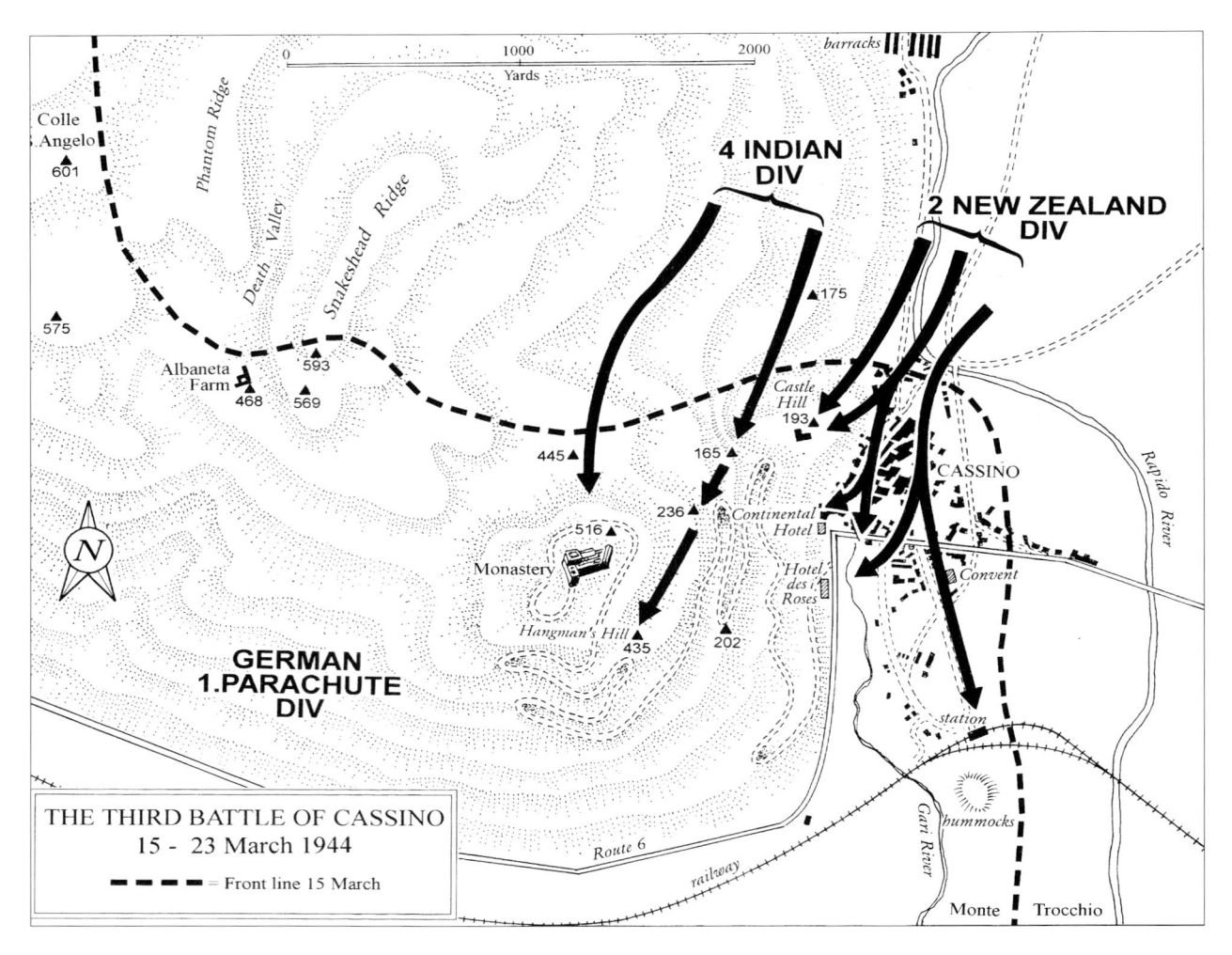

It was now that things began to go astray. One of the great lessons that had been learned from the previous NZ Corps battle was that infantry must quickly follow up the effects of air bombardment before the enemy can reorganise himself. For Freyberg's plan to be effective, he had to get troops into Cassino quickly and move on to the lower slopes of Monastery Hill behind the town as soon as possible. With the capture of Castle Hill by D Coy, 25th Bn at 1645 hours in the afternoon, 5 Indian Brigade should have been called forward at once to pass through and continue the attack. For some reason this did not happen; the leading battalion, 1/4th Essex Regiment, did not start out for the hill to relieve the New Zealanders until 1900 hours. No one had told the brigade that Castle Hill had been captured; no signal, visual or otherwise, had been received, despite the fact that the strongpoint was in perfect view from almost every part of the corps' lines.

To this failure was added the slowness of 6 NZ Brigade to commit more troops into the town. From 1200 hours, and for the next five hours, the 2nd NZ Division's attack on Cassino consisted of the efforts of just three companies of infantry and a few tanks that had managed to reach the outskirts of the town. The brigade's second unit, 26th Bn, released a company to help clear out the resistance around a large turreted house near the base of Castle Hill at 1700 hours. Half an hour later the remainder of the battalion was committed to carry out the movement that it had planned to make at 1400 hours.

It was originally envisaged that the battalion would advance with tank support in a 'left hook' to cross over Route 6 and capture the railway station. Three and a half hours late, it was ordered to make the attack - but without the aid of tanks, in total darkness and in driving rain. When it did finally fight its way into the town it failed to get anywhere near the station, being halted three hours later on the line of Route 6. Here its troops scratched themselves some cover for the night and stayed put. The rain had turned the brick dust and rubble into mud; the enemy strongly resisted every forward move; the engineers could not clear the blocked roads to get tank support forward; and 25th Bn, to the right, was now in serious trouble under enemy fire from a series of bunkers around the Continental Hotel. Up on the foothills to the right, 5 Indian Brigade was trying to push its men forward. Down below on the two parallel roads all was chaos as men, tanks and mules tried to move forward, or backward, in the rain, the mud and the darkness. German artillery fire crashed down onto the congested routes as the enemy locked in on what they knew to be the only possible supply roads.

It took until 2330 hours for the 1/4th Essex to get established on Castle Hill and the lower hairpin bend on the road that led up to the monastery, relieving D Coy of the NZ 25th Battalion. Following closely behind them were the men of 1/6th Rajputana Rifles, who had suffered many casualties and had become disorganised by enemy shellfire during their move towards the town. They were glad to be free from the confines of the deadly roads on the valley floor, but this mood soon changed when they found that the way forward was hazardous in the extreme, with an enemy machine gun persistently firing down the only rocky track that led up to the castle. Out on the hills they gathered together those men that they could find and sent two companies on up to Castle Hill to begin their attack on the upper hairpin bend located by Point 236.

Next onto the hills were 1/9th Gurkha Rifles. This battalion's task was to establish itself on Point 435, 'Hangman's Hill', so named because of a metal pylon which stood out starkly against the skyline and reminded those below of a gallows. The Rajputs and the Gurkhas were supposed to use the positions of the 1/4th Essex located around Castle Hill as a firm base from which to launch their attacks.

The Gurkhas waited for news of the Rajputs' attack before moving forward; but, having heard nothing by 0200 hours, Col Nangle decided to press on with their assault. He was acutely aware of the short time he had left before the light of dawn exposed his men to the enemy from all sides. He ordered his two lead companies to make separate moves along two tracks which led onwards from the castle, both apparently heading in the right direction, while he arranged for the rest of the battalion to establish defensive positions just north of the town. Of the two companies that moved off into the night, the first was immediately halted by accurate enemy fire while the other seemed to be swallowed up by the darkness.

The Rajputs had a disastrous night. One of the companies managed to get close to the upper hairpin bend and put in an attack, but it lacked sufficient punch and was beaten back. The battalion tried again later with a two-company attack which met with the same results. As they closed for the final assault a mortar bomb knocked out the battalion HQ and the whole of the command post, including the CO and the adjutant. The attack failed and the remainder of the battalion withdrew to the castle.

By the end of the first day and night of the third battle for Cassino, the opening moves could not be considered a great success. Apart from the capture of Castle Hill, the NZ Corps had not stamped its authority on the defenders of Cassino. Even this small gain had not been exploited to the extent that it should have been. General Freyberg had only five battalions in action: two in the town and three strung out on the foothills above Cassino. There were legitimate reasons, excuses, why this was so; but to those watching from their lofty positions of higher command the NZ Corps' exploitation of the great bombing raid seemed very sluggish. If the commanders on the ground did not get to grips with the problems that were slowing their troops down, then the enemy would use their guile and expertise to once again destroy any hope of engineering a breakthrough.

The second day

The morning of 16 March saw a resumption of the previous day's local battles. In the town, 25th and 26th NZ Bns attempted to come to terms with their problems. The whole area was in such a ruinous state that the old layout of streets and houses no longer existed. Clawing their way through this three-dimensional puzzle of stone, brick, timber and twisted metal, the Kiwis had to drive the enemy

Staged photographs taken on 8 April after the third battle, reconstructing the attack on the 'Turreted House' area of the town on 15 March. This quarter was situated between Castle Hill and the northern edge of the town, and was hotly contested; German occupation of the buildings enabled the castle to be kept under constant fire. For this media opportunity the actual units which had taken part in the attack returned; although staged, the photos give a realistic idea of the ground that NZ 6 Bde had to fight across on the first day of the battle. (Imperial War Museum)

from one devastated ruin at a time. Often they were clearing the smashed upper floors with grenade and Tommy gun while German paratroopers were still fighting from the cellars, or vice versa. Painfully they edged forward to Route 6, pressing the enemy back as they went. It was a slow process, costly in both time and lives. During the morning 26th Bn pushed on, veering to the left and striving to reach the railway station. Very little progress was made in that direction, but 25th Bn had more success in forcing the paratroopers back towards the right hand edge of the town. It soon became clear that Heidrich's men were making a fighting withdrawal back into the south-western part of Cassino, an area of buildings backing on to the lower slopes of Monastery Hill. Here resistance stiffened considerably around the rubble that marked the site of the Continental Hotel.

This particular ruin had been turned into a fortress. It was slightly elevated above its surroundings, overlooking Route 6 as it turned left and skirted the base of the hill. The

The stark ruins of Cassino castle sit defiantly on Castle Hill surrounded by the rubble that once was the town. The only way up the hill was over a steep rock face - a stiff climb, needing the use of both hands to pull oneself up. The bombed-out ruins of the town can be seen here to offer countless perfect defensive hides for Hauptmann Foltin's paratroopers. (US National Archives)

hotel had been converted into a network of interlocking concrete bunkers and weapons pits. Machine guns bristled from every available opening; riflemen covered every approach. From the collapsed lobby a stationary tank dominated the roadway in front. Linked to the hotel were several other buildings, including a large palazzo called the Baron's Palace and the equally formidable Hotel des Roses. This row of wrecked buildings now held the main line of German resistance in the town. The New Zealanders soon learned that any frontal approach on this series of strongpoints was suicidal, as was the ground to their rear. The lesson was made very clear to the leading troops of 25th Bn when they had the misfortune to come within sight of them during the latter part of the morning.

Up on the hills that morning, the CO of the 1/9th Gurkhas received some good news. The second of his companies, C Coy, which had seemingly disappeared the previous night, was found to be on its objective, Hangman's Hill. The Gurkhas had threaded their way between the Rajputs' battle for the upper hairpin bend on their right and the firefight involving the New Zealanders down in the town on their left, and had pressed on to their objective. A faint radio message from Maj Drinkall now confirmed that C Coy had rushed the summit during the darkness and had ejected the German defenders after a short fight. The CO radioed back to Drinkall asking him hang on through the day, telling him that the rest of the battalion would move up to join him that night.

The second day passed for the NZ Corps in a series of small gains wrenched from the paratroopers against bloody-minded resistance. In the town the two battalions fought their way through a few more broken buildings, while the Indian Division endured German artillery and mortar fire on the hills as it held on tightly to the ground taken the night before. Movement during daylight, even under a protective cloud of smoke, was perilous. New gains and consolidations would have to wait for the cover of darkness.

The night of 16/17 March saw Col Nangle leading the rest of his battalion of the 9th Gurkhas up to Hangman's Hill to relieve his isolated company. At the same time the Rajputs made another attack on the upper hairpin bend - the division's first objective for the previous day. This effort helped to divert enemy attention from the Gurkhas; further distractions down in the town were provided by the New Zealanders as they resumed their attack on the Continental Hotel. Between the two battles, Nangle and his stocky, muscular Nepalese riflemen threaded their way up the steep slopes in single file, each platoon tentatively picking a way forward in the darkness over the loose rocks and through the gorse scrub, following closely on the heels of the one in front under a cold, driving rain. It took almost the whole of the hours of darkness for the battalion to negotiate the narrow goat tracks and get all of its men up to the summit, arriving complete just before dawn. Their arrival was very timely, for just as daylight broke the Germans launched their first counter-attack on Hangman's Hill. Fortunately the area had been made secure and the entrenched Gurkhas easily beat off this assault.

Further down the hill the Rajputana Rifles at last achieved some success when they actually gained possession of the upper hairpin bend. Unfortunately, before they could consolidate this gain the enemy launched a dawn counter-attack and drove them off it. The Rajputs once again retired back down the hill to their start line.

The enemy had also been active that night, and had filtered men back into the northern sector of the town to cut the connection between the New Zealanders in Cassino and the Indians on Castle Hill. This new threat to the rear of the two battalions in the town made their hold on Cassino extremely precarious. It also made supplying the Gurkha outpost on Hangman's Hill with ammunition and rations an even more difficult proposition.

The third day
On 17 March the commander of 6 NZ Brigade, Brig Bonifant, introduced his 24th Bn into the town. This new unit moved to the right and helped 25th Bn attack the Continental Hotel area. By this time some tanks had got through the outskirts of Cassino and were giving welcome support to the hard-pressed infantry. The Shermans had entered the town from the east, across a bridge over the Rapido erected by US Army engineers. However, despite this reinforcement for the Kiwis in the town the paratroopers holed up in the strongpoints in the south-west quarter were still proving very difficult to dislodge. The attack could get no closer than 200 yards from the hotel. It did, however, succeed in creating a diversion for its neighbouring battalion. During the afternoon 26th Bn made another, more powerful push for the station, this time supported by tanks. With dash and determination, the lead companies pressed home their attack and evicted the German defenders from the station buildings, even managing to push on to take the engine sheds and the 'Hummocks' from a startled enemy section. At long last some material gains were beginning to emerge from the battle.

General Freyberg now considered whether it might be time to commit more battalions into Cassino. He still had 5 NZ Brigade or one of the brigades from the British 78th Division at his disposal, waiting to be called into the battle. He declined to use either, deciding that should a breakthrough be achieved these fresh troops would be needed to exploit it. He also thought that there was still plenty of fight left in the three battalions of 6 Brigade, enough at least to finally clear the town. Route 6 had been reached, and once the south-western strongpoints round the Continental Hotel had been eliminated the Liri valley was just around the next bend. Once more, the commander of a battle for Cassino had been lured into believing that just one more determined push would win him the long-denied breakthrough – and thus, into holding back reinforcements which were desperately needed. It was to prove, once again, just wishful thinking.

Earlier that day there was a meeting of the senior German commanders to discuss the situation in Cassino. General Heidrich conceded that the situation in the town was critical, although he was certain that his paratroopers could hold on to the centre; casualties were severe, but morale remained high. He needed more reinforcements to help bolster the line. His corps commander, Von Senger, agreed that the sector required more assistance and offered to send in troops from Panzer-Grenadier-Regiment 115, part of 15.Panzer-Grenadier-Division, the corps reserve. Heidrich insisted that the battle for Cassino itself should continue to be fought by parachute troops alone. He wanted the reinforcements used to hold 'quiet' sectors of the line in order to free more of his paratroopers to fight in the town and on Monastery Hill. He knew that his men would

Troops from 5 Bde, 4th Indian Division move through the northern outskirts of Cassino on 16 March, the second day of the third battle. They are probably from 1/6th Rajputana Rifles, coming out of the line after their abortive attempt on Points 165 and 236 the night before. (Imperial War Museum)

hold on regardless as long as they controlled the whole sector; they trusted no other troops on their flanks, but had complete confidence in themselves.

It was clear to the NZ Corps staff that the most important objective of the whole operation was now the capture of the Continental Hotel area. Until this was free of the enemy the flanks of any troops moving across Monastery Hill to support those already on Hangman's Hill would be exposed to fire from those strongpoints. Indeed, if an attack was actually put in on the monastery, as was being planned, then the defenders of the ruined hotels could fire into the backs of the Indian infantry as they moved up the mountain. They had to be cleared; but any concerted assault by the New Zealanders on the hotel area would need tank support. It was therefore necessary for the engineers to redouble their efforts to clear paths for the tanks to be brought right up to the German strongpoints and blast a way in for the final infantry assault.

During the night of 17/18 March the first priority was to get ammunition and food up to the Gurkhas on Hangman's Hill and to resupply the troops on Castle Hill. A supply train was organised, consisting of porters from the Bengal Sappers & Miners for Castle Hill and a Pioneer company to take supplies further up the slopes to the Gurkhas. Two companies of 4/6th Rajputana Rifles would act as escort. The column moved out after dark and immediately began to take casualties. The stumbling, heavily-loaded porters eventually reached Castle Hill at 2200 hours after much difficulty – and there were still another 1,000 yards of open slope to be covered in the face of many enemy guns. The prospect was too much for the Pioneers, who refused to go any further. The Rajputs, however, were made of sterner stuff; they took on the dual tasks of carrying supplies up to their exposed comrades on Hangman's

A relaxed New Zealander, hand in pocket, escorts a group of Fallschirmjäger captured on 16 March - who appear to be equally relaxed. They show no signs of serious combat exhaustion, and their morale appears to be good. They wear the characteristic long, camouflaged jump-smocks - see colour plate B. They are being escorted northwards out of the town along the road which leads towards the ruined Italian barracks. Parked by the road is a Sherman from NZ 4 Armd Bde, waiting to be called forward to support the infantry of 6 Bde who are trying to clear the town. (Imperial War Museum)

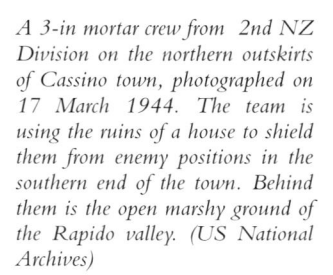

A 3-in mortar crew from 2nd NZ Division on the northern outskirts of Cassino town, photographed on 17 March 1944. The team is using the ruins of a house to shield them from enemy positions in the southern end of the town. Behind them is the open marshy ground of the Rapido valley. (US National Archives)

Hill, and acting as fighting troops as they went. It took from 0200 hours until just before first light at 0625 hours for the whole of the supply column to gain the relative safety of the Gurkha positions, having lost eight men on the way.

Other men were also out on the mountains between the town and the monastery that night. C Company of 24th NZ Bn moved along the lower slopes to gain a knoll overlooking another of the hairpin bends on the road leading up to the monastery. This one was situated at Point 202, just below Hangman's Hill and behind the area of German strongpoints on the west side of Cassino. The company established itself under cover of darkness, and at dawn on the 18th they made an attack on the rear of the Hotel des Roses. They managed to get within a hundred yards of the building before being turned back by withering machine gun fire from the jumble of ruins. With little cover and no hope of gaining their objective, the survivors of the raid withdrew back on to Point 202 and strengthened their exposed position on the hill. With the Gurkhas and Rajputs on Hangman's Hill, there were now two lonely pockets of the NZ Corps isolated on the bare slopes of Monte Cassino.

The fourth day
The rest of 18 March was also frustrating for Gen Freyberg. During the night the sappers had worked hard to provide new routes for the tanks, but it was still very difficult to clear away the rubble close to the western strongpoints and exposed to their fire. Another bridge had been put over the Rapido, and a makeshift route established along the embankment into the railway station enabled some tanks to be brought forward into the town, although unfortunately not in the area where they were most needed.

A counter-attack by men from the Parachute Motorcycle Company - a reconnaissance element of Heidrich's division - was put in against the station area, but was beaten off with relative ease. Vengeance was now taken for the Maoris of 28th Bn; from solidly established positions the New Zealanders loosed a remarkable volume of fire into the ranks of the screaming enemy, whose flanks were also exposed to the dug-in troops on the Hummocks. Only nineteen paratroopers returned from this disastrous attack.

Elsewhere in the town, 25th Bn continued its frustrating attacks towards the Continental Hotel. Three separate efforts were launched, and some small success was gained during the last push when one of the enemy strongpoints was eventually cleared. The tariff paid for this one gain was equal on both sides: in the attack both lost 17 men dead, injured or captured. This single house was the sole achievement for the NZ Corps in a whole day of battle. General Freyberg's great offensive was in danger of grinding down into a stalemate. The survivors of the battalions committed to the fighting were now chronically short of sleep, cold, wet, hungry, their nerves shredded by the constant tension of days and nights of fighting and fearful vigilance.

Disheartened by the efforts of the day, Freyberg planned to add some weight to the resumption of the attack on 19 March. He ordered 28th (Maori) Bn to join 6 NZ Brigade and told Brig Bonifant to use this reinforcement to make an all-out attack on the Continental Hotel area, beginning at 0300 hours. At the same time the Gurkhas on Hangman's Hill, reinforced by 1/4th Essex, were to attack the monastery - the depleted 1st and 4th Bns of 6th Rajputana Rifles were first to relieve the Essex battalion from their garrison duties on Castle Hill. Complimentary to these two attacks, a tank force would cross the mountains to the north-east of Monte Cassino and strike towards the monastery along a newly completed circuitous track ('Cavendish Road') which had been laid across the mountains by the engineers.

The fifth day
The first disappointment came in the early hours when only two companies of the Maori battalion joined the battle, making little impression on the defenders of the Continental Hotel and the Hotel des Roses. Armoured support was minimal as the Shermans found their way still blocked by rubble and water-filled craters.

Next, the complicated plan for the 1/4th Essex Regiment to join the isolated Gurkhas on Hangman's Hill began to go awry just after the battalion had handed over the responsibility of holding Castle Hill to the combined Rajputs. The change-over was delayed by the darkness and enemy mortar fire, and it was not until 0530 hours that the Essex battalion moved out via Points 236 and 202 towards the Gurkhas. There was still time for them to get up on to Hangman's Hill before daylight, but unforeseen events interfered with their progress. General Heidrich chose this very hour to launch a counter-attack on Point 165 and Castle Hill.

German paratroopers charged down the mountainside out of a barrage of well directed mortar and machine gun fire. The attack split the 1/4th Essex, meeting some of the battalion head-on while passing to the rear of others. The paratroopers swept over Point 165 and closed on the castle. A mixed force of Essex and Rajputs tried to contain the enemy and bar their way into the medieval fortress. A furious, close-quarter struggle for possession of the hill developed, and every officer of the Essex battalion on Castle Hill was killed or wounded. German casualties were also heavy, and eventually the attack began to falter. The paratroopers withdrew a short distance, continuing to harass the depleted garrison in the castle for the remainder of the day.

Of those troops of the 1/4th Essex Regiment who escaped the German attack, seventy reached Hangman's Hill later that morning. News of their arrival and of their depleted numbers did not arrive at Divisional HQ until 1015 hours. By that time it was clear that any attack on the monastery would lack the necessary strength to carry the position, and Brig Bateman decided to postpone the attempt until the progress of the armoured thrust to the rear of the monastery became clear. If the tanks could get close to the monastery then the Gurkha and Essex infantry would attack from the east in unison.

'Cavendish Road' had been carved out of the mountains by the Sappers & Miners of 4th Indian Division. For weeks the engineers, plus a field company of New Zealand sappers, had been working on a track which led up from Cairo village on to the northern slopes of the Colle Maiola. Freyberg ordered that this path be widened and reinforced to make it capable of carrying tanks up into the mountains. From Maiola the tanks could pick their way across the ridge towards Albaneta Farm, Point 593, and down on to the monastery. The armoured force under the command of Lt Col Adye began its advance at 0600 hours, and by 0900 had reached Albaneta Farm. The column was a combined group from 7 Indian Infantry Brigade's reconnaissance squadron

(Main) This picture was not staged: taken on 18 March, the fourth day of the battle, it shows infantry of NZ 6 Bde in action in the streets. (Imperial War Museum)

(Inset left) 'Kiwis' from 24th Inf Bn of NZ 6 Bde crouch behind rocks near Castle Hill and look out towards the heights of Points 445 and 450. Monastery Hill is just out of sight to the left. Smoke shells are falling on the upper slopes in an attempt to shield the New Zealanders from enemy machine guns. (Imperial War Museum)

(Inset right) A signaller lies prone, attempting to restore a field telephone land line as tanks move past him on their way into Cassino town on 24 March, the ninth day of the third battle. Land lines were constantly being cut by shellfire and passing vehicles, and were as constantly repaired. Given the limitations of the fairly unreliable No 18 back-pack radio sets carried by infantry company headquarters in 1944, field telephone lines had to be laid whenever the nature of the fighting allowed. (Imperial War Museum)

and 20th NZ Armoured Regiment in M4 Sherman medium tanks, with light M5 Stuarts from the US 760th Tank Battalion. The appearance of 40 tanks, guns blazing, on top of the mountains came as something of a shock to the German defenders. The farm was taken and the notorious enemy stronghold on Point 593 was subdued. Next came the final push towards the monastery. The last 1,000 yards were only possible along a narrow, well-defined path which the paratroopers had expertly covered. Attempts were made to disperse the tanks off the track, but loose rocks and the steep slopes close beside the pathway made this impossible. Heavy small arms fire peppered the tanks and forced the commanders to close down the hatches. This resulted in the tanks grinding forwards virtually blind (visibility from a 'buttoned-up' tank has been described by veterans as like peering through the slit of a letterbox filled with a glass brick). German paratroopers now closed on the tanks and stalked them with bazookas. Without friendly infantry to keep the probing enemy away, the close-quarter attacks by the paratrooper tank-killer teams soon began to take a toll. Several tanks were knocked out and others stalled while trying to get past them on the narrow track. It was clear that without supporting infantry to give close protection and engineers to widen the route the tanks could advance no further. By 1730 hours the armour had been pulled off the mountains and back into the lines in the valley below. With the failure of this armoured attack there was no point in the infantry on Hangman's Hill putting in their assault on the monastery. Once again the offensive had stalled with virtually no new gains made that day.

The appearance of tanks on the mountains overlooking the monastery alerted XIV Panzer Corps to a substantial new threat, however, and Gen von Senger felt some relief when the attack failed. In response to this Allied introduction of armour on the high ground Gen von Vietinghoff of Tenth Army sanctioned the release of fifteen Panther tanks to Von Senger for use in the defence of Cassino. (The paratroopers were being bolstered by the best German armour available, however small the numbers; skilfully used in defence, the Panther could face several times its weight in Shermans with confidence.)

Heidrich's troops in the town were by now in a critical state and needed reinforcement; he planned to bring the 3rd Bn, Parachute Rifle Regiment 4 down off the mountains to form a strategic reserve. He replaced them with the reconnaissance battalion from 15.Panzer-Grenadier-Division. Heidrich now gradually extricated tired men from the town and brought them into reserve, replacing them with fresh troops in rotation. Far from being content with just holding the line, the commander of the 1.Fallschirmjäger-Division was intent on counter-attacking to regain lost ground. He was determined to wrest Castle Hill back from the Indian Division, and to clear the area between that strongpoint and the town.

The sixth to twelfth days

With the complete failure of all three attacks on 19 March, Freyberg was forced to introduce fresh troops into the battle. He now turned to Gen Keightley's British 78th Division, and ordered its 11 Brigade, commanded by Brig Arbuthnot, to take over the southern part of the line from 5 NZ Brigade; the latter was to enter Cassino town to join 6 NZ Brigade. Freyberg also gave the 4th Indian Division a battalion from 78th Division - 6th Royal West Kents - to take over the garrison of Castle Hill. These moves were ordered for the night of 19/20 March so that new dispositions to continue the offensive might be effected immediately. The plan was for the 2nd NZ Division to continue to slog it out with the paratroopers in the town; the 4th Indian Division would hold on to the key points of Castle Hill, Hangman's Hill and Point 202, and was to recapture Points 165 and 236, while preventing the enemy reinforcing his men in the town via the deep ravines that ran down Monastery Hill.

The sixth day of the battle was just a continuation of the previous five. This regrouping and further attempts to grind down the opposition had little real effect. The Indian Division made another attempt on Point 165 with those troops of 6th Royal West Kents who were not holding the castle, and Point 445 was attacked by a single company of 2/7th Gurkhas, but both attempts failed; they were simply too weak to cause the paratroopers much alarm. The New Zealanders continued to batter themselves against the defences of the south-western part of the town, again without success. Attempts to enlarge the lodgement on Point 202 and to provide a line to link up with the Gurkhas on Hangman's Hill also failed.

These seemingly futile attempts continued throughout 21 and 22 March, as infantry and a few tanks tried again and again to make some impression in the town. On the foothills behind Cassino the 4th Indian Division could do little but hold on to the few gains that it had made. As an offensive formation it was a spent force; the troops were tired, overstretched, and in no fit state to continue the struggle. Bravery was simply not enough to sustain the division any longer.

On 23 March, Gen Freyberg conferred with his three divisional commanders. Parkinson of the 2nd NZ Division had to admit that there was no likelihood of the strongpoints he had hoped to gain changing hands in the near future. General Galloway - who had replaced Brig Dimoline in command of the 4th Indian Division - knew that his battalions strung out on the hills behind the town and across the mountains to the north of Monte Cassino had to be relieved; his men had fought themselves to a standstill. General Keightley still had two fresh brigades in his 78th Division, but this was not enough with which to resume the offensive on such an awful battlefield. Bernard Freyberg had to admit that his New Zealand Corps had exhausted its strength. With great regret he called his army commander, Gen Clark, and asked for permission to break off the offensive. Clark immediately agreed, and reported this to Alexander. The commander of Fifteenth Army Group came forward to see things for himself, and concurred with his subordinates. He decided that the offensive battle should cease forthwith and a strong defensive line be created covering those gains that might be successfully held against enemy incursions.

Aerial view of Monte Cassino and the town looking north. On the left, the white hulk of the monastery commands the battlefield, at the end of the zig-zag road whose hairpin bends were specific objectives during the Allied assaults; on the right, Cassino town lies shattered at the foot of the mountain. In the centre of the picture, emerging from behind the shoulder of the hill, the parallel blocks of buildings in the old Italian barracks can be seen on the edge of the Rapido. (US National Archives)

All that remained was to call back the men holding the isolated enclaves won and held at such cost on Point 202 and Hangman's Hill, and to establish the actual lie of the front line. Freyberg dictated that the general disposition of the forward areas would be along a line from the eastern slopes of Point 593, through Point 175, Castle Hill, the north-western part of Cassino town, the railway station, the Hummocks, and down to the junction of the River Rapido with its tributary, the Gari. General Keightley's 78th Division would take over in the mountains, holding the sector Monte Castellone, Point 593, Castle Hill, while the 2nd NZ Division held the town and the Rapido. The 4th Indian Division was to be pulled completely out the line and moved across to 5 Corps on the Adriatic coast for a rest. With this reorganisation the role of New Zealand II Corps came to an end; Freyberg's corps was disbanded on 26 March and the responsibility for the Cassino sector passed to Gen Kirkman's British XIII Corps of Eighth Army, who were now beginning to arrive in the area. The third battle for Cassino was over.

CHAPTER EIGHT

An Infantry Division in the Line: March–April

It was now the turn of the British 78th Division, commanded by Maj Gen Charles Keightley, to learn to live on the exposed mountains of the Cassino massif. Since joining New Zealand II Corps after its arrival from Eighth Army's front the division had done little but hold the line along the Rapido opposite the Liri valley. One of its battalions, 6th Royal West Kents, had briefly joined the 4th Indian Division when it was given the responsibility of holding the castle. Its commander, Lt Col Paul Bryan, recalled the take-over:

'On the morning of 19 March my battalion moved to the village of San Michele while I and the company commanders went forward to the mountainside overlooking Castle Hill. We were to take over this feature from a battalion of the Essex Regiment in 4 Indian Division. As we neared the battalion headquarters I left my company commanders behind in the shelter of a hollow and climbed up the craggy slope to find the Essex CO, who had established himself under the cover of an overhanging rock. After brief greetings he got down to the business of describing the situation and we stepped out on to a ledge to survey the scene. As we stood together looking at his map I heard a sharp crack, he fell at my side – yet another victim for yet another German sniper.'

Colonel Bryan rejoined his company commanders and they started back to rejoin the battalion, picking their way through the craters across the open ground near the Rapido. Throughout the long walk the small group were under constant shellfire. One particularly accurate salvo straddled the officers and two of them were killed by shrapnel. It was a very sobering start for the battalion.

The remainder of the division was held in reserve waiting to exploit the elusive breakthrough which never came. When the 2nd NZ and 4th Indian Divisions were both finally pulled out of the line for rest and reinforcement, the task of holding the whole of the Cassino sector in defence was given over to this relatively fresh division. Its line ran from Cassino station, through part of the town, up to the castle and over the mountains until it reached the heights of Monte Castellone.

The 78th ('Battleaxe') Division was as much at home in the wretched mountains around Cassino as any division would ever be: its men were no strangers to precipitous terrain. It had landed at Algiers in November 1942 as the only formation of British First Army in the assault wave, and had later fought a series of major battles in the final North African campaign. Almost all of its fighting had been conducted in the hills and mountains of Tunisia and Sicily, where it had performed resolutely against German paratroopers and the 'Hermann Göring' Division. It already included accomplished muleteers who had organised four-legged supply trains along almost vertical tracks through barren mountains. It had spent most of the present winter

British troops move warily through Cassino. Even though Castle Hill is now in safe hands, observation is still possible from the German-held high ground beyond. (Imperial War Museum)

high in the Apennines, often completely snowbound and isolated. It had already broken through the Gustav Line to a distance of seven miles on the Adriatic coast when it made an assault crossing of the River Sangro, fighting head-to-head with the 16.Panzer-Division. The 78th was probably the most accomplished 'mountain' division in the British Army.

The first of the locations to be taken over by the 'Battleaxe' Division's 11 Brigade were the forward positions of the 4th Indian Division in the area of Snakeshead Ridge and the infamous Point 593. Next, 36 Brigade moved into Cassino station and the remainder of the town to relieve the last of the New Zealanders; finally, 38 (Irish) Brigade took over Monte Castellone and the adjacent peaks to the northeast of Monastery Hill. These change-overs took several days to complete.

On 24 March, 11 Brigade, commanded by Brig R.Arbuthnott, began its move up into the mountains. The difficult terrain, most of which was under enemy observation, made the relief a long drawn out affair. It took at least two days to get just one battalion out and another in. The final part of the journey for the men of 11 Brigade started in the village of San Michele, situated a few miles back from the Rapido, opposite the ruined Italian barracks. San Michele was the logistics centre and supply dump for all the infantry deployed on the Cassino sector. From this vast storehouse trains of supplies were made up, loaded and sent up the line each night. Most of the stores were carried on mules, though some were taken part way by jeep, depend-

A mechanical smoke generator operated by a US Army Chemical Smoke Company belching out its acrid fumes across the battlefield. These generators operated throughout the hours of daylight both in the Cassino area and the Anzio beachhead, to screen all operations and movements from the enemy. (US National Archives)

ing on their destinations. When the road or track ran out the loads were carried forward by porters. Every bullet, mortar bomb and ration pack had to be manhandled into the line. The whole process of sending up stores and reinforcements had to be organised to a fine degree; the tracks and paths into the hills were so narrow that log-jams of jeeps and mules, foot soldiers and porters had to be avoided at all costs. Virtually the whole of the route forward was vulnerable to German shell and mortar fire.

Under the cover of darkness the first of 11 Brigade's battalions - 5th Bn, Northamptonshire Regiment - began its move up to the front line. Files of infantry trudged silently out of the ruined village; followed by a long train of pack mules carrying their kit, they marched across the Rapido valley, over the river and along the dirt road that led to Cairo village. After a short distance they veered to the left on to a narrow track and began the long climb up through the mountains. After several hours' hard slog they reached a deep, steep-sided valley carved out of the mountain, forming the partial shape of a bowl. It was here that Battalion HQ was located and the mules were off-loaded, for the rear of the sheer-sided valley faced the enemy and offered some protection from his artillery fire. By this time it was too late to go any further forward to effect a relief of the battalion in the line; the rapidly approaching hours of daylight made such moves much too hazardous.

The battalion rested up throughout the next day until darkness had crept over the jagged mountains. It was then relatively safe to moved further forward to exchange responsibilities with the battalion holding the line. Such take-overs were nerve-wracking and dangerous, as men groped their way among loose rocks and steep-sided gullies to find their allotted hole in the ground. The enemy was often just a short distance away and any sudden noise could bring forth a stream of bright German tracer probing the air to find the source of the disturbance. Flares would go up, bathing the rock face with stark light, and mortar fire came crashing down on any chance sighting.

When the 5th Northamptons were established it was the turn of the 2nd Lancashire Fusiliers to come into the line. The fusiliers' CO, Lt Col John Mackenzie, gave an account of his battalion's take-over from 4th Indian Division:

'We left our vehicles and proceeded on foot along a mule track up the steep mountainside to a halfway assembly area in a natural hollow called the 'Bowl'. Here we slept fitfully and remained all the next day. My three vivid impressions were, the intermittent enemy shells exploding on the rim of the 'Bowl', the Gurkha cemetery with tiny black boots at the foot of each grave and, lastly, the herd of mules with their Indian and Italian muleteers waiting for the night to complete their journeys'.

Colonel Mackenzie and his battalion were given one of the most forward sectors of all to hold, the front overlooking the ground running through Points 445 and 450 to Point 593. The Lancashire Fusiliers were as close as anyone could be to the German advance positions, just fifty yards often separating the two sides. It was virtually impossible to make the change-over in silence, since the noise made by hobnailed 'ammunition boots' crunching over loose stones was hard to disguise. Mackenzie called on some help to mask the sound of his relief:

'Artillery harassing fire was laid on to drown sounds of soldiers making their way across the rock-strewn surface. It was an agonising strain for everyone: success and disaster were close bedmates that night. I sighed with relief when the handover was completed. In our hovel the Gurkha commanding officer shook hands and wished us luck. His RSM, unsteady from an overdose of rum, shook hands with me and babbled a short speech. The CO translated: 'He wished you all a safe return to your families or a warm welcome by your ancestors!'

Life and death in the sangars

In the line next to the Lancashire Fusiliers were the 5th Northamptons, holding the long Snakeshead Ridge which culminated in the infamous Point 593. The third of 11 Brigade's battalions, 1st East Surrey Regiment, was kept in reserve, but rotated companies and responsibilities with the 5th Northamptons during their long stay on the mountains in order to save men from too long an exposure on the barren hillsides. The conditions endured by the rifle companies were appalling, as Maj John Horsfall, the second-in-command of an adjacent battalion - 2nd London Irish Rifles - remembered:

'Digging in along the tops of the mountains was virtually impossible as the key parts of the feature were the living rock. Because of this our pickets and observation posts had to lie up behind rough sangars built out of loose boulders. Most of these were pushed together during the night in the vain hope of protecting our men from small arms fire. Certainly they provided for nothing else and new ones had to be built most nights, if only to mislead the enemy as to which ones were occupied. The Germans had no such problems on the opposite crags, having had months to prepare their positions with explosives'.

The same was true for John Mackenzie's fusiliers. It was

impossible to 'dig in' on the mountains because of the solid rock. Blasting shelters was out of the question because of the nearness of the enemy, who overlooked every movement. Shelter was contrived by piling rocks and boulders around any cleft or depression in the ground to give protection from enemy fire. These 'sangars' were deepened, strengthened and made less uncomfortable by their occupants every time darkness provided cover for them to move about in the open. But the sangars had to be kept to a modest size lest the enemy spot them among the jumble of boulders that littered the mountainside. Life inside these holes was grim in the extreme, as Maj Horsfall explains:

'The soldiers had to lie in cramped positions in their two-man sangars, often wet and cold. They took it in turns to sleep by day; at night they had to be alert and occasionally take turns in patrolling. There was a steady dribble of casualties with nightly evacuation of stretcher cases from the Regimental Aid Post. It was agonising to see a fine fighting team wasting away.'

The discomfort felt by the exposed infantry was common to all on the hills above Cassino, as recalled by the adjutant of 5th Northamptons, Capt Ian McKee:

'Holding dominating positions the enemy was able to employ snipers with good effect. The slightest movement on the part of anyone occupying a sangar was greeted by a sniper's bullet. In consequence it was soon learned that during daylight it was essential to remain under cover. Lookouts had to be alert, however, as the enemy was only 90 yards away. Periscopes were used, but were often spotted by snipers and their positions frequently had to be changed. Boxes had to suffice as latrines. Interior economy was carried out after dark when it was possible to get up hot dinners which had been cooked further back. Rats infested the area and could be heard at night tearing at the bodies lying around. As the weather grew warmer so the stench increased and the flies grew more prolific.'

During the day the only sustenance that the troops could call upon was dried 'Compo' rations swilled down with tea brewed on their tiny 'tommy cookers'. Wherever possible, great pains were taken to get at least one hot meal up to the exposed troops during the night. It was important to the men's morale that they be given something warm and filling. John Mackenzie recalls that 'By experiment, it had been found that the most practical and popular hot meals were meat pies and pasties. These were kept warm by wrapping them in paper and straw. They were carried in sandbags with other items for distribution to individual sangars.'

The 78th Division had taken over a mountain line that twisted through a series of peaks and valleys. There was no 'front line' because many of the positions had the enemy overlooking and even behind the British forward troops; indeed, the whole battlefield was dominated by the enemy-held Monte Cairo, from which German observation posts looked down into both forward and backward areas from the rear. The 'front' was a series of strongpoints scattered about the mountainsides in a seemingly haphazard way. But these positions had been won through great sacrifice and their retention was a tactical necessity should the offensive ever get underway again, as Col John Mackenzie found out when he questioned the dispositions of his troops:

'The forward defensive layout was tactically unsound, almost untenable. The Germans held the high points on a rocky ridge overlooking our soldiers in their stone shelters

Lieutenant Colonel John Mackenzie, CO of the 2nd Bn, Lancashire Fusiliers, displaying on his shirt the 'Battleaxe' Division's sign. (Imperial War Museum)

who were more vulnerable to bombs from light mortars and even thrown grenades. Furthermore, we were all overlooked by distant enemy observers around the towering Monastery and by those on Monte Cairo. It was dangerous to move during daylight; toilets had to be performed within the sangars. My request for adjusting the defensive layout was refused; the reason given was that positions won at such great cost during the previous battle must not be relinquished. It seemed illogical to have to defend such vulnerable positions.'

The close proximity of the enemy made everyone very nervous. The troops felt extremely vulnerable knowing that German soldiers, and paratroopers at that, were just a few yards away. The enemy often sent patrols out to try to snatch men from their sangars at night, hoping to gain information in the process. Both sides tried to strengthen their immediate front, laying mines and barbed wire to stifle raids and prohibit patrols, but the nearness of the opposing side meant that a determined attack could be amongst the forward positions before the alarm could be raised. The strain placed on the men clinging to their rat-holes amongst the barren rocks was often intolerable, as the CO of 2nd Lancashire Fusiliers recalls:

'Under these appalling conditions six fusiliers, recent reinforcements to the battalion, attempted to desert. They abandoned three adjacent sangars leaving a defenceless gap that jeopardised the lives of their comrades. This was plain cowardice, but I felt that arresting them and sending them for court-martial was not a practical option. I had already made it clear that only wounded would be permitted to leave the battle area. A battle patrol was detailed to intercept the men and force them to return to their sangars. There was a sharp scuffle in the dark before they were led back to the front line. News of this spread round the battalion and I was told that the outcome was considered just. A similar incident occurred in a neighbouring unit and some soldiers were evacuated with 'battle fatigue' that induced others to emulate them. There was, however, a happy outcome for our six. They worked hard and fought well to redeem themselves in the eyes of their comrades. Some months afterwards the men asked to see me; they said how sorry they were for the incident below the Monastery and expressed their relief that they had not had to face a court-martial. I assured them that I had confidence in them and reminded them of the motto that our founding General Evelegh had recommended to the division in 1942: 'It all depends on me'.

For the Irish Brigade, further back on the slopes of Monte Castellone, there was a wide valley separating the two sides and the presence of the enemy was not so keenly felt; but his counter-fire certainly was, as Maj John Horsfall outlines:

'Life in the line was not particularly dangerous, and the enemy shelling of the forward positions was largely a waste of time providing one sat tight. The real hazards only existed for those who were above ground, or on the move at night, owing to the German habit of intermittently shelling the approaches. It was of course the first essential to cut all movement at night, or at any other time, to a minimum, and this was the main objection to the frequent reliefs of the forward companies. This latter practice was also very frustrating for our soldiers, who I knew by quite long experience to be adaptable in virtually all conditions. In consequence I also knew that once safely in the line they were best kept there until tactical or other necessities determined the matter. By such a policy, an unavoidable one in the past, the troops acquired an intimate knowledge of their sector and, above all, of their opponents, which could never be achieved in any other way.'

To prevent the enemy becoming too daring, the 'Battleaxe' Division stamped its authority on the mountainside. Apart from the question of casualties, there was no 'live and let live' approach to its stay on the Cassino massif. When the Irish Brigade took over from the French on Monte Castellone it had been surprised at the attitude which prevailed in its sector. The French did not appear to go in for patrolling and had allowed the Germans to wander about on the mountains at will. Colonel 'Bala' Bredin and his 6th Royal Inniskilling Fusiliers soon put a stop to that, punishing any Germans who set out into no man's land with a shower of mortar bombs and grenades. His men patrolled the area vigorously, swept German mines from in front of their positions, and harassed the enemy by every possible means at their disposal.

To keep the paratroopers at bay, a programme of interdictory fire was implemented; however, only certain areas could be covered by artillery fire, for several reasons. The proximity of the two sides near the monastery made shelling of the enemy's advance positions equally hazardous to those of the 'Battleaxe' Division. The distance and placements of the guns with relation to the forward areas often meant that the trajectory of incoming shells was too shallow to clear many of the high points, leaving some areas in a 'shadow'.

(Left) German paratroopers dressed in tropical khakis waiting in a courtyard ready to attack; the picture is dated 21 April. The relatively undamaged buildings put the location in an isolated farmhouse or in one of the villages in the lee of Monte Cassino, shielded from Allied artillery fire by the mountains. *(Imperial War Museum)*

(Right) Royal Artillery signallers working from their dug-out in a Forward Observation Post, relaying information back to the field guns in the rear. *(Imperial War Museum)*

Finally, the vulnerability of forward troops resulted in fewer Forward Observation Officers being available to direct artillery fire.

One weapon that was very effective during this type of close-quarter warfare was the mortar. Each of the battalions in the line had its own platoon of 3-inch mortars sited close by. In the case of the 5th Northamptons, theirs were situated in a deep ravine behind the 'Bowl' at the foot of the hills. The mortars were well dug into the steep sides of the valley, and field telephones linked each section's position to the command post, which in turn was linked to the forward companies and Battalion HQ by wire and radio. Captain Ian MacKee describes how these mortars operated:

'It was impracticable to have Forward Observation Posts, so that all firing was done direct from infantry observers. Where possible the forward company commanders gave corrections direct by telephone. The 'defence fire' tasks amounted to twelve in number. All of these tasks covered the area immediately in front of the forward companies and all known German mortar positions. Individual single targets were also engaged. In the area of 100 square yards, 150 bombs, each weighing ten pounds, could be brought down in one minute. Thus for each German bomb sent over ten British bombs went back. Up to ten mortars fired at one time. During the month, 3,639 rounds were fired.'

Apart from the individual infantry battalions' support platoons, heavy mortar and machine gun support was provided by companies from the division's support battalion - 1st Bn, Kensington Regiment. The 4.2-inch tubes manned by the Kensingtons had a greater range and heavier punch than the smaller 3-inch mortars of the battalions. These larger weapons were located still further back near the village of Cairo. With the assistance of aerial photographs and sound-ranging equipment, together with the registration of flash and other indicators seen by the forward troops, all known enemy mortar and machine gun positions and paths used by the enemy in maintaining forward troops were plotted and labelled with code names. Whenever a barrage of mortar bombs was required to be brought down on any particular enemy location, the appropriate code flashed back to the mortar detachments in the rear was sufficient to bring fire down on the enemy without having to provide exact co-ordinates and other data. This placed the full weight of supporting fire at the disposal of every company commander in the line. Every gully or ravine in front of the division was covered by at least one platoon of 4.2-inch mortars. Unfortunately, due to ammunition shortages, a maximum use of only 24 rounds per mortar per day was in force during the division's stay in the mountains.

Incoming fire

The enemy had also had ample time to register his guns and mortars, and was not short of plotted and labelled targets. He was also aware of the routes up to the forward positions, and knew at which times of the day and night traffic was to be found on the roads and tracks leading through the hills. Everyone in the division can recall that their stay in the mountains was punctuated throughout 24 hours of the day by intermittent shell and mortar fire. Sometimes just a single random missile would crash into a company position,

A Vickers .303in medium machine gun in action near Cassino. This team, from an MG platoon of NZ 22nd Motorised Inf Bn, were part of a 'hit and run' raid sent out on 4 March to isolate enemy machine guns overlooking Route 6. In the foreground, a range-finder gives details of the target to the 'number one' who is firing his weapon in an elevated position, with an effective range of 4,000 yards. Since the Great War the Vickers had been famous for its ability to lay down accurate indirect fire, creating lethal 'beaten zones' at long range. (Imperial War Museum)

(Right) *On the left, a leutnant from 5.Gebirgs-Division - note the* Edelweiss *sleeve badge, common to all mountain troops - in discussion with two Fallschirmjäger. (Bundesarchiv)*

seeking a target of opportunity; sometimes a full blown barrage would be brought down on a track to interfere with the movement of infantry making a relief. Often the enemy would have a go at the known positions of support weapons, hoping to catch them fully manned and kill their crews. Captain McKee recalls one such barrage against the 5th Northamptons:

'On 17 April the enemy brought down a very heavy stonk, one shell landed on an ammunition dump. This went up, rapidly engulfing other dumps nearby. The whole hillside caught on fire as red hot metal landed in the gorse. The damage amounted to one mortar blown to pieces and 600 bombs blown up. The lost mortar was replaced the next day, but the resupply of wasted bombs was another matter and it took many nights of mule trains to restock'.

The continual sniping and enemy artillery and mortar fire inevitably caused casualties among the troops on the mountain. Often it was not the forward troops who suffered most, for anyone on the hillsides was susceptible to enemy fire. John Horsfall recalls that whenever the positions of the 2nd London Irish Rifles were being blasted, many low trajectory shells whistled over their heads and landed amongst the staff of Brigade HQ in the rear around Cairo village. Death came completely at random, with no place being completely safe for long.

The problems of dealing with casualties were magnified by the terrain. There was little enough room to shelter individuals on the rocky slopes, let alone to provide beds and medical services. Nevertheless, through often Herculean efforts and great bravery the wounded and maimed were cared for by their comrades. Ian McKee explains how this was carried out by the Northamptons:

'In B Company area there was a farm building. Although no roof was left, there was a certain amount of cover on the ground floor. This was utilised as a Regimental Aid Post and cookhouse for the forward companies. Here was cooked the food for the men manning the sangars. The enemy often fired close to the door of this building making entry very difficult. Captain Richardson, the Medical Officer, thought that a live doctor was better than a dead one, and stayed indoors for a fortnight. Due to his taste for tea, the sooty fires made him look black when he finally emerged. At no time was the Regimental Aid Post further back from the forward troops.

'The medical arrangements were noteworthy. Stretcher bearers were constantly on the scene whenever a casualty occurred. Protected by the Red Cross Flag, the wounded were placed on a stretcher and taken to the Regimental Aid Post (RAP). The enemy respected the Red Cross and in turn his was respected. Numerous are the stories of comradeship between stretcher bearing parties of both sides. From the RAP, the stretcher was carried down the mountains by teams of men stationed along the track at 200 yard intervals to the Advance Dressing Station. Evacuation continued through Main Dressing Station, Casualty Clearing Station to General Hospital. The journey from the front line to the General Hospital could be as much as 100 miles and was often completed within 24 hours.'

The valley and the castle

Down on the valley floor, in and around the town and its castle, 36 Brigade was holding the line. The castle was still garrisoned by 6th Royal West Kents, while the 5th Buffs (the traditional title of the Royal East Kent Regt) were covering the station, and 8th Argyll & Sutherland Highlanders the remainder of the captured part of the town. Just as up in the mountains, Heidrich's paratroopers were very close by, probing and niggling to add to the discomfort and danger of these static positions. To give some relief from the dominance of enemy observation a continual smokescreen was maintained over the town throughout the day.

The 5th Buffs held a line of about 1,000 yards from the railway station to the edge of the town. Major Cox occupied the railway station area with B Company, his HQ being located in one of the inspection pits in the engine sheds. Bren light machine guns were sited in the cabs of derelict locomotives. He recalls of his time at the station: 'We were so close to the enemy positions that they could hear the slightest movement we made on the rubble. Any noise and we were immediately mortared. So near were they that you could hear the "pop" of the mortars as they fired.' During their stay in this part of the line the Buffs lost sixty casualties to mortar fire alone.

Holding the area of the castle was Lt Col Paul Bryan with his 6th Royal West Kents. The only access to the castle from the friendly side was via a precipitous ridge of rock, each man needing to use both hands to haul himself up the steep face. To the north was a narrow gorge with a short spur behind it on which Bryan located his battalion HQ. He held the position with one company in the castle and two companies on the spur. He was well aware of the importance and vulnerability of his location:

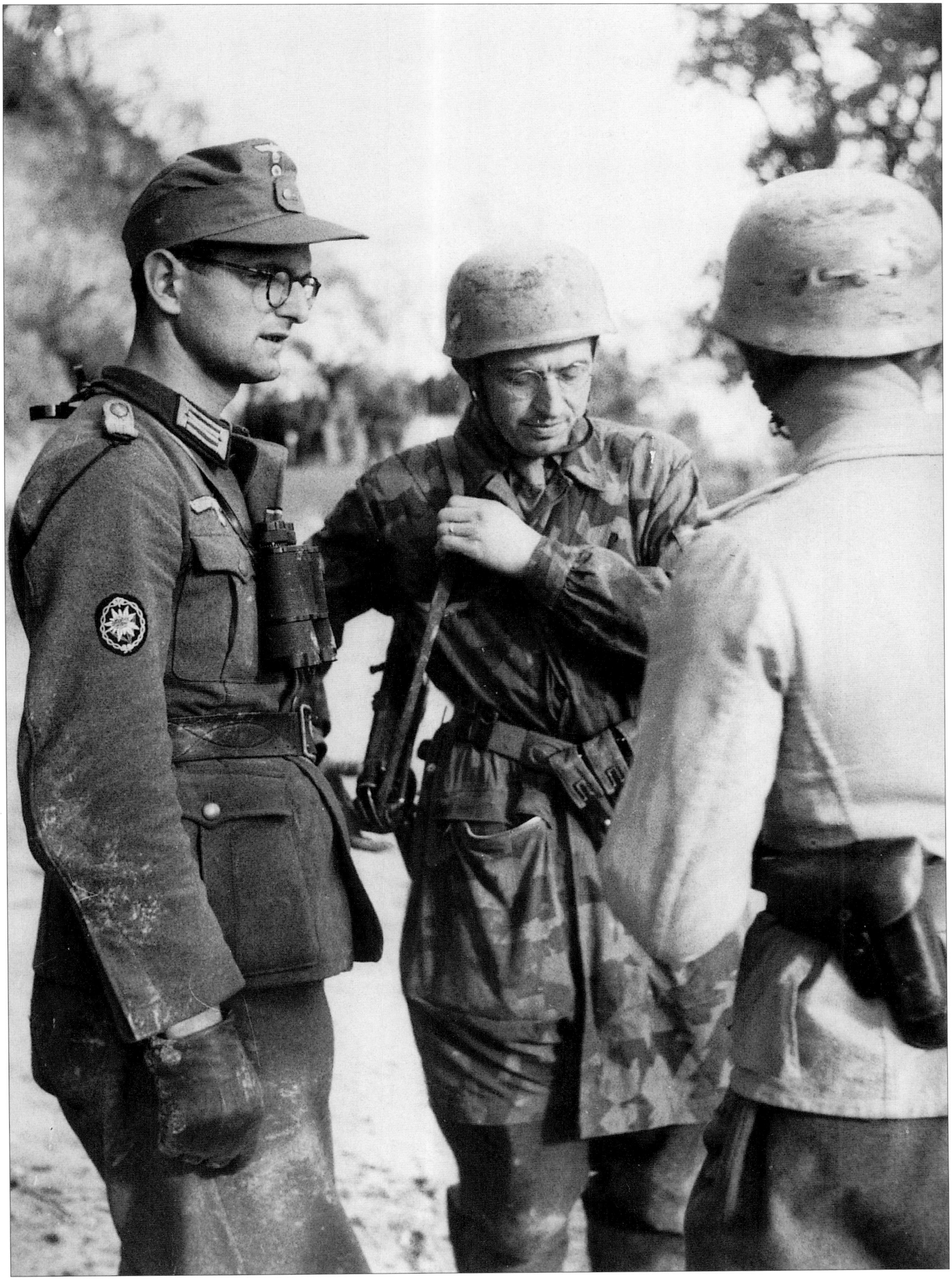

(Left) An American GI surveys the shattered Cassino area after the battle. The picture gives a remarkable view of the dominating high ground that made Cassino such a difficult town to attack. In the foreground is Castle Hill; immediately behind is Monte Cassino, 'Monastery Hill', with the ruined monastery overlooking everything; to the left of this is Hangman's Hill, and to the right the heights of Points 445 and 450. (US National Archives)

(Right) Major General Keightley's 78th Division headquarters outside Cassino during a visit by Lt Gen Anders to arrange the hand-over of the sector to his Polish II Corps. From left to right: Lt Col Hodgson, GSO1 78th Division; Brig Thrith; Maj Gen Keightley; Lt Gen Anders, and a Polish interpreter. (Imperial War Museum)

'It was clear to me that as the capture of the castle was one of the few Allied successes, there was bound to be a counter-attack. I therefore had the two most obvious approaches carefully registered by the guns of the corps. On the code word "Ginger Rogers" 600 guns would shower their shells on one area, on the code word "Fred Astaire", on another. Sergeant Major Dixon from our side of the valley had his machine gun platoon with their guns on fixed lines ready to back up the artillery'.

One morning the inevitable and expected enemy counter-attack came in against the castle. Colonel Bryan was quick to react:

'I gave the code word – I can't remember which. All hell broke loose. It was too much even for the famous parachutists and forty of them came up to the castle with their hands above their heads. We were in need of that sort of a tonic.'

The Royal West Kents manned this sector for a week until relieved by the Argylls; their losses during those seven days were eleven officers and 120 men. Major Denis Forman was one of the eleven:

'I was leading a counter-attack out of the castle against a German force only about sixty yards away when I saw a smoke canister from a supporting New Zealand battery land in a shellhole. "Lightning never strikes twice in the same place", I yelled to my batman Rutherford; "let's get in there." But we were no sooner in than lightning did strike again, in the shape of a second smoke canister which landed on, and shattered, my lower left leg. By impressing some stretcher bearer members of the neighbouring Indian Division, Rutherford managed that night to lower me, still woozy from a heavy intake of morphine, down the precipitous cliff to the town below. But every time a shell landed close by the bearers dispersed and poor Rutherford had to recruit a fresh squad. Later I was told that my leg was amputated in an Indian field hospital at the base of the rock. I have fleeting memories of a seemingly endless nightmare trip in a field ambulance with five other wounded men, all of us screaming for water, of which there was none.'

Colonel Bryan was able to visit his company commander a few days later in a hospital near Caserta: 'His description of his journey by stretcher, jeep and ambulance over bumpy mountain tracks and roads to hospital made one shudder. Literally thousands of our casualties went through the same torture.' Forman regarded himself as being lucky, for although he had lost a leg he knew that very few officers survived intact in the front line through the North African campaign and Italy. He was also lucky in another way: 'As septicaemia spread up my limb, I had access to plasma and penicillin. Penicillin was new. There was only enough for a few dozen cases, and as an officer of field rank, I was one of those that got it. Other ranks died'.

The responsibility for holding the castle area was rotated so that each battalion of 36 Brigade held the sector for a few days at a time. Two companies remained on the hillside, one was responsible for the castle itself and one was held in reserve. The exposed, but extremely important position in the castle was held by two platoons at any one time. During the day the troops lay low among the ruins, but vigilantly watching for any enemy attack. They gathered in cellars watching the single entrance lest the German paratroopers should burst through it. Those who were able to tried to sleep, others just stared out through a few broken gaps in the wall at the barren hillside hiding the enemy. Each night one of the two platoons was relieved and the garrison was resupplied, so that no platoon spent more than forty-eight hours in the medieval stronghold.

The castle was under almost constant fire; the Germans peppered it with mortar and small arms throughout the day. Sometimes heavier calibre weapons straddled the area with their fire. On one occasion a direct hit killed an officer and eight men from the Argylls; another wiped out three of the four men from an observation party of 138 Field Regiment, Royal Artillery. Every day individuals were picked off by snipers if they happened to show some small part of themselves as they moved within the castle courtyard. Just as in the Anzio beachhead, the day-to-day ordeal of holding these positions would have been entirely familiar to soldiers of 1915-18.

For six weeks the 'Battleaxe' Division continued to hold the line. At the end of April it began to be pulled out of the sector for rest and retraining in order to be ready for its part in the coming spring offensive. British Eighth Army was now gathering its strength on the Cassino front; Gen Kirkman had disengaged his XIII Corps from the Adriatic side of the country and brought it across the mountains to come into the line alongside US Fifth Army, together with Gen Burns' Canadian I Corps. Also on the move was Polish II Corps; and it was this formation which relieved the 78th Division as Gen Anders sent his two Polish infantry divisions to take over the high points alongside Monastery Hill and to familiarise themselves with the topography. The Americans and Indians had tried, and failed; soon it would be the Poles' mission to attempt to seize the monastery.

One by one, the battalions of the 78th Division out on the hills were relieved and brought down into the valley for onward travel to a rest camp. The Irish Brigade was one of the first to exchange its exposed positions with the Poles. It was a complex operation, taking three nights before the brigade had pulled out and the Polish 6th Lwowska Brigade was in place. The relief could only take place during the hours of darkness, which were barely sufficient to allow one battalion of Poles time to get across the Rapido valley and into their mountain positions, and an Irish battalion to get out and back before daylight. Major Horsfall recalls the handing over of the 2nd London Irish Rifles' positions to the Poles:

'Some of their officers could talk French, and a few English, but there was no way of communicating with their NCOs and their soldiers. However, their motives were as clear as they were simple. They only wished to kill Germans, and they did not bother at all about the usual refinements when taking over our posts. They just walked in with their weapons and that was that. They were quite imperturbable.'

For 11 Brigade the task was even more complex and dangerous; it was located right under the monastery, its positions the most exposed of all. Whereas its take-over of the sector had been done with stealth, the Poles entered the battle zone with bravado and disdain. They had come to kill Germans, not to cower in holes in the ground. Their main idea was to find out where the nearest Germans were and go after them. Colonel John Mackenzie was apprehensive of this belligerent attitude, lest the Poles bring down German retribution during their take-over of the positions held by his 2nd Lancashire Fusiliers:

'That night was an agony of suspense. Somehow the Germans sensed that something was up and started harassing fire across our front; our own artillery was also firing. The relief took longer than expected and it left little time for the battalion to descend and cross the Rapido valley before daylight. It was a nightmare march with occasional shelling en route; we had to dive for cover several times. As dawn approached we were forced to hurry; men took turns in carrying the heavier loads. Then came the worst part: the "Mad Mile" across the valley. Thank God the smoke canisters had thickened the mist to hide us from Monte Cassino and Monte Cairo. Eventually we reached San Michele where transport was waiting for us. The Divisional Commander watched the utterly exhausted fusiliers, some aiding sick and limping men. Their dirty faces showed a firm jaw line, grim determination and a touch of pride. Once in the vehicles they were soon fast asleep. The general was moved and quietly said: "They are great chaps, and I am proud of them."'

CHAPTER NINE

The Fourth Battle – Operation 'Diadem': 11–18 May

With the arrival of British Eighth Army in front of Cassino, US Fifth Army finally laid down its sole responsibility for the task of breaking through into the Liri valley. The dispositions of the major formations facing the Gustav Line were now radically changed. British X Corps left the Garigliano front and came across to the right of the line, taking over the mountains to the north of Cassino in the sector previously held by the French. McCreery's corps was due for a rest, and took little part in the coming battle. General Juin, in turn, moved his CEF over to the left to replace X Corps, thus bringing together both of Clark's corps. General Oliver Leese's Eighth Army took over the middle sector and continued with the plans for the fourth and final battle for Cassino.

The German defences facing the British were stronger than ever; for all the expenditure of blood, hope and time the battles of January to March had done little to weaken their grip on the Cassino sector. Work had continued fortifying the Liri valley and the land behind the Rapido. Further back, nine miles behind the Gustav Line, construction continued on a second line of defences which were carefully sited to shut off the valley if Cassino should fall. This new system was called the 'Hitler Line' (but for obvious propaganda reasons was later renamed the 'Senger Line' when it seemed likely that it would be overrun). Should the Gustav Line break, or the northern hills and the monastery be taken by the Allies, then XIV Panzer Corps would fall back into the Hitler Line.

At its strongest point this defensive system was designed to be an even tougher proposition than the Gustav Line. Its construction had been undertaken over a long period; out of sight of Allied observation and interference, thousands of conscripted workers had laboured over the interlocking bunkers and concrete gun emplacements. An anti-tank ditch was created by strengthening the banks of the small River Aquino in front of the line and sowing its approaches with mines. At the centre of the defences were great underground bunkers that could hold large numbers of defending troops safe from bombs and shellfire. Concrete machine gun posts half buried in the ground and crowned with steel cupolas were sited to sweep all approaches. Interlocking with these anti-personnel weapons were turrets taken from Panther tanks, mounted on buried concrete emplacements; their long 75mm gun was capable of penetrating the armour of all Allied tanks at 1,000 yards, while their own frontal plate was invulnerable at 150 yards. The line was designed to be as near impregnable as possible.

Meanwhile, up on the heights around the monastery,

Exhausted engineers from 8th Indian Division rest after a hard night's work mine-clearing and bridge-building through the Gustav Line on day two of Operation 'Diadem'. The Indian division had crossed the Rapido south of San Angelo and was the first formation of British XIII Corps to establish a secure bridgehead over the river. (Imperial War Museum)

108

(Below) A well-camouflaged Pzkw V Panther tank in the Liri valley in May. The long-barrelled 75mm gun was more than a match for any Allied tank. Apart from the Panther turrets mounted on concrete blockhouses as static guns, many tanks were used in a static role on the Hitler Line, dug-in 'hull down' so that only the exposed turrets presented a small target to the attacking Allies. Note the cross-hatched Zimmerit plaster coating on the turret, to prevent enemy infantry attaching magnetic explosive charges; in the last year of the war this was applied to German tanks in the factories. (Bundesarchiv)

units. On the right, Gen Anders' Polish II Corps would take the monastery heights with its two divisions, then break through to the village of Piedimonte on the flank of the Hitler Line. Depending on the success of the breakthrough, Gen Burns' Canadian I Corps would either pass its two divisions - one of which was armoured - through XIII Corps, or would swing around the left to drive at the main Hitler Line. Supporting Burns' attack would be another three independent armoured brigades. General Leese had more than 2,000 tanks available to make and exploit the attack, and behind him were the massed ranks of division, corps and army artillery, totalling 1,060 pieces. Even after the disappointments of the winter, all serious opinion agreed that this time the Allies had assembled enough men, steel and high explosive to bludgeon their way through; this battle just had to be a success. And if it was a success, and Cassino fell, then the race for Rome would end in victory, for the Germans had staked everything at Cassino.

The British attack would be undertaken in conjunction with US Fifth Army. General Clark was putting six-plus divisions into the offensive - four, with an attached force of 12,000 Moroccan *goumiers* irregulars, from Juin's French Expeditionary Corps, and two from Keyes' US II Corps. The American/French attack across the Garigliano would be launched from the bridgehead won by British X Corps in the first battle back in January. The US II Corps would attack on the extreme left of the line along the narrow

(Below) Three days into Operation 'Diadem' a small stream is bridged just outside San Angelo by a Scissors tank. The Canadian host tank which carried the bridge can be seen in the foreground, surrounded by empty shell packing tubes discarded by the crew of the Sherman behind it. Further back on the left, in the small stream over which the bridge passes, a Stuart light tank has come to grief while trying to negotiate the obstacle. (Imperial War Museum)

Heidrich's paratroopers still controlled the northern hills. The interlocking fire missions of pre-registered artillery, mortars and machine guns criss-crossed every open space, sited to counter all possible Allied routes forward. German observation across the approaches to Cassino town, the Rapido and the mouth of the Liri valley was still all-encompassing, bringing shells down on any unfortunate caught in the open without the protective covering of smoke. The lull in the offensive since the failed operations by New Zealand II Corps in March had been exploited energetically, and the defences of the Cassino feature were now many times stronger than when Gen Walker's Texans had suffered their first bloody defeat trying to cross the Rapido four months previously.

General Alexander's plan for his Fifteenth Army Group's spring offensive, Operation 'Diadem' - designed by his chief-of-staff, Gen John Harding - depended not upon any dazzling manoeuvre or cunning misdirection, but upon brute force. Any renewed attempt to break into the Liri valley could only be successful if undertaken by an overwhelmingly large force with a punch too heavy for the German defenders to absorb. The final design executed by Gen Leese involved two corps in the centre and one on the flank. General Kirkman's British XIII Corps would cross the Rapido with one armoured and three infantry divisions, supported by tanks from additional British and Canadian

coastal plain, with two new divisions fresh from the United States, the 85th and 88th (Keyes' old 34th and 36th Divisions had been transferred to Anzio). On the right of the US corps Juin's French and North Africans would take to the mountains with the aim of swinging right into the upper Liri valley. General Juin's corps had been reinforced by the arrival of the 4th Moroccan Mountain Division, and the 1st Motorised Infantry Division – this latter was basically the retitled 1st Free French Division, the hard core of Gaullist volunteers who had been fighting alongside British Eighth Army for two years.

General Leese was able to plan Eighth Army's part in the breakthrough battle from a position of strength. He had six infantry and two armoured divisions, together with three independent armoured brigades. A third armoured formation, South African 6th Armoured Division, was also in reserve to be used as required. The plan was for Kirkman's British XIII Corps to attack across the Rapido either side of San Angelo over the same ground that the 'Texas' Division had tried, but this time with two divisions. Two more divisions would follow, ready to move into the bridgehead immediately it was possible to do so. The corps would then split: two divisions would veer to the north to link up with the flanking attack being put in on the right by Polish II Corps, while the other two pressed on to the Hitler Line through the centre of the valley. The Polish Corps would be attacking the monastery and northern heights across the same route tried successively by the US 34th and Indian 4th Divisions during previous battles; but Gen Anders would have at his disposal two divisions committed simultaneously – divisions whose character could fairly be described as bloodthirsty.

The German appreciation

On the German side, the six weeks of relative inactivity around Cassino had allowed Kesselring to give many of his units some respite. The mobile divisions were pulled back from the front for rest and refit, leaving the infantry to hold the line. As the stalemate continued Kesselring became convinced that the Allies would not attempt another major attack until the summer weather hardened the ground and made the going more suitable for tanks. He allowed his commanders to release up to a third of the defenders at a time for rest, so sure was he that the front had stabilised. His intelligence staff had detected the movement of divisions from Eighth Army's Adriatic front over to the west, and it was obvious that they would be brought into the attack when the time came. But this also reassured him that he too could weaken his Adriatic front without fear of being attacked there.

To reinforce the western sector he moved Gen Feurstein's LI Mountain Corps HQ over the Apennines to face the Eighth Army, and gave it the responsibility of holding the northern mountain line including Cassino and the monastery. This corps now took command of the three divisions already in the line there: Ringel's Bavarian 5.Gebirgs-Division, Bayer's Austrian 44.Infanterie-Division, and Heidrich's paratroop 1.Fallschirmjäger-Division.

This left Gen von Senger und Etterlin with a shortened

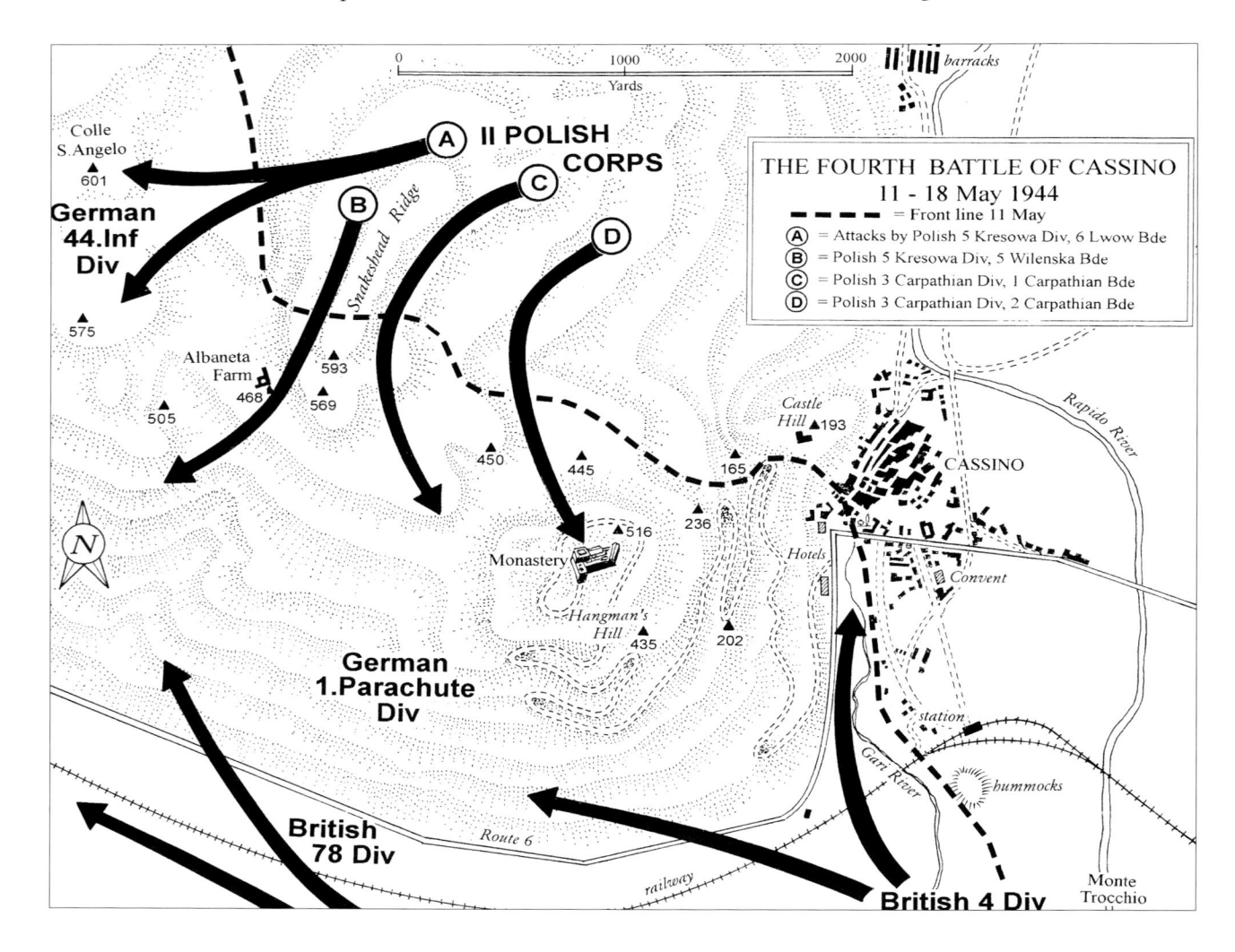

Polish infantry begin the grim task of bringing their dead off the mountains around Cassino. The bodies are collected beside a small farmhouse alongside the track leading up to Snakeshead Ridge. All along the pathway are telephone lines running up to the forward positions. (Imperial War Museum)

sector of the line to cover, and finally relieved the commander of XIV Panzer Corps of responsibility for Cassino - much to his annoyance. His 15.Panzer-Grenadier-Division, which had held the valley floor below Cassino in the San Angelo sector for three long months, was finally relieved and pulled back into reserve. It was replaced by a force called the 'Bode Blocking Group', made up from two battalions of 305.Infanterie-Division, two from 15.Panzer-Grenadier-Division, and the machine gun battalion of 1.Fallschirmjäger-Division. The rest of Von Senger's section of the Gustav Line was held by Gen Raapke's 71.Infanterie-Division, which had given a good account of itself in the earlier fighting north of Cassino, and Gen Steinmetz's 94.Infanterie-Division, which had been holding the Garigliano area for some time.

If the Allies were bold enough to again attack the strongest point of the front, Kesselring believed that Von Vietinghoff and his Tenth Army were strong enough to hold them on the formidable defensive systems of the Gustav and Hitler Lines. Moreover, when the Allies finally did move against him in the south, Kesselring believed that it would be no more than a holding attack to divert attention from their main effort, which would come on the Anzio front. He was sure that Alexander would not repeat his earlier failures for a fourth time by making another attack against the main German positions around Cassino. He believed that because the Allies had held on to the Anzio beachhead at great cost, they were certain to make the best use of such a valuable threat to the rear of Tenth Army.

Kesselring was content to leave Gen von Mackensen to face this threat, believing that the dispositions and strength of his Fourteenth Army were solid enough to contain and stifle any Allied expansion from the lodgement. Fourteenth Army had five divisions holding the perimeter: 4.Fallschirmjäger, 3.Panzer-Grenadier, 65., 362. and 715.Infanterie-Divisions. In addition, Kesselring's mobile reserves were available for deployment either at Anzio or Cassino as needed. This powerful force consisted of 29. and 90.Panzer-Grenadier, 26.Panzer and 92.Infanterie-Divisions.

Crucially, the German C-in-C Italy was also of the opinion that a new Allied amphibious landing would be made north of Rome. He feared this most of all, and this fear was reinforced by an elaborate Allied deception plan. Moves were made to simulate the arrival of the Canadian Corps in the Naples area, where it rehearsed amphibious techniques alongside the US 34th Division. The mass of shipping in the harbour and the activities around the dockyard led German intelligence to assume that landings in the Civitavecchia region were imminent. Back in January, when the Anzio landings took place, Kesselring had already committed his mobile reserve against British X Corps on the Garigliano and was unprepared to counter the amphibious assault; he was not about to make the same mistake again. When the Allies next attacked he would wait to see just where the main blow fell before he released his reserves. He did not, however, expect the attack to come for a while yet. The concealment of British Eighth Army well back from the front, and the quiet nature of the rear areas, led German intelligence to assume that the coming offensive would not start until June. When it was unleashed late on the night of 11 May it caught the entire enemy camp by surprise, with three of their leading commanders - Von Senger, Von Vietinghoff, and Baade of 90.Panzer-Grenadiers - absent on leave.

Tenth Army targeted for destruction

Alexander's new plan for operations in Italy involved a departure from the strategy which had been employed in the theatre up until then. The struggle forward from Salerno and along the Adriatic coast had been measured in terms of gaining ground and occupying territory. After each river was crossed, there had been another barring the way; the taking of every range of mountains had revealed another overlooking them. While the object of Operation 'Diadem' was to get to Rome and beyond, it also had a more important purpose: Alexander wanted to kill Germans. This coming battle was planned in progressive phases so as to draw the enemy in and annihilate him. Alexander wanted to destroy the German Tenth and Fourteenth Armies rather than just pushing them back to the next stop line.

The first phase was to break through and destroy the Gustav Line: and this was the most difficult task of all. It had to succeed swiftly enough to achieve a penetration before Kesselring realised that it was the main Allied effort and that the amphibious threat was a ruse. It was important that he was prevented from committing his mobile reserves before the Gustav Line was broken. The second phase would be the destruction of the Hitler Line. By this time Kesselring would have appreciated the situation and would be moving his reserves against the attack. As these mobile forces came south, the perimeter around Anzio would be vulnerable. At a moment of his choosing, Alexander would then give the order to Truscott for US VI Corps to break out of the Anzio lodgement and cut the rear lines of German Tenth Army at Valmontone on Route 6. With US Fifth and British Eighth Armies pushing up Routes 6 and 7 from the south, and US VI Corps attacking inland from Anzio, there was every chance that the bulk of Tenth Army would be caught in a trap.

★ ★ ★

Operation 'Diadem' began with an immense artillery barrage at 2300 hours on 11 May 1944. All along the front, from Cassino to the sea, 1,600 Allied guns laid down the heaviest artillery preparation of the war in Italy. Behind this deluge of shellfire, the Americans were the first to move off; US II Corps attacked out of the Garigliano bridgehead, with the 88th Division trying for Santa Maria Infanta and the 85th making diversionary thrusts on its left. The German 94.Division resisted this American advance with great determination and withstood the pressure better than Gen von Senger had expected.

To the right of US II Corps, Juin's French Expeditionary Corps began its offensive with the 2nd Moroccan Division attacking towards Monte Maio, the great height that overlooked the Liri valley from the south. Making a supporting attack on its left, the 4th Moroccan Mountain Division swept up into the trackless mountains. Behind them, the 3rd Algerian Division waited to come forward and outflank Castelforte, while the 1st Motorised Infantry Division acted as reserve. Confronting the French corps and slowing the impetus of its attack was the German 71.Division, which also fought with remarkable resilience.

In the centre, at the mouth of the Liri valley, British XIII Corps began its assault across the Rapido. On the left, next to the French, the 8th Indian Division crossed the river below San Angelo; to the north, the British 4th Division pitched itself against the river above that village. Both of these divisions had to traverse the deadly ground over which the US 36th Division had struggled in January. The enemy had lost none of his resolve since then, and resistance was ferocious. The Indian Division secured a precarious bridgehead over the river during the night of 11/12 May and by first light had two tank bridges in place. During the morning of the 12th the Indians absorbed frequent counter-attacks by the Bode Group, and gradually their foothold south of the village.

To the north the British 4th Division fared less well. Attacking the strongest section of the river line, close to and beneath Monte Cassino, it suffered from enemy interference from the moment its leading battalions moved off. During the day determined efforts enabled it to get two small bridgeheads over the Rapido, but it was unable to begin any bridging operations due to its lethal exposure to the enemy above. Each time the engineers began their work they were

The Fourth Battle - Operation 'Diadem': 11-18 May

(Left) A smokescreen laid by generators smothers the Liri valley on 17 May during Operation 'Diadem'. By this time, a week into the fourth battle, British Eighth Army had broken into the valley and were approaching the second system of German fortifications - the Hitler (or Senger) Line. (US National Archives)

[Right] Troops of 6th Bn, Royal Inniskilling Fusiliers advance into the Liri valley, passing through the positions of 2nd Bn, London Irish Rifles. Both battalions served with 38 (Irish) Bde, part of British 78th Division. (Imperial War Museum)

beaten off by accurate enemy shellfire.

In the mountains to the right of British XIII Corps, the Poles began their attempt to take Monte Cassino and drive down behind it on to Route 6. In the early hours of 12 May, Gen Anders unleashed his Polish II Corps against the German defenders in the hills around the monastery, attacking not the monastery itself but the high ground close to it. Inevitably taking the same routes as had the US 34th and 4th Indian Divisions before them, the Poles intended to achieve in strength what those divisions had failed to gain through using 'penny packets'. What had stopped previous attempts was the enemy's ability to bring fire down from mutually supporting heights on any of its strongpoints under attack; whenever one feature was being pressed, other hill positions, including the monastery, could sweep its approaches with covering fire. General Anders planned to overcome this difficulty by attacking all of these strongpoints simultaneously, hoping that each would be too busy defending itself to help any of the others.

Unlike the Indian Division in its abortive attack on the monastery, the Polish Corps had had time to bring up considerable quantities of stores, create ammunition dumps and establish itself in great strength prior to the assault, even though each of the two Polish divisions consisted of only two brigades rather than the usual three. The corps had also had sufficient time in the fine early summer weather to improve supply routes and to extend the tracks crossing the lower hills so that they would be able to take tanks. Among Gen Anders' Polish soldiers confidence and determination were high.

At 0100 hours both divisions attacked across the slopes and ridges of the barren mountainside into the face of the usual murderous machine gun fire. Using Snakeshead Ridge as its starting point, the 3rd Carpathian Division attacked along the stony backbone of the feature towards the infamous Point 593. On its right the 5th Kresowa Division assaulted Phantom Ridge, Colle San Angelo and Point 575. Casualties were severe, just as they had been in all previous attempts; the German counter-fire had lost none of its venom during the intervening weeks. The strength of the Polish onslaught was such that as the infantry fell, others were there to take their places. Throughout the night the Poles pushed home their attacks with great energy and bravery. The Carpathian Rifles gained a foothold on Point 593 and the Kresowa Division established itself on Phantom Ridge. By dawn, after a night of bitter fighting, the gains had been small but the preliminary objectives had been taken. But, as before in the tragic history of all the Cassino battles, it was not enough just to take ground by night; it had to be held by day.

As daylight swept across the high mountains on the morning of the 12th the enemy observation posts plotted the exposed Polish infantrymen. One by one, they were picked off by German snipers; groups were cut off and destroyed by machine gun fire; slowly but ever so surely, the lead battalions of the two Polish infantry divisions were isolated and decimated. It was impossible to move openly on the stony hillsides; every manoeuvre brought down retaliatory fire. The infantry could not be reinforced or resupplied. They were on their own, fighting off the enemy as best they could.

By early afternoon it was clear to Gen Anders that the attack had failed in its objectives. He gave orders for the infantry to withdraw from the exposed features back behind their start line. In little more than fourteen hours the two Polish divisions had been stopped dead and driven back; once again the German paratroopers holding the mountains had proved too strong. General Leese visited Anders later that day and consoled the Polish commander. Anders was concerned that the failure of his troops would effect the overall plan, and anxious that his corps should not jeopardise 'Diadem'. He told Leese that he would try again immediately, but Leese replied that he should take his time. The Eighth Army commander knew that the problem of taking Monte Cassino and its neighbouring heights would become easier the further XIII Corps moved up the Liri valley. He asked Gen Anders to ready his corps for another attempt, but not to strike until the troops in the valley could wheel to the right and envelope the rear of Monastery Hill. He then planned a pincer movement that would finally excise the tumour of Monte Cassino, and Heidrich's paratroopers with it.

113

A few jubilant Polish infantry (right) inside the ruins of the great Benedictine monastery the day after the fortress had finally fallen to the 3rd Carpathian Division. The destruction of the abbey was total; nothing remained but the foundations and a few roofless walls. (Imperial War Museum)

Although Ander's attack in the mountains achieved little material success, it did ease some of the pressure being applied to the British 4th Division down on the Rapido, as Heidrich's paratroopers found themselves occupied on both faces of their sector. The bridgeheads gained by the 4th Division gradually expanded, and a bridge was put across during the night of 12/13 May. The situation was still very precarious, however, as Gen Feurstein had deployed some troops from LI Mountain Corps' divisions in the northern hills. Elements of the 44.Infanterie and 5.Gebirgs-Divisions now found themselves fighting on the floor of the valley in an effort to stifle the Allied bridgehead across the Rapido.

★ ★ ★

At the end of the second day of 'Diadem' successes were few. British XIII Corps had gained a lodgement in the Liri valley, but its two divisions were contained in tight bridgeheads still overlooked by a German-held Monte Cassino. A smokescreen, established by generators and topped up with smoke shells, shrouded most of the ground, but it was impossible for the whole area to be completely covered at all times; gaps inevitably opened up as the slight wind dispersed the haze. German artillery observers pounced on any marked and vulnerable target, calling down a torrent of shells on to the exposed infantry or engineers. Progress was slow and consolidation difficult; every time it seemed that a route had been blasted by the artillery and supporting tanks and that some move forwards was possible, a determined enemy counter-attack would seal off the gap. Up on the mountains to the right the Poles moved back into a defensive role, counting the cost of their attack and trying to regroup their two mauled divisions. On the left hand mountains, however, across on the south side of the Liri valley, there was some success to mark on the command maps.

The French Corps had started slowly, but by noon on 12 May had gained the intermediate objective of Monte Faito on the way to the strategically important Monte Maio. Once established on Faito, the Berber *tirailleurs* of the 2nd Moroccan Division saw off the inevitable German counter-attack and then pressed on with their advance with their characteristic energy. On their left the 4th Moroccan Mountain Division and their attached force of Goums snaked relentlessly forward through the hills, and arrived to overlook Castelforte. This flanking movement helped the Americans with their attack, and the US 88th Division took the village of Damiano, for so long a target of McCreery's X Corps.

The third day of 'Diadem' saw continued savage fighting, but with a greater measure of success. The French continued their advance and the Moroccans seized the heights of Monte Maio, the left hand pillar guarding the gates to the Liri valley. On the opposite side a German flag still flew over the other great bastion of Monte Cassino; but for the first time Allied troops were finally able to look down on the Germans holding the valley floor below. By nightfall the Moroccans were already moving along the western slopes of the mountain, seeking to envelop those units of the German 71.Division which they had outflanked. To their right, the way forward was now open; the Free French troops of the 1st Motorised Infantry Division were filtering down the northern face, moving alongside the 8th Indian Division on the other side of the Liri.

The taking of Monte Maio had pierced the line held by 71.Division. A number of gaps now began to open up in the hills, through which columns of Moroccan and Algerian riflemen from the 4th Mountain and 3rd Algerian Divisions exploited forward. Across the barren hillsides and up the stony gullies, units of *goumiers*, camouflaged in their drab-striped gowns, loped like wolves over impossible ground, out-manoeuvring isolated pockets of the enemy and dispatching those that they caught in their own bloody way.

Down near the coast to the left of the French, the Americans took advantage of the progress made by Juin's colonial troops. Their advance so far had been slow against the surprisingly dogged German 94.Division. After two days the US 88th Division was still battering itself against Santa Maria Infante; but the presence of the French on the enemy's left flank increased the pressure felt by the Germans, and their defence began to weaken.

In front of British XIII Corps the way forward was no easier, but the weight being applied by the gradual build-up of troops in the bridgeheads was beginning to tell on the Bode Blocking Group and its adjacent units. On the evening of 13 May the two bridgeheads linked up and formed a continuous Allied lodgement along the Rapido around San Angelo. It was almost time for Gen Kirkman to introduce his reserves into the battle, but there was so much congestion on both banks of the Rapido that there was no room for them to manoeuvre. On 14 May a second bridge was put across the river in the 4th Division's area, and the extra armour that came over helped the division to press inland, veering to the right under the noses of the paratroopers on Monastery Hill. This brought them closer to the strongest part of German LI Corps' defences, and the enemy response was savage.

The third full day of the battle, 14 May, saw more of what had gone before. Enemy resistance was still resolute, but was beginning to weaken, while more and more units of Fifteenth Army Group were fed into the attack. For British XIII Corps there was the additional problem of space. General Kirkman was trying to introduce a mass of infantry, armour and supplies into a very small area; he had the fist, but lacked the room to swing it. His bridgehead was expanding gradually as the inexorable weight of the two attacking divisions was brought to bear, but things were not

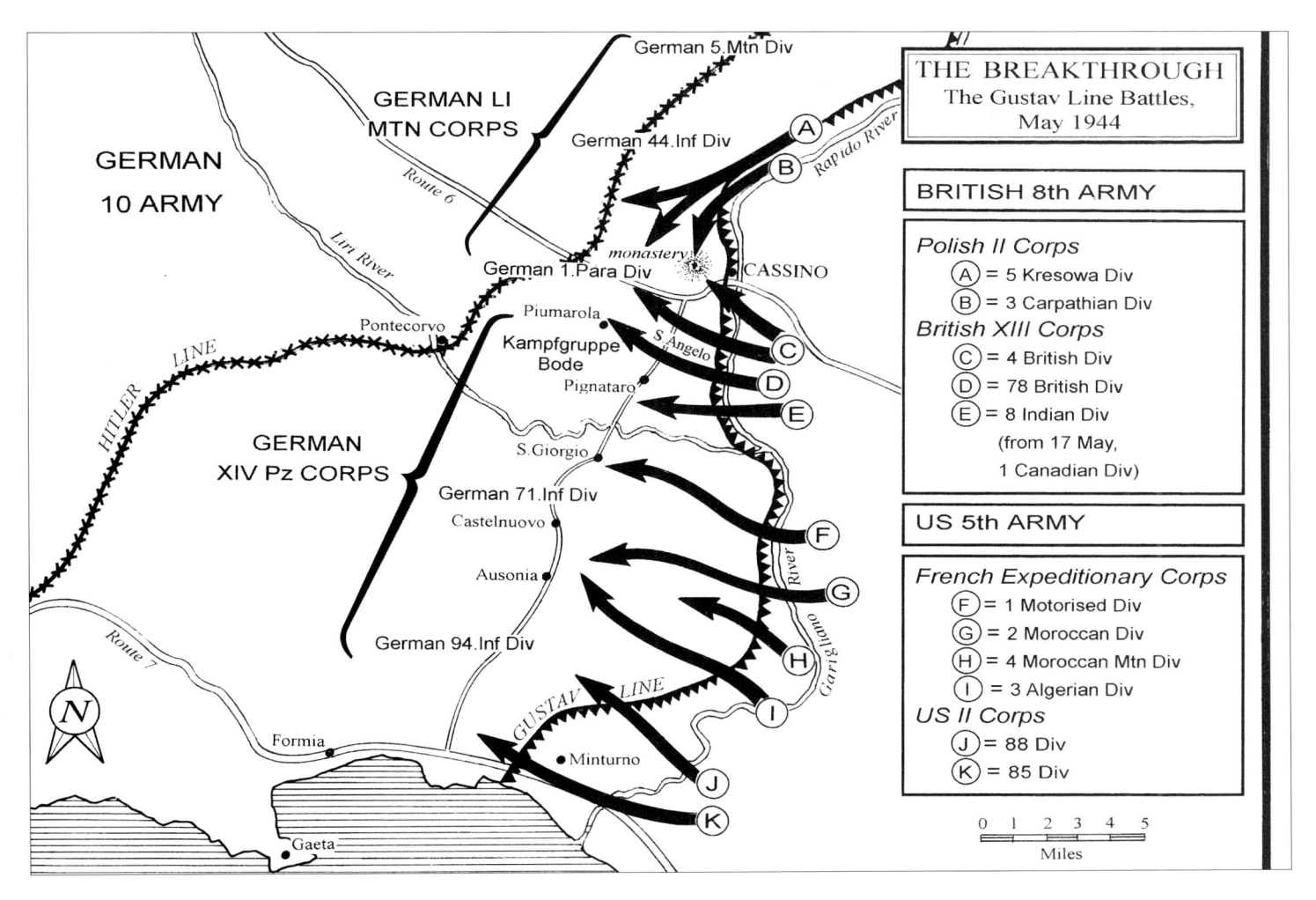

THE BREAKTHROUGH
The Gustav Line Battles, May 1944

BRITISH 8th ARMY

Polish II Corps
- Ⓐ = 5 Kresowa Div
- Ⓑ = 3 Carpathian Div

British XIII Corps
- Ⓒ = 4 British Div
- Ⓓ = 78 British Div
- Ⓔ = 8 Indian Div
  (from 17 May, 1 Canadian Div)

US 5th ARMY

French Expeditionary Corps
- Ⓕ = 1 Motorised Div
- Ⓖ = 2 Moroccan Div
- Ⓗ = 4 Moroccan Mtn Div
- Ⓘ = 3 Algerian Div

US II Corps
- Ⓙ = 88 Div
- Ⓚ = 85 Div

---

moving fast enough. General Fuerstein was making very good use of his local units in slowing the Allied attack, and he could hope for better when the German mobile reserves were committed. Kirkman had to blast his way through the Gustav Line before Kesselring released his tanks and mechanised infantry.

On 15 May, the British 78th Division was put over the Rapido and joined in XIII Corps' battle. General Keightley's division was fed through the bridgehead on the left of the 4th Division and directed to wheel right and cut Route 6 beyond Monte Cassino. Moving forward in stages, the 'Battleaxe' Division was introduced into the fighting a brigade at a time. While 11 Brigade moved to cut Route 6, the Irishmen of 38 Brigade advanced to cover its left flank. Against fierce enemy resistance, it took most of the day and part of the 16th to arrive within 1,000 yards of the highway; but progress had been good, and it allowed the infantry to look up and see, through the gaps in the smokescreen, that the towering heights of Monastery Hill were finally behind them.

The Poles on Monastery Hill

This attack was one of the claws of Gen Leese's pincer movement to encircle Monastery Hill; and it was now time for the Polish Corps to try once more. General Anders launched his attack at 1800 hours on 16 May. Again he committed both of his divisions, but this time with intervals between the launching of each assault. Two battalions from the 5th Kresowa Division opened the operation on the right flank with an attack along Phantom Ridge, and succeeded in capturing it early the next morning. Two further battalions continued the advance towards Colle San Angelo, taking the fight right into the heart of the German defences. Although Heidrich's paratroopers had been seriously weakened by being engaged on both sides of the battlefield as well as down in the valley, their resistance seemed just as fierce as ever.

Anders' other division, the 3rd Carpathian, began its attack by once again assaulting Snakeshead Ridge and Point 593. At 0730 hours on the 17th the division's fresh and untried 2 Brigade advanced over the bloody stones where so many had died before them. The lead battalion lost its CO almost immediately along with many of its riflemen, but they persisted with their attack and took the eastern side of the ridge by early afternoon. Tanks and infantry from the Polish Armoured Brigade lent support, sweeping down the slopes on to Albaneta Farm; the fighting here was ferocious, but the Poles inched their way forward and by nightfall had seized the farm. On their right the 5th Kresowa Division continued its push along Phantom Ridge and on to Colle San Angelo.

The next day, 18 May, Gen Anders committed everything that he had to the attack, including those units that had been badly mauled in the first abortive attempt on Monastery Hill. He even managed to organise two small extra battalions from men of the anti-tank regiment, motor transport drivers, workshop personnel, and reconnaissance commandos from the 15th Poznan Lancers. After the relentless fighting of the past few days Wladislaw Anders believed that the Germans must be as exhausted as his own men, and that final victory was within his grasp. He was right.

On the morning of 18 May the Poles renewed their attack. With the dominating heights now in their possession, the riflemen of 3rd Carpathian Division fought their way across the final few hundred yards that had been the graveyard of so many battalions before them. The previous day's fighting had been too much for the enemy; the ground lost, and the relentless progress being made by the Poles on the mountains and the British around the base of the hill had persuaded Gen Heidrich to pull out most of his troops before they were surrounded. With only covering forces left in front of them, the Poles moved inexorably across the northern slopes of Monastery Hill. At 1020 hours on 18 May 1944, men of the 12th Podolski Lancers hoisted the red and white flag of Poland over the battered ruins of the monastery of Monte Cassino. The second great pillar guarding the entrance to the Liri valley had fallen at last.

Down in the valley below, the Tommies of both the 4th and 78th Divisions had swung across to Route 6. The 4th Division now pressed forward and occupied the town, and all the lower slopes of Monte Cassino. General Heidrich

Two regimental commanders from 3rd Algerian Infantry Division pose in front of an abandoned Panther tank marked '331'; like most CEF personnel they wear a mixture of mainly US uniform with French badges. (Left) Col Bonjour, CO of the division's armoured reconnaissance regiment, 3rd Algerian Spahis (3e RSA); (right) Col van Heoki, CO of the tank-destroyer regiment, 7th Chasseurs d'Afrique (7e RCA). The M10 tank-destroyers were sometimes tactically assigned to the divisional artillery to thicken up barrages. (Imperial War Museum)

had managed to extricate most of his paratroopers from possible envelopment during the night of 17/18 May, harassed all the way by British artillery fire. The survivors of the dreadfully mauled but still defiant 1.Fallschirmjäger-Division now withdrew into the established fortifications of the Hitler Line. In the centre of the Liri valley, the 8th Indian Division was enlarging its lodgement to open the way for Canadian 1st Division to be introduced into the battle. General Alexander's Operation 'Diadem' was beginning to gain momentum. The door to the road to Rome was, at last, beginning to swing open.

CHAPTER TEN

Break-Out: 19 May–4 June

Field Marshal Kesselring was in great danger of being outmanoeuvred by Alexander's offensive. Hitler's Commander-in-Chief Italy had watched the slow crumbling of Gen von Vietinghoff's Tenth Army in the Gustav Line with increasing frustration. The first of his mobile reserves to be committed against the offensive were Gen Baade's 90. and Gen Rodt's 15.Panzer-Grenadier-Divisions, the veterans of the earlier Rapido battles, which were both sent forward into the Liri valley to counter-attack British XIII Corps. The valley was seen to be the centre of the Allies' main effort and it was here that Kesselring thought the offensive could be held.

However, the situation on XIV Panzer Corp's sector was also becoming dangerous as the French pushed on through the mountains behind the Garigliano. The corps commander, Gen von Senger und Etterlin, did not return from leave until 17 May; his deputy had not handled the challenge well, and by that time things had got out of control. The gap opened up between the 94. and 71.Divisions had allowed the French to get into the Liri valley, and they were approaching the Hitler Line before it could be properly manned. The momentum of this Allied attack on Kesselring's right flank threatened to undermine the planned orderly withdrawal of Tenth Army behind the Hitler Line defences.

As Alexander's offensive rolled on, Kesselring was having trouble with the strong personalities of his subordinate commanders. The 1.Fallschirmjäger-Division should have made a timely withdrawal off the mountains in order to echelon to the right flank of Baade's 90.Panzer-Grenadiers in the valley; but Gen Heidrich had been reluctant to let go of 'his' Monte Cassino. This delayed LI Corps' retirement into new positions in the Hitler Line, and through Piedimonte in the mountains. This in turn meant that XIV Panzer Corps had to cling to intermediate positions longer than had been planned.

Kesselring also had problems with Gen von Mackensen of Fourteenth Army. When it was known that the Canadian Corps - which was supposedly embarking at Naples for a landing on the coast north of Rome - was in the Liri valley, it became clear that another Allied amphibious operation was unlikely. Kesselring could now safely release more of his mobile reserve to help stem Alexander's attack in the south. On 19 May he ordered Fourteenth Army to release 29.Panzer-Grenadier-Division and send it to Tenth Army to close the gap that was opening up between Von Senger's and Feurstein's corps. General Fries had his division positioned north of Rome as the immediate reaction force to counter any further Allied landing; when Kesselring ordered it south, Von Mackensen protested and delayed the move. Fourteenth Army's commander was reluctant to part with such an important component of his reserves at a time when a break-out from the Anzio beachhead was imminent.

A tired section from D Coy, 7th Bn, Cheshire Regiment take cover from snipers in a captured German trench. This battalion provided Vickers machine gun and 4.2in mortar support for the infantry brigades of the British 5th Division; these men, armed with rifles and Thompsons, came under fire while reconnoitering new gun positions. (Imperial War Museum)

Kesselring did not learn of this delay until he reached his battle headquarters on 20 May, and it enraged him. While he sympathised with Von Mackensen, he also realised that if the Allied tide were not stopped in the south, Fourteenth Army would be swept aside in its turn whether the Americans broke out of Anzio or not. This disobedience, stemming from just one of many disagreements over the preceding months, was intolerable to Kesselring, and after the battle Von Mackensen was relieved of his command.

The leading elements of the 29.Panzer-Grenadier-Division did not arrive on the southern front until 21 May, and by then it was too late. They were fed into the battle piecemeal, fighting from unprepared positions. Worse was to come, for 26.Panzer-Division, stationed on the Alban Hills to prevent US VI Corps breaking out for Rome, also had to be committed into the Liri valley. Kesselring had thus been forced to use all of his mobile reserves in response to Alexander's strategy, leaving Anzio covered only by the units which Von Mackensen had stationed along the perimeter.

General Leese now informed Alexander that his Eighth Army would be ready for the major assault on the Hitler Line on the night of 21/22 May. This attack, and the pressure it would apply to the already weakened German Tenth

Private Mornington Sutton, 1st Bn, Green Howards, is carried back from his battalion's attack on the River Moletta by captured German paratroopers from 4.Fallschirmjäger-Division. Private Sutton's left foot had been blown off by a Schu anti-personnel mine during his company's passage through a thick minefield on the German side of the river. The Green Howards' attack was part of a British 5th Division diversionary assault on the extreme left of the Anzio beachhead, launched on the night of 22 May just before US VI Corps' main break-out attack through Cisterna. (Imperial War Museum)

Army, signalled that the time had arrived for Gen Truscott to break out of the Anzio beachhead with his US VI Corps. At the same time Juin's storming French corps was to swing to the right into the rear of those enemy divisions holding the Hitler Line, cutting Route 6 behind them at Ceprano. General Keyes' US II Corps would continue its coastal advance up Route 7 to link up with the forces at Anzio.

Flushed with their success on Monte Cassino, the Poles swept across the mountains towards the towering Monte Cairo and then swung down on to the fortified village of Piedimonte, which guarded the extreme right of the Hitler Line above Route 6. Across the valley to the south the French did the same, closing on the defensive line and getting behind its interlocking positions. With both flanks turned, the Canadians attacked the centre together with the British 78th Division. The first few days' fighting were brutal and costly; every attack ran into strong resistance from an enemy bolstered by the arrival of their reserves; but as the composite line was gradually prised open by so many simultaneous assaults, German Tenth Army began to give way. It soon became clear to both Kesselring and his army commander that unless he began to pull out the Tenth Army it was in danger of being encircled and annihilated. The great German retreat was starting. Little by little, Von Vietinghoff's troops began to disengage, conducting an orderly and defended withdrawal back towards Rome.

The reprieve of Tenth Army
Sixty miles to the north, US VI Corps began its fight to break free of the beachhead. The principle objective of Operation 'Diadem' was to destroy German forces rather than to take ground. Accordingly the direction of Lucian Truscott's attack, as ordered by Alexander, was to be towards Valmontone on Route 6, to try to cut the lines of communication and main axis of retreat of German Tenth Army.

Mark Clark saw things differently, however. He believed that Rome was the main objective, and he was anxious to ensure that his US Fifth Army liberated the 'eternal city'. He felt very strongly that after a grim winter's fighting his army deserved this militarily empty but highly symbolic prize. He was not about to let the city slip from his grasp, or be taken by troops other than his own.

The battle for the break-out began on 23 May when the US 3rd Division, together with 1st Armored Division and the Special Service Force, attacked Cisterna. The intention was for the two attacking divisions to breach the German defences and allow the 36th Division to pass through and make for Valmontone. The US 45th Division would then widen the gap and protect the northern flank of the advance which faced the Alban Hills. At the same time, the British 1st and 5th Divisions would hold the northern side of the beachhead and prevent any flanking counter-attacks by German I Parachute Corps.

The attack ran into fierce resistance almost immediately it left the start line and heavy fighting continued during the first two days of the operation. The combined opposition of the 362. and 715.Infanterie-Divisions was reinforced by paratroopers from the northern part of the perimeter as Von Mackensen threw fresh troops into the Americans' path. By 25 May, however, Cisterna had been taken and the leading troops were in contact with elements of US II Corps driving up from the south. After four months of separation, US Fifth Army was at last united into a continuous front. German resistance reached its peak when the 'Hermann Göring' Panzer-Division arrived to join the battle. This strong formation had been earmarked by German High Command to go to France in expectation of the Allied invasion there, but had been diverted back to Anzio. So great was the need to get this crack division into the line that it risked moving south during daylight, and consequently suffered heavy punishment from Allied aircraft. When it arrived at Anzio it was too weak to stop the break-out.

Late on 25 May, Gen Mark Clark changed the orders given to him by his Army Group commander, Gen Alexander, and switched the weight of his advance away from Valmontone and towards Rome. He ordered Gen Truscott to keep the exhausted 3rd Division heading for Valmontone, but to swing the bulk of his forces to the left, using Route 7 as their axis and pushing through the Alban Hills. Four US divisions - the 34th 'Red Bull', 36th 'Texas', 45th 'Thunderbird' and 1st Armored - now mounted a concentrated thrust on the Italian capital, leaving just the tired 3rd 'Marne' Division to close on Valmontone and cut Von Vietinghoff's axis of retreat along Route 6.

When the 3rd Division got within three miles of Valmontone they were stopped dead by a combined force from the 'Hermann Göring', 334. and 92.Divisions, who were firmly established in front of this key position to hold open Tenth Army's escape route. In the meantime, Clark's drive on Rome had met with very stiff resistance on a hastily erected defence line - the 'Caesar Line' - south of the city. For four days US VI Corps pounded the enemy, achieving very little progress for their heroic efforts.

In the south, British Eighth Army pressed on the heels of the retreating German XIV Panzer and LI Mountain Corps. General Leese had sent two of his armoured divisions - the British 6th and Canadian 5th - in pursuit of the fleeing enemy, but each time they approached the tail of Tenth Army they suffered a bloody riposte. The redoubtable 1.Fallschirmjäger and 90.Panzer-Grenadier-Divisions fought determined delaying actions all along Route 6. Traffic jams in the rear hindered the British progress to an alarming degree; there was just not enough room on the narrow roads to deploy the ponderous armoured divisions and their supply columns. The Italian countryside once again demonstrated that it was not the place in which to conduct modern mechanised warfare.

On 29 May, Gen Clark regrouped his forces and tried again to break through the Caesar Line; he now brought US II Corps up to strengthen his weakened VI Corps. By a stroke of luck, a patrol from 36th Division found an unoccupied gap in the line and two regiments were quietly passed through during the night. The next day the breach was widened and, despite a counter-attack by 'Hermann Göring' units, the 36th Division broke through. At the same time every available man in both US corps joined in a concerted attack, including the two British divisions from the Anzio beachhead. It was too much for the enemy; the eleven Allied divisions were unstoppable. Reluctantly, Kesselring ordered another withdrawal to the north and declared Rome to be an 'open city'.

On 4 June, just two days before the Allied landings in Normandy, Gen Mark Clark's personal ambition was fulfilled as he and his US Fifth Army entered Rome. General Juin's French Expeditionary Corps wheeled close around and into the eastern side of the city, while Gen Oliver Leese's British Eighth Army cut across the hills and continued to pursue the enemy up the east bank of the River Tiber. Even with two more armoured divisions added to Eighth Army's pursuit the enemy still managed to elude any final confrontation. The three corps of US Fifth Army, all pressing down on Rome, would take days to clear the city, choked by ever-growing traffic congestion and confusion; meanwhile, Kesselring's bloodied but still dangerous forces escaped northwards to fight another day.

Even so, 'Diadem' had been a memorable victory for Gen Alexander and his chief-of-staff, John Harding. German Fourteenth Army had been routed and Tenth Army thoroughly beaten, suffering heavy losses of men and matériel - though certainly not as much as might have been expected if US Fifth Army had closed the escape route at Valmontone. The German High Command (OKW) had been intent on blocking 'Diadem' from its outset and had offered Kesselring a number of new divisions to counter the offensive, even though they knew that the cross-Channel

The desolation surrounding the monastery at the end of the four battles for Cassino. After the Allies had done their worst, it seemed as though every building had been destroyed, every rock turned over, every tree stripped of its foliage. (US National Archives)

invasion was imminent. As already noted, the formidable Panzer-Division 'Hermann Göring' had been held back in Italy. During the battle, but too late to make a difference, three new infantry divisions, 16.Panzer-Division, and the weak 19. and 20.Luftwaffe Field Divisions were sent to Italy, as well as tank and artillery reinforcements. General Alexander had thus fulfilled one of the prime objectives of the war in Italy – to draw into the theatre divisions that might otherwise have been committed against the 'Overlord' operation in northern France.

After the fall of Cassino and the breaking of the Gustav Line, the struggle for the possession of Italy continued. Faced by a supreme strategist in Kesselring, Alexander's task proved no easier after June 1944. The Germans continued to fight their rearguard actions until well north of Rome, where they made a series of stands, all the while delaying Fifteenth Army Group while they built yet another line of defences across the mountainous north of the country. This new system, the 'Gothic Line', was in many ways as complete and formidable as the Gustav Line had been. By the time the Allies reached it the summer sunshine had given way to foul rain and cold winds as winter once more closed in around them, forcing Alexander's men to endure another freezing season of static warfare in the barren mountains of Italy.

Changes in command took place during this period. Henry Maitland Wilson left the Mediterranean, to be replaced by Harold Alexander, who took over as Supreme Commander and was made a field marshal. Mark Clark was given another star and made Commander Fifteenth Army Group, and Lucian Truscott replaced him in command of US Fifth Army. Oliver Leese went to the Far East, with McCreery rising to become Commander British Eighth Army in his place.

Early in 1945, even though Fifth Army had been reduced in size by having to provide divisions for the 'Anvil' landings in southern France, Clark and Alexander planned and implemented another successful major offensive. This smashed the Gothic Line and the defences along the River Po, annihilating all German forces in Italy. On 2 May 1945, five days before the cease-fire that ended the war in Europe, the German forces in Italy finally surrendered.

Field Marshal Albrecht Kesselring, the genius of the German defence in Italy, was not there to see it. In March 1945 the Führer, flailing around for some 'white hope' to save the collapsing Third Reich, appointed him Commander-in-Chief West to replace Field Marshal von Runstedt. His task was, of course, hopeless, and he surrendered to US forces on 6 May. In 1947 a British Military Court in Venice held him responsible for atrocities committed by troops under his command in Italy. He was sentenced to death; but Field Marshal Alexander was only one of several senior Allied commanders who intervened to save his life. His sentence was commuted to life imprisonment, but he was released on grounds of ill-health in 1952. During the remaining eight years of his life he was active in the German ex-servicemen's association.

APPENDIX I
Allied Orders of Battle

Note: Only major infantry, machine gun, armoured and field artillery units integral to Divisions are listed here. Infantry Divisions also incorporated reconnaissance, anti-tank, anti-aircraft, signals, ordnance, quartermaster, engineer, medical, and other supporting units. Many armoured, tank-destroyer, artillery, engineer and other specialist units were Corps or Army assets, assigned to operate alongside Divisions according to tactical necessity.

CASSINO

US FIFTH ARMY
Lt Gen Mark Clark

US II CORPS
Maj Gen Geoffrey Keyes

US 34th Infantry Division (to Anzio, April 1944)
Maj Gen Charles Ryder
133rd Infantry Regiment
135th Infantry Regiment
168th Infantry Regiment
125th, 151st, 175th, 185th Field Artillery Battalions

US 36th Infantry Division (to Anzio, April 1944)
Maj Gen Fred Walker
141st Infantry Regiment
142nd Infantry Regiment
143rd Infantry Regiment
131st, 132nd, 133rd, 155th FA Bns

US 85th Infantry Division (joined II Corps for Op. 'Diadem')
Maj Gen John Coulter
337th Infantry Regiment
338th Infantry Regiment
339th Infantry Regiment
328th, 329th, 403rd, 910th FA Bns

US 88th Infantry Division (joined II Corps for Op. 'Diadem')
Maj Gen John Sloan
349th Infantry Regiment
350th Infantry Regiment
351st Infantry Regiment
337th, 338th, 339th, 913th FA Bns

US 1st Armored Division
Maj Gen Ernest Harmon
1st Armored Regiment (1st, 4th, 13th Tank Bns)
6th Armored Infantry Regiment (6th, 11th, 14th AI Bns)
27th, 68th, 91st FA Bns
(Only Combat Command B employed by II Corps; later moved to Anzio, April 1944)

BRITISH X CORPS
Lt Gen R. McCreery

British 5th Infantry Division (to Anzio, March 1944)
Maj Gen G. Bucknall to 22 Jan 1944; thereafter Maj Gen P. Gregson Ellis
13 Infantry Brigade:
    2nd Battalion, Cameron Highlanders
    2nd Bn, Royal Inniskilling Fusiliers
    2nd Bn, Wiltshire Regiment
15 Infantry Brigade:
    1st Bn, Green Howards
    1st Bn, King's Own Yorkshire Light Infantry
    1st Bn, Yorkshire & Lancashire Regiment
17 Infantry Brigade:
    2nd Bn, Royal Scots Fusiliers
    2nd Bn, Northamptonshire Regiment
    6th Bn, Seaforth Highlanders
(Machine gun) 7th Bn, Cheshire Regiment
91st, 92nd, 156th Field Regiments Royal Artillery

British 46th Infantry Division
Maj Gen J. Hawkesworth
128 Infantry Brigade:
    2nd Bn, Hampshire Regiment
    1/4th Bn, Hampshire Regiment
    5th Bn, Hampshire Regiment
138 Infantry Brigade:
    6th Bn, Lincolnshire Regiment
    2/4th Bn, KOYLI
    6th Bn, Yorks & Lancs Regiment
139 Infantry Brigade:
    2/5th Bn, Leicestershire Regiment
    5th Bn, Sherwood Foresters
    16th Bn, Durham Light Infantry
(MG, mortar) 2nd Bn, Royal Northumberland Fusiliers to March 1944; thereafter 9th Bn, Manchester Regiment
70th, 71st, 172nd Field Regiments RA

British 56th (London) Infantry Division
(to Anzio, Feb 1944)
Maj Gen G. Templer
167 Infantry Brigade:
    8th Bn, Royal Fusiliers
    9th Bn, Royal Fusiliers
    7th Bn, Oxfordshire & Buckinghamshire Light Infantry
168 Infantry Brigade:
    1st Bn, London Scottish
    1st Bn, London Irish
    10th Bn, Royal Berkshire Regiment
169 Infantry Brigade:
    2/5th Bn, Queen's Royal Regiment
    2/6th Bn, Queen's Royal Regiment
    2/7th Bn, Queen's Royal Regiment
(MG) 6th Bn, Cheshire Regiment
64th, 65th, 113th Field Regiments RA

NEW ZEALAND II CORPS
Lt Gen Bernard Freyberg

New Zealand 2nd Division
Maj Gen Howard Kippenberger to 2 March 1944; thereafter Brig G. Parkinson
4 NZ Armoured Brigade:

18th, 19th, 20th NZ Armd Regiments
22nd NZ Motorised Battalion
5 NZ Infantry Brigade:
   21st, 23rd, 28th (Maori) NZ Infantry Battalions
6 NZ Infantry Brigade:
   24th, 25th, 26th NZ Infantry Battalions
(MG) 27th NZ Battalion
4th, 5th, 6th NZ Field Regiments,
11th, 17th Field & 66th, 80th Medium Regiments RA

Indian 4th Infantry Division
Maj Gen F.Tuker to 4 February 1944;
Brig H.Dimoline to 9 March 1944;
Maj Gen A.Galloway to 25 March 1944; thereafter
Maj Gen A.Holworthy
5 Indian Infantry Brigade:
   1/4th Bn, Essex Regiment
   1st Bn, 6th Rajputana Rifles
   1st Bn, 9th Gurkha Rifles
7 Indian Infantry Brigade:
   1st Bn, Royal Sussex Regiment
   4th Bn, 16th Punjab Regiment
   1st Bn, 2nd Gurkha Rifles
11 Indian Infantry Brigade:
   2nd Bn, Cameron Highlanders
   4th Bn, 6th Rajputana Rifles
   2nd Bn, 7th Gurkha Rifles
(MG) 5th Bn, 5th Rajputana Rifles
1st, 11th, 31st Field Regiments RA

British 78th Infantry Division
(to British Eighth Army for Op. 'Diadem')
Maj Gen Charles Keightley
11 Infantry Brigade:
   2nd Bn, Lancashire Fusiliers
   1st Bn, East Surrey Regiment
   5th Bn, Northamptonshire Regiment
36 Infantry Brigade:
   6th Bn, Royal West Kent Regiment
   5th Bn, Buffs (Royal East Kent Regiment)
   8th Bn, Argyll & Sutherland Highlanders
38 (Irish) Infantry Brigade:
   1st Bn, Royal Irish Fusiliers
   2nd Bn, London Irish Rifles
   6th Bn, Royal Inniskilling Fusiliers
(MG, Mtr) 1st Bn, Kensington Regiment
17th, 132nd, 138th Field Regiments RA

FRENCH EXPEDITIONARY CORPS (CEF)
Lt Gen Alphonse Juin

2e Division d'Infanterie Marocaine (2e DIM)
Brig Gen André Dody
4e Régiment de Tirailleurs Marocains (Moroccan Rifles)
5e Régiment de Tirailleurs Marocains
8e Régiment de Tirailleurs Marocains
63e Régiment d'Artillerie d'Afrique
(attached) 4e Groupement de Tabors Marocains

3e Division d'Infanterie Algérienne (3e DIA)
Maj Gen de Goislard de Monsabert
3e Régiment de Tirailleurs Algériens
4e Régiment de Tirailleurs Tunisiens
7e Régiment de Tirailleurs Algériens
67e Régiment d'Artillerie d'Afrique
(attached) 3e Groupement de Tabors Marocains

4e Division de Montagne Marocaine (4e DMM)
(joined CEF for Op. 'Diadem')
Brig Gen Sevez
1er Régiment de Tirailleurs Marocains
2e Régiment de Tirailleurs Marocains
6e Régiment de Tirailleurs Marocains
69e Régiment d'Artillerie de Montagne

'Mountain Corps'
In May 1944 Gen Sevez commanded a task group comprising his 4e DMM and the assembled Groups of Moroccan Tabors:
Goums Morocains
Brig Gen Guillaume
1er GTM: 2e, 3e, 12e Tabors (joined CEF for Op. 'Diadem')
3e GTM: 9e, 10e, 17e Tabors (from 3e DIA, above)
4e GTM: 5e, 8e, 11e Tabors (from 2e DIM, above)

1st Motorised Infantry Division (1re DMI)
Maj Gen Diego Brosset
(joined CEF for Op. 'Diadem' – the reorganised and retitled Gaullist 1st Free French Division; its British-style brigades corresponded to US regiments)
1ere Brigade:
   1er & 2e Bns Légion Étrangère
   22e Bn de Marche Nord-Africain
2e Brigade:
   4e, 5e & 11e Bns de Marche
4e Brigade:
   Bn d'Infanterie de Marine & Pacifique
   21er & 24e Bns de Marche
1er Régiment d'Artillerie

ANZIO

US VI CORPS
Maj Gen John Lucas to 22 Feb 1944; thereafter
Maj Gen Lucian Truscott

US 3rd Infantry Division
Maj Gen Lucian Truscott to 22 Feb 1944; thereafter
Maj Gen O'Daniel
7th Infantry Regiment
15th Infantry Regiment
30th Infantry Regiment
9th, 10th, 39th, 41st Field Artillery Bns

US 34th Infantry Division (from US II Corps, April 1944)
See above under CASSINO

US 36th Infantry Division (from US II Corps, April 1944)
See above under CASSINO

US 45th Infantry Division
Maj Gen William Eagles
157th Infantry Regiment
179th Infantry Regiment

180th Infantry Regiment
158th, 160th, 171st, 189th FA Bns

US 1st Armored Division
See above under CASSINO

US Ranger Force
Col William O. Darby
1st, 3rd, 4th Ranger Battalions

US/Canadian 1st Special Service Force
Brig Gen Robert T. Frederick

British 1st Infantry Division
Maj Gen W. Penney
2 Infantry Brigade:
    1st Bn, Loyal Regiment
    2nd Bn, North Staffordshire Regiment
    6th Bn, Gordon Highlanders
3 Infantry Brigade:
    1st Bn, Duke of Wellington's Regiment
    2nd Bn, Sherwood Foresters
    1st Bn, King's Shropshire Light Infantry
18 Infantry Brigade (arrived Anzio, 24 Feb 1944):
    1st Bn, Buffs (Royal East Kent Regiment)
    14th Bn, Sherwood Foresters
    9th Bn, KOYLI
24 Guards Brigade (withdrawn to Naples, 7 March 1944):
    5th Bn, Grenadier Guards
    1st Bn, Scots Guards
    1st Bn, Irish Guards
(MG, Mtr) 2/7th Bn, Middlesex Regiment
2nd, 19th, 67th Field Regiments RA

British 5th Infantry Division
(from British X Corps, March 1944; see above under CASSINO)

British 56th Infantry Division
(from British X Corps – see above under CASSINO – until March 1944, when withdrawn to Egypt for refit)

OPERATION 'DIADEM'

BRITISH EIGHTH ARMY
Lt Gen Sir Oliver Leese

BRITISH XIII CORPS
Lt Gen Sidney Kirkman

British 4th Infantry Division
Maj Gen Dudley Ward
10 Infantry Brigade:
    2nd Bn, Bedfordshire & Hertfordshire Regiment
    2nd Bn, Duke of Cornwall's Light Infantry
    1/6th Bn, East Surrey Regiment
12 Infantry Brigade:
    2nd Bn, Royal Fusiliers
    6th Bn, Black Watch
    1st Bn, Royal West Kent Regiment
28 Infantry Brigade:
    2nd Bn, Somerset Light Infantry
    2nd Bn, King's Regiment (Liverpool)
    2/4th Bn, Hampshire Regiment
(MG, Mtr) 2nd Bn, Royal Northumberland Fusiliers from March 1944
22nd, 30th, 77th Field Regiments RA

British 78th Infantry Division
(from New Zealand II Corps, April 1944; see above under CASSINO)

Indian 8th Infantry Division
Maj Gen Dudley Russell
17 Indian Infantry Brigade:
    1st Bn, Royal Fusiliers
    1st Bn, 12th Frontier Force Rifles
    1st Bn, 5th Gurkha Rifles
19 Indian Infantry Brigade:
    1/5th Bn, Essex Regiment
    3rd Bn, 8th Punjab Regiment
    6th Bn, 13th Frontier Force Rifles
21 Indian Infantry Brigade:
    5th Bn, Royal West Kent Regiment
    1st Bn, 5th Mahratta Light Infantry
    3rd Bn, 15th Punjab Regiment
(MG) 5th Bn, 5th Mahratta Light Infantry
3rd, 52nd, 53rd Field Regiments RA

British 6th Armoured Division
Maj Gen Vivian Evelegh
26 Armoured Brigade:
    16/5th Lancers
    17/21st Lancers
    2nd Lothian & Border Horse
1 Guards Brigade:
    3rd Bn, Grenadier Guards
    2nd Bn, Coldstream Guards
    3rd Bn, Welsh Guards
61 Infantry Brigade:
    2nd Bn, Rifle Brigade
    7th Bn, Rifle Brigade
    10th Bn, Rifle Brigade

CANADIAN I CORPS
Maj Gen E. Burns

Canadian 1st Infantry Division
Maj Gen C. Vokes
1 Canadian Infantry Brigade:
    Royal Canadian Regiment
    Hastings & Prince Edward Regiment
    48th Highlanders of Canada
2 Canadian Infantry Brigade:
    Princess Patricia's Canadian Light Infantry
    Seaforth Highlanders of Canada
    Loyal Edmonton Regiment
3 Canadian Infantry Brigade:
    Royal 22e Regiment
    Carleton & York Regiment
    West Nova Scotia Regiment
(MG) Saskatoon Light Infantry
1st (RCHA), 2nd, 3rd Field Regiments RCA

Canadian 5th Armoured Division
Maj Gen B. Hoffmeister
5 Canadian Armd Brigade:
    2nd Armd Regiment (Lord Strathcona's Horse)
    5th Armd Regiment (8th Princess Louise's New
      Brunswick Hussars)
    9th Armd Regiment (British Columbia Dragoons)
    (Mot inf) Westminster Regiment
11 Canadian Infantry Brigade:
    Perth Regiment
    Cape Breton Highlanders
    Irish Regiment of Canada
Royal Canadian Artillery

POLISH II CORPS
Lt Gen Wladyslaw Anders

3rd Carpathian Infantry Division
Maj Gen Duch
1 Carpathian Rifle Brigade:
    1st, 2nd, 3rd Carpathian Rifle Battalions
2 Carpathian Rifle Brigade:
    4th, 5th, 6th Carpathian Rifle Battalions
(MG) 3rd Machine Gun Battalion
1st, 2nd, 3rd Artillery Regiments
(recce) 12th Podolski Lancers

5th Kresowa Infantry Division
Maj Gen Sulik
5 Wilenska Infantry Brigade:
    13th, 14th, 15th Wilenska Rifle Battalions
6 Lwowska Infantry Brigade:
    16th, 17th Lwowska Rifle Battalions
(MG) 5th Machine Gun Battalion
4th, 5th, 6th Artillery Regiments
(recce) 15th Poznan Lancers

Polish 2 Armoured Brigade:
Maj Gen Rakowski
    4th Polish Armd Regiment 'Skorpion'
    1st Krechowiecki Lancers
    6th Polish Armd Regiment 'Dzieci Lwowskie'

ARMY RESERVE

South African 6th Armoured Division
11th SA Armoured Brigade:
    Prince Alfred's Guard
    Pretoria Regiment
    Special Service Battalion
    (Mot Inf) Imperial Light Horse/Kimberley Regiment
12th SA Motorised Infantry Brigade:
    1st Royal Natal Carbineers
    1st City/Cape Town Highlanders
    Witwatersrand Rifles/ De La Rey Regiment
    1/6th, 4/22nd Field, 7/23rd Medium Regiments,
    SA Artillery

British 24 Guards Brigade (from May 1944)
See above under ANZIO

APPENDIX II
German Order of Battle

NOTE: Many of these German divisions were swapped between corps and sectors during the sequence of battles, and their component units did not always fight together as complete divisions.

ARMY GROUP 'C'
General Field Marshal Albrecht Kesselring

TENTH ARMY
General of Panzer Troops Heinrich von Vietinghoff-Scheel

LXXVI PANZER (ARMOURED) CORPS
Gen of Pz Troops Traugott Herr
On Adriatic front against British Eighth Army
(not at Cassino); HQ moved to Anzio, 4 Feb 1944.

XIV PANZER CORPS
Lt Gen Fridolin von Senger und Etterlin

44. Infanterie-Division (Reichsgrenadier-Division 'Hoch und Deutschmeister')
Lt Gen Dr Franz Bayer
Grenadier Regiment 131
Fusilier-Grenadier Regiment 132
Grenadier Regiment 134
Artillerie Regiment 96

3. Panzer-Grenadier-Division
Lt Gen Fritz-Hubert Gräser
Panzer-Grenadier Regiment 8
Pz-Gren Regiment 29 (to Anzio, late Jan 1944)
Panzer Abteilung (battalion) 103 (to Anzio, late Jan 1944)
Artillerie Regiment (Mot) 3

71. Infanterie-Division
Maj Gen Wilhelm Raapke
Infanterie Regiment 191 (to Anzio, late Jan 1944)
Infanterie Regiment 194 (to Anzio, late Jan 1944)
Infanterie Regiment 211
Artillerie Regiment 171

15. Panzer-Grenadier-Division
Maj Gen Eberhard Rodt
Pz-Gren Regiment 104
Pz-Gren Regiment 129
(later redesignated Pz-Gren Regt 115)
Panzer Abteilung 115
Artillerie Regiment (Mot) 15

94. Infanterie-Division
Maj Gen Bernard Steinmetz
Infanterie Regiment 267
Infanterie Regiment 274
Infanterie Regiment 276
Artillerie Regiment 194

29.Panzer-Grenadier-Division
Maj Gen Walter Fries
Pz-Gren Regiment 15 (to Anzio, late Jan 1944)
Pz-Gren Regiment 71 (to Anzio, late Jan 1944)
Panzer Abteilung 129
Artillerie Regiment (Mot) 29

5.Gebirgs-Division
Maj Gen Julius Ringel
Gebirgsjäger (Mountain Rifle) Regiment 85
Gebirgsjäger Regiment 100
Gebirgs Artillerie Regiment 95

90.Panzer-Grenadier-Division
Maj Gen Ernst Baade
Pz-Gren Regiment 200
Pz-Gren Regiment 361
Panzer Abteilung 190
Artillerie Regiment (Mot) 190

1.Fallschirmjäger-Division
Maj Gen Richard Heidrich
Fallschirmjäger (Parachute Rifle) Regiment 1
Fallschirmjäger Regiment 3
Fallschirmjäger Regiment 4
Fallschirm Maschinengewehr (Para MG) Btl 1
Fallschirm Artillerie Regiment 1

LI MOUNTAIN CORPS
Gen Valin Feurstein
From Adriatic front:

5.Gebirgs-Division
From XIV Pz Corps - see above

44.Infanterie-Division 'Hoch und Deutschmeister'
From XIV Pz Corps - see above

1.Fallschirmjäger-Division
From XIV Pz Corps - see above

FOURTEENTH ARMY
Colonel-General Eberhard von Mackensen

LXXVI PANZER CORPS
Gen of Pz Troops Traugott Herr
From Adriatic front:

71.Infanterie-Division
From XIV Pz Corps - see above

92.Infanterie-Division
Lt Gen Werner Goeritz
Grenadier Regiment 1059
Grenadier Regiment 1060
Artillerie Regiment 192

362.Infanterie-Division
Lt Gen Heinz Greiner
Grenadier Regiment 954
Grenadier Regiment 955
Grenadier Regiment 956
Artillerie Regiment 362

715.Infanterie-Division
Lt Gen Hans-Georg Hildebrandt
Grenadier Regiment 725
Grenadier Regiment 735
Artillerie Regiment 671

114.Jäger-Division
Maj Gen Alexander Bourquin
Jäger Regiment 721
Jäger Regiment 741
Artillerie Regiment 661

3.Panzer-Grenadier-Division
Lt Gen Fritz-Hubert Gräser
Pz-Gren Regiment 29
Infanterie Lehr Regiment
Panzer Abteilung 103
Artillerie Regiment (Mot) 3

(Fallschirm) Panzer-Division 'Hermann Göring'
Lt Gen Paul Conrath
Panzer Regiment 'Hermann Göring'
    (two Pz bns & one Assault Gun bn)
Pz-Gren Regiment 1 'HG'
Pz-Gren Regiment 2 'HG'
Pz-Artillerie Regiment 'HG'
    (five bns & Werfer mortar bty)
Flak Regiment 'HG' (three bns)

26.Panzer-Division
Maj Gen Smilo von Luttwitz
Panzer Regiment 26
Pz-Gren Regiment 9
Pz-Gren Regiment 67
Pz-Artillerie Regiment 93

29.Panzer-Grenadier-Division
From XIV Pz Corps - see above

I PARACHUTE CORPS
Gen of Paratroops Alfred Schlemm

65.Infanterie-Division
Lt Gen Georg Pfeifer
Grenadier Regiment 145
Grenadier Regiment 147
Artillerie Regiment 165

4.Fallschirmjäger-Division
Maj Gen Heinrich Trettner
Fallschirmjäger Regiment 10
Fallschirmjäger Regiment 11
Fallschirmjäger Regiment 12
Fallschirm Artillerie Regiment 4

BIBLIOGRAPHY

Adleman, Robert, H. & Walton, Col George, *Rome Fell Today* (Leslie Frewin, London, 1969)

Alexander, Field Marshal Earl of Tunis, *The Alexander Memoirs* (Cassell, London, 1962)

Anders, Lt Gen W., *An Army in Exile* (Macmillan, London, 1949)

Anon, *Anzio Beachhead 22 January - 25 May 1944* (Center of Military History, United States Army, Washington DC, 1990)

Barber, Laurie & Tonkin-Covell, John, *Freyberg: Churchill's Salamander* (Hutchinson, London, 1990)

Blaxland, Gregory, *Alexander's Generals* (William Kimber, London, 1979)

Blumenson, Martin, *Bloody River: Prelude to the Battle of Cassino* (George Allen & Unwin, London, 1970)

Blumenson, Martin, *Mark Clark* (Jonathan Cape, London, 1985)

Blumenson, Martin, *Salerno to Cassino* (US Army in World War Two, Government Printing Office, Washington, 1969)

Bryan, Paul, *Wool, War and Westminster* (Tom Donovan, London, 1993)

Clark, Mark, *Calculated Risk* (Harrap, London, 1951)

Connell, C., *Monte Cassino* (Elek, London, 1963)

Darby, William O., *Darby's Rangers* (Presidio, Novato, CA, 1993)

Edwards, Roger, *German Airborne Troops* (Macdonald & Janes, London, 1974)

Ellis, John, *Cassino: The Hollow Victory* (Andre Deutsch, London, 1984)

Fergusson, Bernard, *The Black Watch and the King's Enemies* (Collins, London, 1950)

Fisher, E.J., *Cassino to the Alps* (US Army in World War Two, Government Printing Office, Washington, 1977)

Ford, Ken, *Battleaxe Division: From Africa to Italy with the 78th Division, 1942-45* (Sutton, Stroud, 1999)

Forman, Denis, *To Reason Why* (London, 1991)

Gaujac, Paul, 'La CEF en Italie 1943-44' (*Militaria* magazine nos.127 & 129, Paris, 1996)

Graham, Dominick & Bidwell, Shelford, *Tug of War: The Battle for Italy 1943-1945* (Hodder & Stoughton, London, 1986)

Hapgood, David & Richardson, David, *Monte Cassino* (Angus & Robertson, London, 1984)

Horsfall, John, *Fling Our Banners to the Wind* (The Roundway Press, Kineton, 1978)

Jackson, W.G.F., *The Battle For Italy* (Batsford, London, 1967)

Kesselring, Albrecht, *The Memoirs* (William Kimber, London, 1964)

Kippenberger, Maj Gen Sir Howard, *Infantry Brigadier* (Oxford University Press, London, 1949)

Kuhn, Volkmar, *German Paratroopers in World War II* (Ian Allen, London, 1978)

Linklater, Eric, *The Campaign in Italy* (HMSO, London, 1951)

Mackenzie, Brig John, *CO 2LF* (privately published, 1997)

Majdalany, Fred, *Cassino: Portrait of a Battle* (Longman, Green & Co., London, 1957)

Majdalany, Fred, *The Monastery* (John Lane, The Bodley Head, London, 1945)

McKee, Ian, *The 5th Battalion Northamptonshire Regiment in Italy* (Tamsweg, 1945)

Mitcham, Samuel W., *Hitler's Legions* (Leo Cooper, London, 1985)

Molony, Brig C.J.C., *The Mediterranean and Middle East, Vol V* (HMSO, London, 1973)

Nicholson, Capt Nigel & Forbes, Patrick, *The Grenadier Guards in the War of 1939-1945, Vol II* (Gale & Polden, Aldershot, 1949)

Phillips, N.C., *The Sangro to Cassino: The History of New Zealand in the Second World War* (Dept of Internal Affairs, Wellington, 1957)

Piekalkiewicz, J., *Cassino: Anatomy of a Battle* (Orbis, London, 1980)

Ray, Cyril, *Algiers To Austria: A History of 78 Division* (Eyre & Spotiswoode, London, 1952)

Rhodes-Wood, Major E.H., *A War History of the Royal Pioneer Corps 1939-1945* (Gale & Polden, Aldershot, 1960)

Ryder, Rowland, *Oliver Leese* (Hamish Hamilton, London, 1987)

Senger und Etterlin, Fridolin von, *Neither Fear Nor Hope* (Macdonalds, London, 1963)

Sicard, Jacques, 'La 3e Division d'Infanterie Algérienne et ses Insignes' (*Militaria* magazine no.10, Paris, 1986)

Sicard, Jacques, 'La 2e Division d'Infanterie Marocaine et ses Insignes' (*Militaria* magazine no,.48, Paris, 1989)

Smith, E.C.D., *The Battles for Cassino* (Ian Allen, Shepperton, 1975)

Stevens, G.R., *Fourth Indian Division* (McClaren, London, 1948)

Trevelyan, Raleigh, *Rome '44* (Secker & Warburg, London, 1981)

Truscott, Lt Gen L.K., *Command Missions* (E. P. Dutton, NY, 1954)

Vaughan-Thomas, W., *Anzio* (Longmans, London, 1961)

Vittiglio, Fred, *Cassino* (Vittiglio, Boston, 1988)

INDEX

Adye, Lt Col, 95.
Alban Hills, 33-35, 43, 79, 117, 119.
Albaneta Farm, 95, 96, 115.
Albano, 35, 43, 44, 48, 49, 64, 78, 80.
Alexander, Gen Sir Harold, 9, 11, 12, 16-19, 36, 43, 47, 52, 54, 55, 58, 79, 80, 81, 83, 86, 98, 109, 112, 117, 119, 120.
ALLIED FORCES:
Allied Fifteenth Army Group, 9, 11, 12, 16-18, 81, 87, 98, 109, 114, 120.
Allied Eighteenth Army Group, 12.
AMERICAN FORCES - see United States Forces
Anders, Lt Gen Wladyslaw, 76, 106, 107, 109, 110, 113-115.
'Anvil', Operation, 18, 120.
Anzio, 13-15, 17-19, 26, 27, 29, 32-36, 43-49, 50-56, 63, 64, 77-80, 82, 83, 112, 117-119.
Apennine Mountains, 8, 116.
Aprilia, 48, 63.
Aquino, River, 108.
Arbuthnot, Brig, 99.
Atina, 19.
Aurunci Mountains, 76.

Baade, Maj Gen Ernst-Günther, 50, 51, 53, 82, 111.
'Barbara' Line, 10.
'Baron's Palace', 92.
Bateman, Brig, 95.
Bayer, Lt Gen Dr Franz, 50.
'Baytown', Operation, 8.
'Bernhardt' Line, 10, 24, 27.
Biferno, River, 10.
Boatner, Col Mark, 38.
Bodoglio, Marshal, 8.
Bondis Group, 76.
Bonifant, Brig, 93, 95.
Bonjour, Col, 116.
Bredin, Lt Col 'Bala', 75, 102.
BRITISH FORCES:
Desert Air Force, 17, 77.
Twenty-First Army Group, 24.
Eighth Army, 7-15, 23, 52, 76, 81, 82, 99, 107, 108, 110, 112, 117, 120.
Ninth Army, 11.
V Corps, 9, 13, 98.
X Corps, 9, 13, 20, 23, 24, 26-28, 34, 36, 39, 41, 50-52, 66, 80, 108, 109, 111, 114.
XIII Corps, 7, 13, 98, 107, 109-115, 117.
1st Airborne Division, 9.
1st Infantry Division, 12, 32, 34, 43, 44, 47-49, 63, 64, 119.
4th Infantry Division, 66, 70, 71, 75, 112, 114-116.
5th Infantry Division, 7, 14, 20, 23, 26, 52, 86, 118, 119.
6th Armoured Division, 79, 119.
46th Infantry Division, 20, 24, 26.
56th Infantry Division, 11, 20, 24, 26, 47, 64, 78, 82, 86.
78th Infantry Division, 71, 75, 82, 93, 97-107, 113, 115, 116, 118.
23rd Armoured Brigade, 10, 43.
24th Guards Brigade, 34, 44, 48.
201st Guards Brigade, 24, 66, 70.
2nd Infantry Brigade, 34.
3rd Infantry Brigade, 4, 48, 63.
11th Infantry Brigade, 97, 99, 100, 107, 115.
12th Infantry Brigade, 66.
13th Infantry Brigade, 24, 86.
17th Infantry Brigade, 24, 26.
28th Infantry Brigade, 75.
36th Infantry Brigade, 99, 104, 106.
38th (Irish) Infantry Brigade, 99, 102, 107, 113, 115.
128th (Hampshire) Infantry Brigade, 26, 75.
167th Infantry Brigade, 64.
168th Infantry Brigade, 47.
Lothian and Border Horse, 66.
North Irish Horse, 76.
46th Royal Tank Regiment, 34, 43, 44.
3rd Bn Coldstream Guards, 66, 70.
1st Bn Irish Guards, 43.
1st Bn Scots Guards, 43.
8th Bn Argyll & Sutherland Highlanders, 104.
6th Bn Black Watch, 66, 70.
5th Bn The Buffs (Royal East Kent Regiment), 104.
1st Bn Duke of Wellington's Regiment, 44, 48.
1st Bn East Surrey Regiment, 100.
1/4th Bn Essex Regiment, 61, 87, 90, 91, 95, 99.
1st Bn Green Howards, 118.
1/4th Bn Hampshire Regiment, 26.
2/4th Bn Hampshire Regiment, 71, 75.
2nd Bn Hampshire Regiment, 26.

5th Bn Hampshire Regiment, 26.
1st Bn Kensington Regiment, 103.
1st Bn King's Shropshire Light Infantry, 44, 48.
2nd Bn Lancashire Fusiliers, 100-102, 107.
2nd Bn London Irish Rifles, 75, 100, 104, 107, 113.
5th Bn Northamptonshire Regiment, 100, 101, 103, 104.
2nd Bn North Staffordshire Regiment, 43.
9th Bn Royal Fusiliers, 24.
2nd Bn Royal Inniskilling Fusiliers, 24.
6th Bn Royal Inniskilling Fusiliers, 71, 75, 102, 113.
1st Bn Royal Irish Fusiliers, 75.
9 Royal Marine Commando, 86.
40 Royal Marine Commando, 86.
2nd Bn Royal Scots Fusiliers, 24, 26.
1st Bn Royal Sussex Regiment, 57, 58, 75.
6th Bn Royal West Kent Regiment, 97, 99, 104, 106.
2nd Bn Sherwood Foresters, 44, 48.
2nd Bn Wiltshire Regiment, 24.
54th Heavy Regiment, Royal Artillery, 26.
138th Field Regiment, Royal Artillery, 106.

Bryan, Lt Col Paul, 99, 104, 106.
Broadhurst, Air Vice Marshal, Harry, 17.
Bucknall, Maj Gen G., 23.
Burns, Maj Gen E., 107, 109.
HMS *Bulolo*, 32.

'Caesar' Line, 119.
Cairo, 39, 100.
Calabria, 8, 10.
Campbell, Brig Lorne MacLaine VC, 86.
Campoleone, 36, 43, 44, 47, 48, 63.
CANADIAN FORCES:
I Corps, 13, 107, 109, 111, 117.
1st Armoured Division, 119.
1st Infantry Division, 7, 10, 73, 76, 116.
2nd Infantry Brigade, 76.
Princess Patricia's Canadian Light Infantry, 73, 76.

Cannon, Gen John K., 17, 87.
Carano, 49.
Carroceta, 44, 63, 78, 83.
Castelforte, 112, 114.
'Castle Hill', 80, 81, 88-93, 95-97, 99, 106.
'Cavendish Road', 95.
Ceprano, 118.
Churchill, Winston, 7, 8, 18, 19.
Cisterna, 35, 36, 43-47, 64, 80, 82, 83, 119.
Civitavecchia, 43, 111.
Clark, Lt Gen Mark, 8, 10, 12, 13, 19-23, 26-29, 33, 36, 39, 41, 43-45, 47, 49, 52, 54, 55, 58, 79-81, 86, 98, 109, 119.
Colle Maiola, 42, 95.
Colle San Angelo, 42, 113, 115.
Colle San Martino, 66.
Conca, 45.
Continental Hotel, Cassino, 90-93, 95.
Cox, Maj G., 104

Damiano, 114.
Darby, Col William O., 32, 45, 79.
Devers, Lt Gen Jacob, 11-13, 24, 55.
'Diadem', Operation, 14, 16, 66, 76, 108-119.
Diamare, Abbot Bishop Gregorio, 56, 58.
Dimoline, Brig Harry, 53-55, 57-59, 98.
Dody, Brig Gen André, 19, 22.
Drinkall, Maj, 92.

Eagles, Maj Gen William, 77, 79.
Eaker, Gen Ira, 17, 55, 87, 88.
Eisenhower, Gen Dwight D., 9, 11, 13 .
Ellis, Maj Gen Gregson, 86.
Evelegh, Maj Gen Vivian, 79, 102.

'Factory, The', 48, 63, 64.
Feurstein, Gen Valin, 83, 110, 114, 115.
Foggia Plain, 8.
Foltin, Capt, 88, 89, 92.
Forman, Maj Denis, 106.
Fowler-Essen, Lt Col, 75.
Frazior, Maj, 29.
Frederick, Brig Gen Robert T., 83
FRENCH FORCES:
French Expeditionary Corps (CEF), 13, 19-23, 27, 36, 39, 41, 50, 54, 74, 76, 80, 108, 109, 112, 114, 118.
1st Motorised Infantry Division, 110, 112, 114.
2nd Moroccan Division, 19, 20, 22, 39, 41, 51, 76, 112, 116.

3rd Algerian Division, 19, 21, 22, 39, 41, 51, 76, 112, 116.
4th Moroccan Mountain Division, 110, 112, 114.
15th Motorised Infantry Division, 20.
7e Régiment de Tirailleurs Algériens, 22.
4e Régiment de Tirailleurs Marocains, 22.
5e Régiment de Tirailleurs Marocains, 22.
8e Régiment de Tirailleurs Marocains, 22.
Goumiers marocains, 20, 21, 109, 114.

Freyberg, Lt Gen Bernard VC, 51, 52, 54-56, 58, 59, 80-82, 87, 88, 90, 91, 95, 98.
Fries, Maj Gen Walter, 117.

Galloway, Maj Gen, 98.
Garigliano, River, 9, 11, 20, 24, 26, 27, 34, 50, 108, 109, 111, 117.
GERMAN FORCES:
Ninth Army, 15.
Tenth Army, 9, 11, 13, 15-19, 23, 34, 35, 51, 52, 79-81, 86, 97, 112, 117-119.
Fourteenth Army, 13, 15, 34-36, 47, 63, 64, 82, 83, 111, 112, 117, 119.
Fifteenth Army, 15.
I Parachute Corps (Fallschirm-Korps), 34, 64, 119.
III Panzer Corps (Korps), 15.
XIV Panzer Corps (Korps), 15, 23, 50, 51, 58, 97, 108, 110, 117, 119.
LI Mountain Corps (Gebirgs-Korps), 83, 110, 114, 117, 119.
XLVI Corps (Korps), 13, 14.
LXXVI Corps (Korps), 15, 64.

1.Fallschirmjäger- (Parachute Rifle) Division, 16, 34, 45, 51, 52, 65, 68, 76, 82, 97, 110, 111, 113-117, 119.
4.Fallschirmjäger-Division, 33, 64, 111, 118.
19.Feld-Division (Luftwaffe), 120.
20.Feld-Division (Luftwaffe), 120.
5.Gebirgs- (Mountain) Division, 20-22, 66, 69, 76, 104, 110, 114.
44.Infanterie-Division, 16, 50, 51, 110, 114.
65.Infanterie-Division, 34, 35, 44, 48, 64, 111.
71.Infanterie-Division, 16, 34, 46, 50, 51, 75, 111, 112, 114, 117.
92.Infanterie-Division, 34, 111, 119.
94.Infanterie-Division, 16, 24, 26, 39, 50, 66, 69, 111, 112, 114, 117.
305.Infanterie-Division, 20, 111.
334.Infanterie-Division, 119.
362.Infanterie-Division, 34, 82, 111, 119.
715.Infanterie-Division, 34, 45, 48, 64, 77, 82, 111, 119.
114.Jäger- (Rifle) Division, 34, 64.
16.Panzer- (Armoured) Division, 9, 99, 120.
26.Panzer-Division, 34, 46, 64, 78, 82, 111, 117.
Fallschirm-Panzer-Division 'Hermann Göring', 14-16, 24, 33-35, 43, 45, 46,56, 63, 64, 78, 99, 119, 120.
3.Panzer-Grenadier- (Mechanised) Division, 16, 34, 35, 43, 44, 48, 64, 111.
15.Panzer-Grenadier-Division, 16, 24, 26, 27, 30, 93, 97, 111, 117.
16.SS-Panzer-Grenadier-Division 'Reichsführer-SS', 34.
29.Panzer-Grenadier-Division, 16, 26, 47, 50, 64, 78, 111, 117.
90.Panzer-Grenadier-Division, 16, 26, 50, 51, 82, 111, 117, 119.
Battle Group Graser, 63.
Bode Blocking Group, 111, 112, 114.
1.Fallschirmjäger-Regiment, 75.
3.Fallschirmjäger-Regiment, 82, 88.
4.Fallschirmjäger-Regiment, 97.
85.Gebirgsjäger (Mountain Rifle) Regiment, 22, 65, 69.
211.Infanterie-Regiment, 76.
Lehr-Infanterie-Regiment, 64, 77.
Panzer-Regiment 'Hermann Göring', 24, 26, 83
15.Panzer-Grenadier-Regiment, 50, 51.
115.Panzer-Grenadier-Regiment, 22, 93
129.Panzer-Grenadier-Regiment, 26
1.Fallschirm-Maschinengewehr-Btl (Parachute Machine Gun Bn), 51, 65, 68, 111.
7.(Luftwaffe) Jäger-Bataillon, 45.
194.Pioniere-Abteilung (Assault Engineer Bn), 66, 69.
508.schwere-Panzer-Abteilung (Heavy Tank Bn), 46.
653. & 654 schwere-Panzerjäger-Abteilungen (Heavy Tank-Destroyer Bns), 15.
1.Fallschirm-Kradschützen-Kompanie (Parachute Motorcycle Co), 95.

Goeritz, Lt Gen Werner, 34.
'Gothic' Line, 120.

127

Index

Gruenther, Maj Gen Alfred, 55.
Guillaume, Gen Augustin, 76.
'Gustav' Line, 9, 10, 11, 16-22, 26, 28, 30, 32-36, 39, 50, 52, 54, 57, 81, 99, 108, 112, 115, 117, 120.

'Hangman's Hill', see 'Monastery Hill'/Monte Cassino
Harding, Maj Gen John, 12, 55, 81, 109, 119.
Harmon, Maj Gen, 36, 44.
Hartnell, Brig, 60.
Hawksworth, Maj Gen J., 24, 26.
Heidrich, Maj Gen (Lt Gen) Richard, 52, 65, 82, 83, 93, 95, 109, 116, 117.
Hewitt, Maj, 89.
Hitler, Adolf, 9, 15, 21, 64.
'Hitler'/'Senger' Line, 76, 108-112, 116-108.
Hodgson, Lt Col, 106.
Hoeki, Col van, 116.
Horsfall, Maj John, 100-102, 104, 107.
Hotel des Roses, Cassino, 92, 95.
'Husky', Operation, 32.

INDIAN FORCES:
4th Infantry Division, 52-58, 60, 72, 75, 81, 87, 88, 90-92, 97-100, 110, 113.
8th Infantry Division, 16, 108, 112, 114, 116.
5th Infantry Brigade, 61, 75, 90.
7th Infantry Brigade, 56, 58, 75, 95.
17th Infantry Brigade, 16.
1st Bn 2nd Gurkha Rifles, 61, 72, 75.
1st Bn 5th Gurkha Rifles, 16.
1st Bn 9th Gurkha Rifles, 61, 75, 91, 92, 95.
2nd Bn 7th Gurkha Rifles, 97.
4th Bn 16th Punjab Regiment, 72, 75.
1st Bn 6th Rajputana Rifles, 90-93, 95.
4th Bn 6th Rajputana Rifles, 60, 61, 93, 95.

Isola Bella, 45, 46, 83.
Italian 1st Armoured Artillery Regiment, 56.

James, Brig, 44.
Juin, Gen Alphonse, 12, 19-23, 36, 39, 41, 51, 108, 110, 118, 119.

Keightly, Maj Gen Charles, 97-99, 106, 107, 115.
Kesselring, Field Marshal Albrecht, 9, 10, 13, 15-18, 24, 26, 33-35, 43, 47, 51, 64, 79, 82, 83, 86, 110-112, 115, 117, 118-120.
Keyes, Lt Gen Geoffrey, 19, 23, 27-29, 36, 39, 42, 51, 55, 109, 118.
Kippenberger, Brig Howard, 52, 59, 60, 62, 82.
Kirkman, Lt Gen Sidney, 98, 107, 109, 110, 114, 115.

Leese, Gen Sir Oliver, 11, 12, 24, 52, 87, 108-110, 113, 115, 117, 119, 120.
Liri, River, 9, 26.
Liri valley, 11, 19, 20, 23, 26, 27, 29, 30, 35, 36, 40, 41, 51, 52, 54, 55, 58, 66, 80-82, 87, 93, 99, 108, 109, 112-117.
Lovett, Brig O., 56, 58, 59, 61.
Lowry, Admiral, 32.
Lucas, Lt Gen John, 32-36, 43-48, 77-80.

Mackensen, Gen Eberhard von, 15, 16, 34, 35, 43-48, 63, 64, 77-79, 82, 86, 111, 113, 119.
Madden, Lt Col, 66.
Manhart, Col, 45.
Marshall, Col, 38, 40.
Marshall, Gen George C., 8.
Martin, Col, 29, 30.
McCreery, Lt Gen Sir Richard, 20, 23, 24, 26, 36, 39, 41, 50, 108, 120.
McKay, Capt William, 78.
McKee, Capt Ian, 101, 103, 104.
McKenzie, Lt Col John, 100, 101, 107.
Messina, 7, 8.
Mignano Gap, 11.
Minturno, 20.
Moletta, River, 34, 35, 49, 63, 118.
monastery, Monte Cassino, 52, 54, 56, 101.
'Monestary Hill', see Monte Cassino
Monna Casale, 65.
Monsabert, Gen Joseph de, 19, 22, 41.
Montaquila, 87.
Monte Albaneta, 41.
Monte Belvedere, 39, 41.
Monte Cairo, 22, 38, 61, 75, 101, 107, 188.
Monte Camino, 11, 66.
Monte Cassino ('Monastery Hill'), 7, 9, 16, 19, 30, 36, 41, 42, 51, 53, 54, 55-59, 61, 62, 75, 80, 82, 86-88, 90-93, 95, 98, 106, 107, 113-116, 118.
Monte Castellone, 40, 53-54, 56-58, 99, 102.
Monte Ceresola, 27.
Monte Faito, 27, 114.
Monte La Difensa, 10, 11, 27.

Monte Maggiore, 10, 11.
Monte Maio, 19, 23, 112, 114.
Monte Manna, 39, 40.
Monte Pantano, 20.
Monte Sammucro, 11.
Monte Trocchio, 19, 20, 23, 27, 30, 38, 60, 82.
Monte Villa, 37.
Montgomery, Gen Sir Bernard, 7, 11, 12.
Mussolini, Benito, 7, 8.
Mussolini Canal, 33-35, 45, 47, 49, 64, 78, 83, 84.

Nangle, Col, 91, 92.
Naples, 8, 10.
Nettuno, 15, 32, 33, 64.
NEW ZEALAND FORCES:
II Corps, 13, 51, 52, 54, 57-59, 75, 76, 81, 82, 86, 87, 90, 91, 93, 95, 98, 99, 109.
2nd Infantry Division, 14, 52, 53, 59, 62, 73, 75, 81, 90, 94, 97-99.
4th Armoured Brigade, 59, 82, 94.
5th Infantry Brigade, 60, 62, 76, 93, 97.
6th Infantry Brigade, 87, 88, 90, 92-97.
19th Armoured Regiment, 89.
20th Armoured Regiment, 96.
22nd Motorised Infantry Battalion, 104.
24th Infantry Battalion, 93, 95, 96.
25th Infantry Battalion, 89-93, 95.
26th Infantry Battalion, 90, 91, 93.
28th (Maori) Infantry Battalion, 60, 62, 73, 75, 76, 95.

O'Daniel, Maj Gen, 82.
Orbetello, 34.
Ortona, 10, 53.
'Overlord', Operation, 11, 13, 18, 32, 120.

Padaglione Woods, 79.
Parkinson, Brig G., 82, 98.
Penney, Maj Gen W., 32, 63.
Petain, Marshal, 20.
Petrella massif, 76.
'Phantom Ridge', 113, 115.
Piedimonte, 117.
Point 56 - 38, 39.
Point 165 - 89, 93, 95, 97.
Point 202 - 95, 97, 98.
Point 213 - 38-40.
Point 236 - 91, 93, 95, 97.
Point 435 - 58, 91, 92, 93, 95, 98, 106.
Point 444 - 59, 61
Point 445 - 59, 75, 96, 97, 100, 106.
Point 450 - 61, 96, 100, 106.
Point 569 - 59.
Point 575 - 113.
Point 593 - 40, 55, 56-61, 75, 81, 95, 96, 98-100, 106, 111, 113, 115.
Point 706 - 40.
POLISH FORCES:
II Corps, 13, 106, 107, 109, 110, 113-115.
3rd Carpathian Division, 76, 113-116.
5th Kresowa Division, 74, 76, 113, 115.
2nd Armoured Brigade, 115.
1st Carpathian Rifle Brigade, 76.
2nd Carpathian Rifle Brigade, 115.
6th Lwowska Infantry Brigade, 76, 107.
12th Podolski Lancers Regiment, 116.
15th Poznan Lancers Regiment, 115.
16th Lwowska Rifle Battalion, 74, 76.

Ponto Rotto, 46, 64.
Po, River, 120.
Pozilli, 87.

Raapke, Maj Gen Wilhelm, 111.
railway station, Cassino, 59, 99.
Rapido, River, 9, 11, 19, 20, 22, 23, 26-30, 36-39, 42, 50, 53, 59, 65, 81, 87, 89, 93, 94, 99, 100, 107-112, 114, 115.
Reese, Col Hal, 53.
Reggio, 7.
Richardson, Capt, 104.
Richthofen, Field Marshal Wolfram von, 17, 83.
Ringel, Maj Gen Julius 'Papa', 20-22, 66.
Rome, 9, 11, 13, 18, 19, 34, 35, 43, 111, 116, 117, 119.
Rommel, Field Marshal Erwin, 9.
Roosevelt, President Franklin D., 8, 19.
Route 6 - 35, 36, 43, 56, 59, 88-93, 104, 112, 113, 115, 116, 118, 119.
Route 7 - 35, 43, 45, 46, 66, 112, 118.
Roux, Col, 41.
Ryder, Maj Gen Charles, 19, 37-39.

Salerno, 8-10, 13, 17, 24, 27, 37.
San Ambroglio, 20.
San Angelo, 27-30, 59, 110-112, 114.
San Giovanni, 26.

Sangro, River, 9, 10, 99.
San Michele, 19, 99.
San Pietro, 11, 27.
Santa Crocce, 66.
Santa Maria Infante, 112, 114.
Schlegel, Lt Col, 56.
Schlemm, Gen, 34.
Senger und Etterlin, Gen Fridolin von, 15, 23, 24, 26, 30, 50, 51, 54, 58, 80, 93, 97, 110-112, 117.
Sicily, 7, 12, 13, 17, 32.
'Slapstick', Operation, 9.
'Snakeshead Ridge' – see Point 593
South African 6th Armoured Division, 110.
Stalin, Joseph, 7.
Steinmetz, Gen, 111.

Taranto, 8-10.
Templer, Maj Gen Gerald, 24.
Thrith, Brig, 106.
Tiber, River, 119.
Todt Organisation, 10.
'Torch', Operation, 12, 13, 20, 32, 37.
Trigno, River, 7, 10.
Troubridge, Admiral Tom, 32.
Truscott, Lt Gen Lucian, 17, 33, 44-47, 79, 82, 83, 112, 117, 120.
Tuker, Maj Gen F., 52-55, 57.
'Turreted House', Cassino, 91.

'Ultra', 16, 52, 54.
UNITED STATES FORCES:
Fifth Army, 8, 10-13, 18, 19, 22, 24, 26, 27, 29, 30, 34, 39, 50, 52, 54-56, 76, 81, 107-109, 112, 119, 120.
Twelfth Tactical Air Force, 17, 57, 77, 87.
Fifteenth Army Air Force, 56.
II Corps, 13, 19, 20, 23, 26-28, 36, 39-41, 50, 51, 53, 55, 57, 80, 109, 112, 117-119.
VI Corps, 9, 13, 17, 19, 32-36, 44-49, 63, 64, 79, 80, 82, 83, 84, 112, 117-119.
1st Armored Division, 19, 36, 43, 44, 48, 59, 64, 77, 78, 119.
3rd Infantry Division, 33, 34, 43-49, 63, 64, 78, 79, 82, 119.
34th Infantry Division, 19, 20, 23, 36-42, 50, 52, 53, 56, 59, 65, 67, 81, 83, 110, 111, 113, 119.
36th Infantry Division, 14, 19, 22, 23, 26-30, 36, 37, 39, 41, 42, 53, 56, 65, 67, 83, 110, 112, 119.
45th Infantry Division, 43, 49, 52, 63, 64, 77-79, 119.
85th Infantry Division, 66, 110, 112.
88th Infantry Division, 110, 112, 114.
1st Special Service Force (US/Canadian), 19, 47, 49, 64, 83, 84, 119.
1st Armored Regiment, 36, 44.
6th Armored Regiment, 44.
7th Infantry Regiment, 45, 46.
15th Infantry Regiment, 45, 46.
133rd Infantry Regiment, 37, 38, 40-42.
135th Infantry Regiment, 38, 39, 41, 42.
141st Infantry Regiment, 28-30, 42, 65, 67.
142nd Infantry Regiment, 22, 39, 40.
143rd Infantry Regiment, 28-30.
157th Infantry Regiment, 63, 64, 77.
168th Infantry Regiment, 38-40, 42.
179th Infantry Regiment, 63, 64, 77-79.
180th Infantry Regiment, 63, 79.
504th Parachute Infantry Regiment, 43, 45.
US Ranger Force ('Darby's Rangers'), 32, 34, 43-45.
151st Field Artillery Battalion, 41.
100th Infantry Battalion, 37, 65, 67.
509th Parachute Infantry Battalion, 32, 34, 82.
1st Ranger Battalion, 32, 45.
3rd Ranger Battalion, 45.
4th Ranger Battalion, 32, 45, 46.
756th Tank Battalion, 37, 39, 40.
760th Tank Battalion, 39, 96.

Valletri, 83.
Valmontone, 35, 43, 112, 119.
Venafro, 87.
Vichy French government, 21.
Vietinghof(-Scheel), Gen Heinrich von, 9, 13, 15, 19, 23, 34, 35, 52, 80, 97, 111, 117-119.
Volturno, River, 10, 37.

Wakeford, Captain R. VC, 75.
Walker, Maj Gen Fred, 19, 27-30, 37, 42, 53, 65.
Westphal, Gen, 35.
Weygand, Gen, 20.
Wilson, Gen Sir Henry Maitland, 11, 13, 55, 120.
'Winter' Line, 11.

Young, Lt Col Russell, 62.